FREE SKIING – HOW TO ADAPT TO THE MOUNTAIN

FREE SKIING

How to adapt to the mountain

CHOUCAS

With deepest gratitude to Hans Karlsson.

Prière du Guide de Montagne

O Père, Maître de l'Univers, apprends-moi à contempler la création avec un regard neuf et un cœur jeune; à puiser dans la richesse de tes dons la générosité à te servir dans mon métier de guide de montagne. Seigneur Jésus, Sommet de l'Univers et Centre des Cœurs. Apprends-moi à lire ta Présence dans le cristal des êtres et à aider la montée de chacun d'eux vers toi. Que par ton Esprit je sois ton témoin à la tête de la cordée: sûr et intrépide à la conduire à l'attaque, capable de l'arrecher à l'envoûtement d'une vie facile pour l'entraîner vers les cimes, fascinée par ta Beauté en elles et soutenue par ta Force et ta Patience en moi. Glorieux saint Bernard de Menthon, notre modèle et protecteur, implore du Seigneur la force de monter comme toi vers le Père avec toute ma vie, avec tous mes frères, avec toute la Création dans l'audace et l'adoration.

Amen

Prière composée pour l'Année des Alpes (1965) par le Chanoine G. Volluz, guide de Montagne.

I still remember all the questions I used to ask myself when I first started skiing full-time. Knowing what I know today, this is the book I wish I'd had but never found back then.

Jimmy Odén, UIAGM Mountain Guide

CONTENTS

Always put food out for the choucas, as the alpine jackdaws (Corvus Monedula) are called. Local legend has it that they are the reincarnated souls of deceased mountaineers.

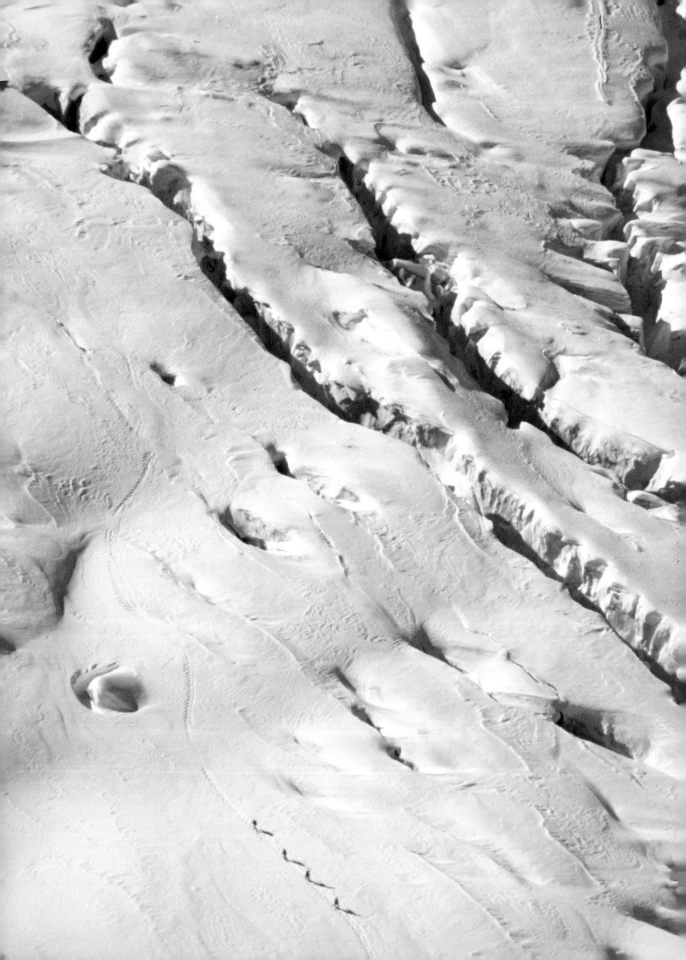

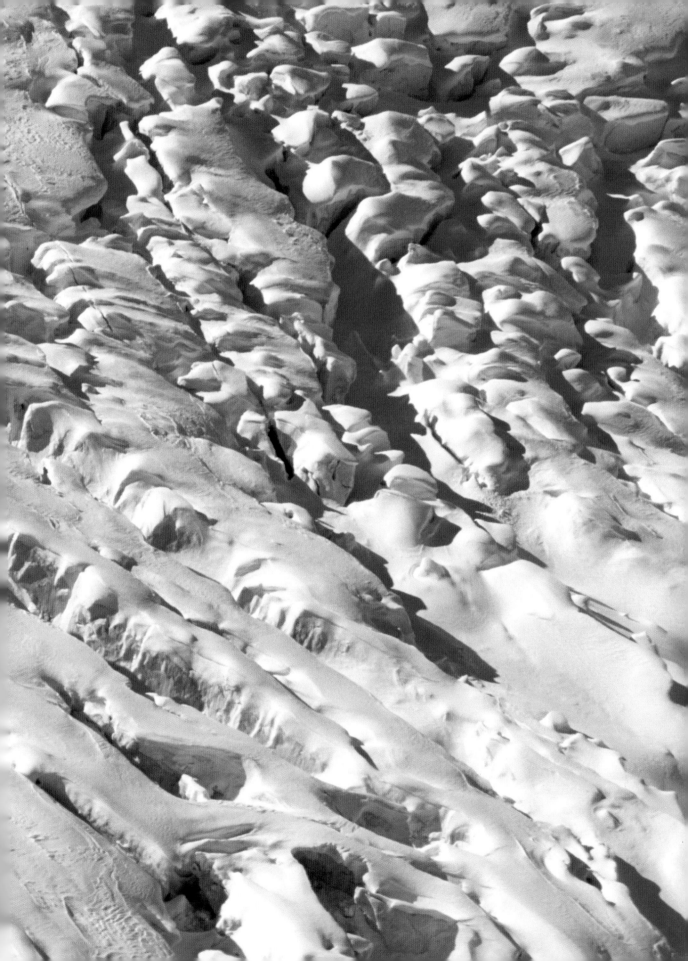

Francine Moreillon in Verbier/Switzerland
Photo Myriam Lang-Willar

Newborn babies living in mountainous areas are lighter than those living at sea level – approximately 100 grams less for every 1000 metres.

24% of the world's surface is mountainous. 10% of the Earth's population live in mountainous regions.

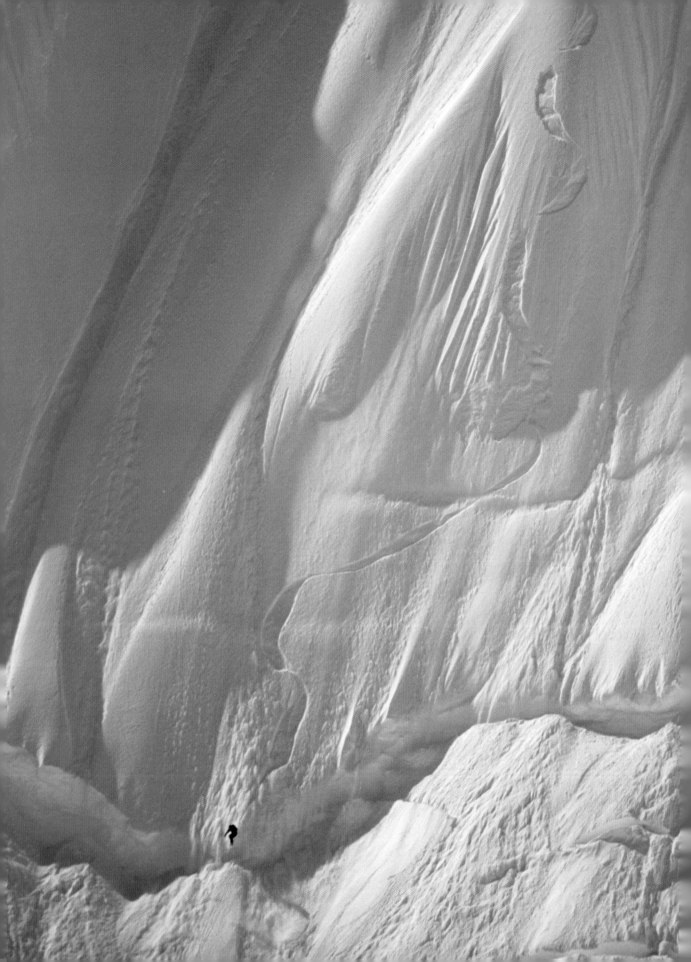

Most slab avalanches occur on 30–45 degree slopes with 38 degrees as the most common angle. In order to assess avalanche terrain, it's important to be able to estimate the angle of a slope's steepest section.

Chapter 3 Snow- and avalanche knowledge

Next page: In 2002, there were 5146 helicopter rescues performed in Switzerland. 264 of those rescued were mothers who were about to give (or had just given) birth.

Life is like a box of chocolates. So is house painting in some places on Greenland. Only one type of colour is delivered each year – you never know what you're going to get.

Kangaamiut/Greenland Photo Hans Solmssen

Avalanche incident, Chapütschin/Switzerland Photo Eidg. Institut für Schnee- und Lawinenforschung, Davos

Niseko/Japan Photo Myriam Lang-Willar

Niseko/Japan Photo Myriam Lang-Willar

Next page: Northern lights, Alaska
Photo Myriam Lang-Willar

Entrée: Tinned ham served on a lid
Main course: Crumbed bread with semi-frozen cheese
Dessert: Freeze-dried tropical fruit soup
The Wine list: Cocoa on chlorine purified creek water

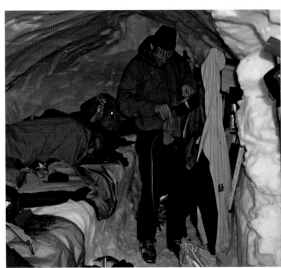

Nature can immediately be understood.

Marie Andrieux, Lebanon
Photo Myriam Lang-Willar

Verbier/Switzerland

01 THE BACKPACK
[See "Skiing".]

Previous page: To relieve pain in case of shoulder joint
dislocation put a soft supporting cushion (like a
rolled fleece jacket) in the armpit before fixation.

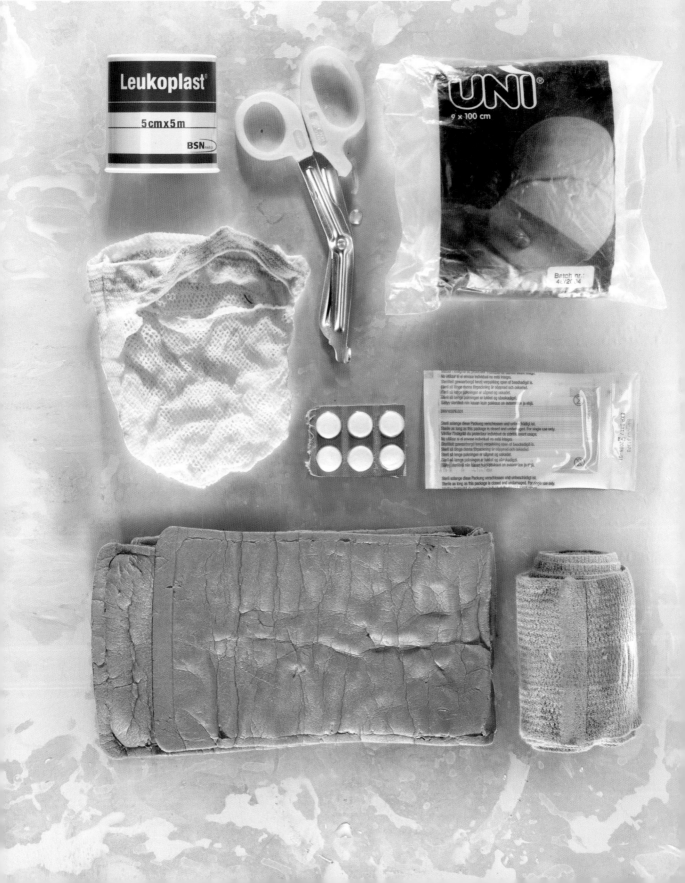

05 THE REPAIR KIT

Multi-tools, head torch, ski wax, scraper, duct tape, wax for the skins, dental floss and needle (for stitching), wire, ski pole repair kit. [See "Skiing".]

THE HYDRATION KIT

Thermos, plastic water bottle, water bag with
energy drink. [See "Ski touring".]

06

THE GLACIER RESCUE KIT
Rope, karabiners, slings, TIBLOCS, mini traxion, block,
ice screws. [See "Glacier skiing".]

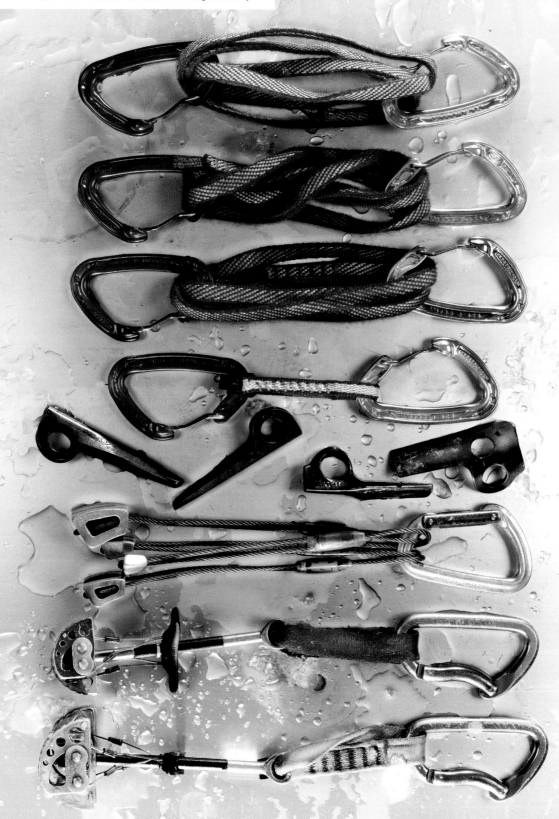

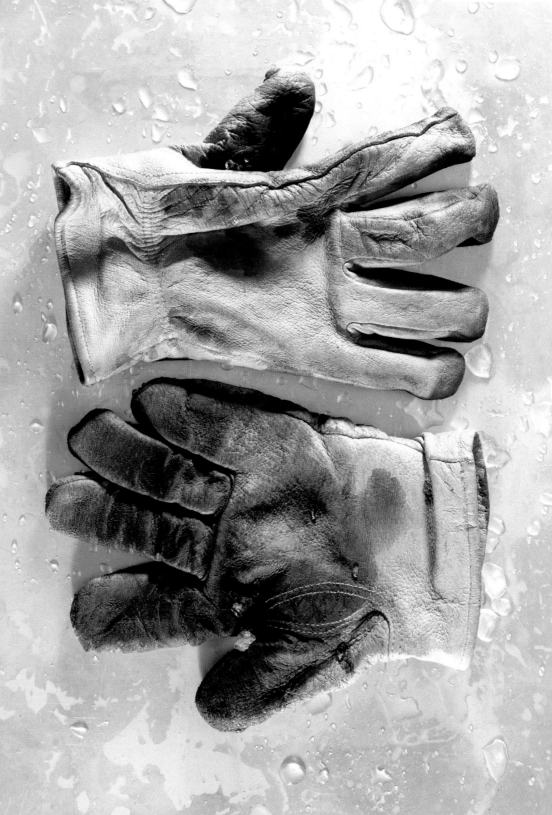

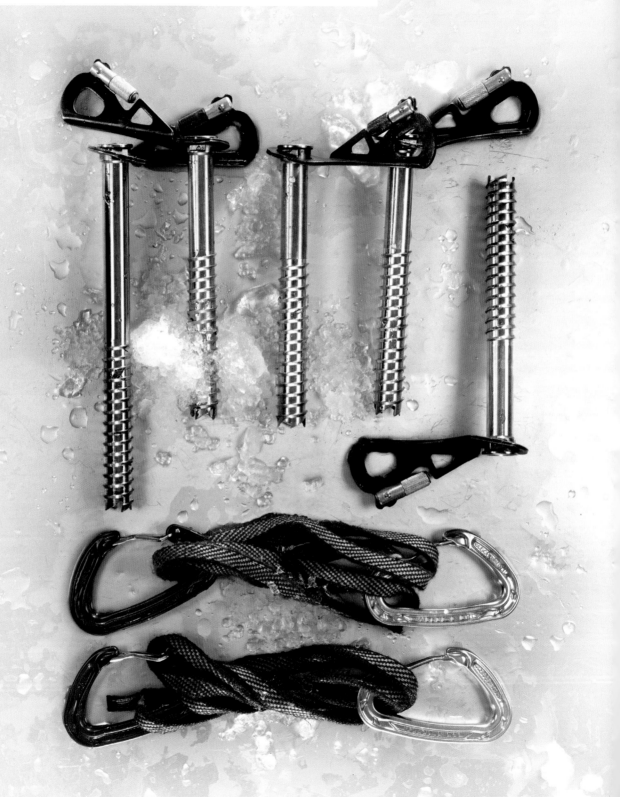

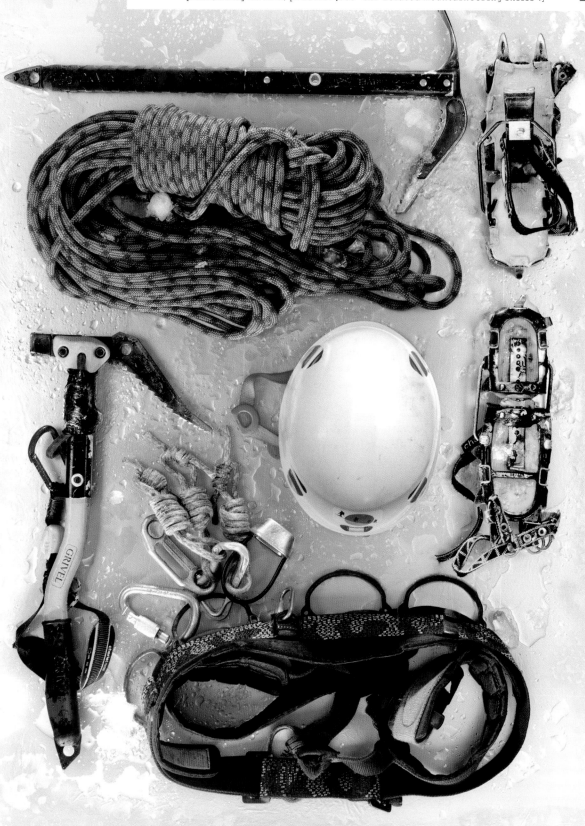

BASIC CLIMBING EQUIPMENT

Ice axe, rope, crampons, helmet, technical ice axe, harness, karabiners, magic plate, belay device, prusiks. [See "Ski-related mountaineering skills".]

12

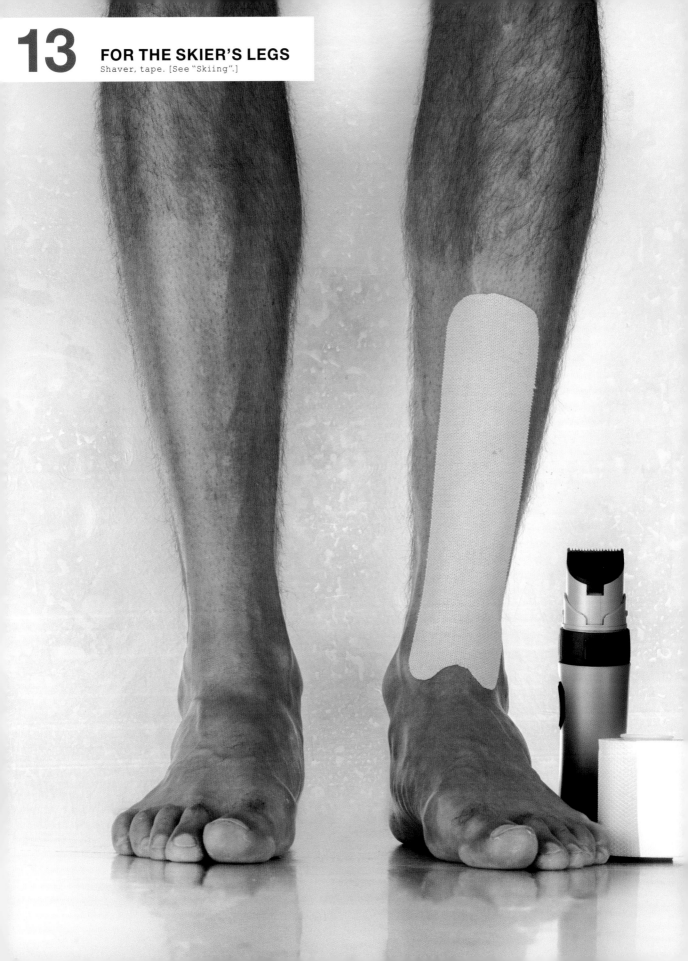

FOR THE SKIER'S LEGS
Shaver, tape. [See "Skiing".]

001

MOUNTAIN SENSE

Even now, some of my past decisions make me feel very stressed. And sometimes I feel even more stressed thinking about decisions I didn't make.

I especially remember one of the first days of my very first season in the Alps. It happened in December 1990. My two friends and I were all keen skiers, and we all had transceivers and backpacks with shovels. But no probes. We figured you didn't need probes, so we spent the money on food and beer instead.

The things we did carry made us seem unusually safety conscious. At that time most ski bums didn't care about that kind of equipment at all. We only had a rough idea about how to use the gear, and no understanding of the mountains whatsoever. But that didn't concern us very much. I was 19, a long way from home, and armed with a secret weapon; the immortality of youth.

The day was sunny, with no wind. There was deep, fresh snow from the previous day. As we were riding a chairlift, we spotted a fantastic bowl off to the side, without a single track. Humble and bright as we were, we wondered why no one else skied there. But we didn't spend too much time thinking about that; we would have it all for ourselves.

Using the little common sense we had, we started to ski on the side of the bowl, one by one. We rode the same chairlift all that day, adding fresh tracks to our old ones. Other skiers saw how much fun we were having, and started to follow our tracks. They probably thought that if we skied there, it must be safe. Perhaps it looked as if we knew what we were doing out there, with our backpacks and all.

On that fantastic carefree day, we did a few minor things right. But in the end that doesn't matter much. We had no idea what we were doing, and made many ignorant decisions. The only reason we made it unscathed through the day was pure luck. And we didn't realise that at the time. Nor did we realise how easily the bowl could have become a giant terrain-trap, with dozens of skiers buried at the bottom under several metres of snow.

In my nightmares, I know the snow conditions weren't favourable that day. And I know that back then I wouldn't have been able to tell the difference.

During my years in the mountains, I've met people who haven't been able to tell the difference, just like the 19-year old version of me.

I was lucky that day. But some skiers have not been so lucky. At the end of the day, a wiser approach (and one I can recommend) is to learn as much as you can from the mountains. This way you can base your future decisions on knowledge.

In the mountains, you have to be able to judge situations and make decisions quickly and efficiently. However, it is not always possible to make a correct decision, so you need to recognise your mistakes, correct them and then learn from them.

When developing as a ski mountaineer it is natural to concentrate on technical skills (such as how to build a rappelling anchor or rope up on a glacier), because you need those skills to get anywhere. That phase is fun and rewarding, tangible and easy to measure. But the skill of applying the right technique at the right time in the right place, takes much longer to develop.

Mountain sense is based on your general knowledge (skills, techniques and knowledge). This is developed by learning and practising new techniques in controlled situations. The greater your general knowledge, the more options you will have for avoiding problems. Mountain sense is difficult to describe, and cannot really be taught. But it can be learned through experience, evaluation, and reflection on experience. Be humble enough to realise that there is always something to be learnt from a day in the mountains. Don't just read this chapter to obtain hard facts. Read it more for formulating an idea and getting a feeling for the process of analysing a situation, and for the ability to apply correct techniques.

DECISION-MAKING More often than not there is no single "right way," but several. When there is only one right way, decision-making is easy because of the lack of choice. You have to be able to recognise which situations only have one reasonable alternative. Be open-minded and flexible. Don't make decisions based on old information, assumptions or protocols.

Take every opportunity to gather, upgrade and update information. Continue to interpret available information all the time. The later you can make a decision, the more information you will have at hand. When following a pre-formed plan, be sure your decisions are based on reality rather than expectations. Along the way you will probably need to adjust and fine-tune the plan. Or even change it completely if unforeseen factors arise.

ERROR CORRECTION It is practically impossible for every decision to be absolutely correct, because of the number of variables and the infinite combinations. It doesn't matter who you are or what you have done before; if you make a wrong decision at the wrong time, you can end up paying the ultimate price. Therefore, one of the most important skills is being able to recognise mistakes early on and correct them efficiently. Constantly thinking about what could go wrong will improve your ability to recognise mistakes early on. This is important, because you will make mistakes. It is inevitable. Experts make mistakes as well, but they admit it and learn from each experience. Don't be afraid to admit that you have made a mistake. Trying to cover up a mistake can often escalate into a chain of mistakes, leading ultimately to an incident or accident. Don't gamble your way out of a situation to protect your ego. Admit the mistake and re-evaluate your options.

Most errors can be corrected with little or no disturbance to the flow of activity. You just need to look at options logically. If an error can be rectified enough to provide an acceptable margin of safety — carry on. If not, create other options. Retreating is also an option, unless it is more hazardous than going on.

Note: "Retreating" should always be regarded as an option before going on, not just as an afterthought or final thought. Remember to reflect upon and evaluate the events of your ski days. It is the only way to learn from your mistakes and to develop and improve for the future.

RISK MANAGEMENT We strive to keep risk at an acceptable level in the mountains. There is no right or wrong level, only your personal level of acceptance, and the consequences of your actions. Know yourself and know what risks you are willing to take. Make sure the risks stay at that level. If you expose yourself to a higher level of risk, this should be a deliberate decision and not due to ignorance.

There is a tendency to accept a greater level of risk:
___ In a group, relying on the judgement of other group members; the problem is often that everyone thinks someone else is making the decisions. Also, a group leader can often overestimate the expectations of the group.
___ It is easy to get a false sense of security close to ski lifts and civilisation.
___ When a person is repeatedly exposed to hazards without any incidents occurring, he or she becomes immune, because nothing has happened so far.

HAZARD RECOGNITION You have to be able to recognise hazards and evaluate them, so as to minimise the risk involved.

Hazards are often divided into two groups. Objective dangers and subjective dangers.
___ Objective dangers cannot be controlled; avalanches, falling seracs, weather, etc.
___ Subjective dangers can be controlled; skill levels, condition, group dynamics, etc.

However, all hazards have both components. All hazards can be controlled by choice.

You can choose not to expose yourself by staying at home, by skiing somewhere else, or by turning back.

On the other hand, all hazards are uncontrollable to a certain extent, because of the number of variables and the infinite combinations involved. When you choose to go into the mountains, you accept potentially exposing yourself to some variables beyond your control. Having said that, you still need to assume responsibility for what happens to you. Accidents can not only be blamed on objective dangers.

For example, most fatal avalanches are triggered by the avalanche victim, or by someone in the group. Even though some accidents are totally unexpected even for the most experienced skier, there will be warning signs to alert you in most cases. It is your responsibility to read and interpret those signs.

SENSE OF DANGER Over time and with experience, you may develop a strong sense of danger and intuitive decision-making. This will allow you to form opinions and take action with a minimum of "conscious" thought. It is developed through complete theoretical understanding, practising skills and techniques hands-on, a vast amount of experience and reflection on the experiences.

All this takes time and does not come easily. Do not confuse it with constantly having a good feeling about everything and an "everything goes" attitude. Analyse uneasy feelings immediately; are they due to internal factors or external factors?

In the beginning it is natural to turn back "too easily" because your perception of risk is greater in a new, unfamiliar environment. This is as it should be. With time you will learn to recognise the various signals and interpret them. Always take note of feeling uneasy. At best going against your feelings will only give you a stressful experience.

MINIMISING RISK Spending almost every day in the mountains I see a lot of strange decisions that could potentially lead to accidents. Usually nothing happens, thanks to luck. When nothing has happened, you get a false sense of security although you actually trusted to luck instead of skill. Then it is just a matter of time before you have an incident or accident. Develop your skills, carry the right equipment and know how to use it.

Avoidance is a way of minimising risk. Avoid hazards whenever practical or possible. Is the hazard related to a location? There are enough hazards in the terrain that you can't judge, so if possible avoid the hazards you do know by route choice, route finding and retreating.

Always strive for a minimum of exposure time. Do this by increasing your speed through exposed areas, by correct timing if the hazard is time related, and sheltering from hazards by using protected stopping points when possible.

Remember that not making a deliberate decision is nevertheless a decision made — you will have to face the consequences. Also, just because something can be done, it doesn't mean you have to do it or should do it.

002

MOUNTAIN WEATHER

The spring snow on the east face of Testa del Rutor had been excellent. But as the snow there got softer, at an altitude of 2700 metres, we started skiing slopes that faced more south, where the snow was still just as great.

Only moments before we got into the helicopter that morning, I had poked the snow with my pole and noticed that only the top layers were frozen, and not all the way to the ground.

Having to change aspects already worried me a bit. I realised, even at 2700 metres, that it was much warmer than it had been for days, which meant that the risk of an avalanche would increase rapidly and dramatically. And I was uneasy, as the group was skiing much more slowly than I had anticipated.

We hit the rotten snow at 2200 metres and in a very short time, the unexpectedly mild temperature had turned the nice spring snow into avalanche terrain. And the snow wasn't frozen on any aspect at this altitude. Luckily, we didn't have too far to go. One more short steep section, roughly 30°, and after that the terrain was flat all the way down to the village.

We traversed to avoid the steepest section, trying to keep at a distance from one another. But as we passed a convex section, the heaviest of my clients set off a small, wet snow slough that went all the way to the ground. Suddenly everyone realised that we really had to get out of there.

We struggled through the rotten snow the last 300 metres down, but at least it was flat enough to be safe. Fortunately we didn't have to call the rescue helicopter.

The sudden rise in temperature had made everything unskiable. We would have hit the rotten snow without doubt, no matter what aspect or altitude we skied at.

Our skiing day was already over at 10.15.

...e of the weather, decisions and plans in the mountains have to be changed
...tly. Therefore, when making your plans, always try to get a forecast that
...cent as possible and covers as small an area as possible. Although most
12-hour weather forecasts are accurate, you still need to bear in mind that they
are predictions and not statements of fact. As long as the atmosphere is stable,
the forecast will be accurate. Unfortunately, accuracy decreases with time when
the weather is unstable, and an accurate forecast is the most important re-
quirement of all.

CONSEQUENCES OF WEATHER

In the mountains, you need to observe developments continuously, assemble the
clues, and make your own short-term forecast. Even more so when doing multiple
day tours in areas that do not have mobile phone coverage or good forecasts.
You also need to understand what the weather does to the mountains, so you can
make decisions accordingly. Analyse what the weather does and how it will affect your plans.

Adverse short-term consequences Avalanche danger increases with heavy snowfall
or rain. And with warmer temperatures. Also, there will be a greater risk of falling rocks.

Colder temperatures mean that it takes longer for the snow to stabilise, and
frostbite and hypothermia are more likely.

Cloud, fog and bad visibility make it difficult to judge the avalanche danger,
and to navigate. And even a small accident can have severe consequences when
it is difficult to get outside help. Clouds prevent the snow pack from re-freezing
during the night.

Wind increases avalanche danger, and frostbite and hypothermia are more
likely. If the wind is strong, getting outside help to evacuate an injured person
can be difficult.

Favourable consequences in the short term Heavy snowfall means fantastic skiing,
with good visibility among the trees, and the glaciers fill in.

Warmer temperatures can give good spring skiing if you are in a spring snow
cycle. Colder temperatures mean that the snow stays cold or frozen even at low
altitude.

Wind causes snow bridges to form on the glaciers.

THE GLOBAL PICTURE

The atmosphere is held to the earth by gravitation. The pressure of the air at a
given point changes over time depending on the height of the column of air above
you. Air pressure is always highest at sea level and decreases with altitude. Atmospheric air pressure is measured in millibars (mb) and the average at sea
level is 1013mb.

Instruments used by skiers that work with air pressure are the altimeter and
barometer. Although it is the same tool with two different scales, the barometer
is mainly used in a valley or when staying overnight in a hut, but it is still useful to understand barometric pressure in order to understand weather charts.

Because you need the altimeter to navigate in the mountains, you will always have it with you; therefore it will be your instrument in the mountains for monitoring air pressure.

Note: With the approach of low pressure the altimeter goes up, and when high pressure is approaching it goes down. The altimeter doesn't know whether you're moving or not. It can only tell that pressure is decreasing, for example, and it will interpret that as you moving uphill as air pressure decreases with altitude. Therefore, it can show you at a higher altitude when in reality you have remained at the same altitude the whole time.

The sun is the engine of all atmospheric phenomena. When the air is being warmed it rises and when it cools, it falls. [See diagram 001.]

Because the world is round, the sun doesn't heat its surface equally. Climate is largely determined by the relationship between solar radiation and cooling radiation.

The distribution of high pressure and low pressure is controlled mainly by these temperature differences. The greatest heat occurs at the equator, where solar radiation hits the earth perpendicularly, and low pressure is formed here.

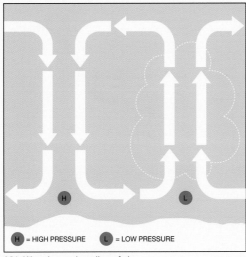

H = HIGH PRESSURE   L = LOW PRESSURE

001 Warming and cooling of air.

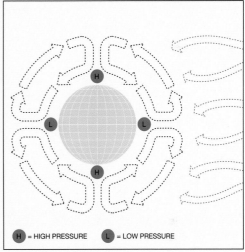

H = HIGH PRESSURE   L = LOW PRESSURE

002 Global circulation.

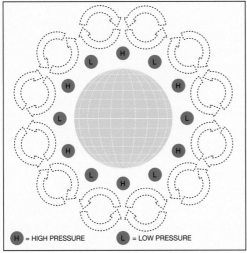

H = HIGH PRESSURE   L = LOW PRESSURE

003 Global circulation.

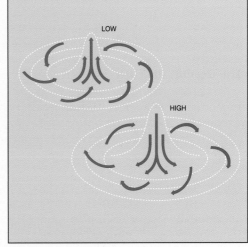

004 High and low pressure.

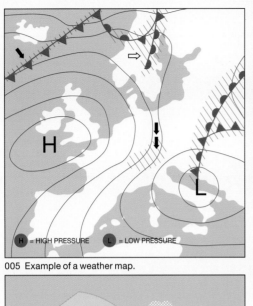

005 Example of a weather map.

H = HIGH PRESSURE   L = LOW PRESSURE

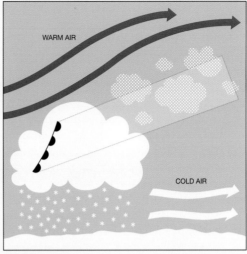

006 Warm front.

WARM AIR

COLD AIR

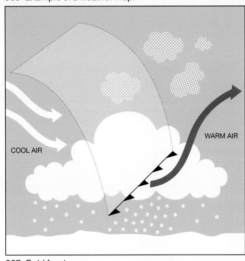

007 Cold front.

COOL AIR

WARM AIR

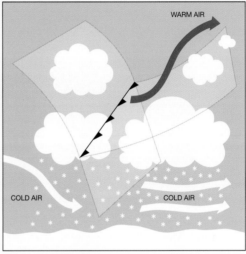

008 Occluded front.

WARM AIR

COLD AIR

COLD AIR

At the poles the opposite is the case, especially during the winter when no solar radiation reaches the surface and higher pressure is formed. If there were no exchange of air mass between these two areas, the temperature at the equator would constantly rise, and at the Polar Regions it would constantly fall. However, since nature strives for balance, differences in pressure are constantly being equalised between high and low-pressure areas. [See diagram 002.]

This is complicated by the tilt and the spin of the earth. [See diagram 003.]

LOW PRESSURE

Atmospheric low pressure is associated with bad weather and much precipitation, especially if the air in it has travelled over a warm ocean.

A boundary between two air masses is called a front. Fronts move with the wind and bring unsettled periods of bad weather. They are associated with low-pressure systems. [See diagrams 004 and 005.]

A WARM FRONT IS ADVANCING An early warning. Skiers need not be taken by surprise; the slow movement of a warm front gives plenty of time for decision-making. Air pressure falls; thin, high clouds are formed that thicken over time and visibility in the mountains decreases.

The result is prolonged snowfalls and bad visibility. When the front has passed, there will be higher temperature, bad visibility and light snowfall. [See diagram 006.]

A COLD FRONT IS ADVANCING Very short warning time. The first sign is that the air pressure falls rapidly, while the wind becomes medium to strong. The front itself is often very cloudy, stormy and with heavy precipitation.

Results are intense precipitation, strong winds, cloud and lower temperatures. When the front has passed, there will be lower temperatures. The clouds rapidly disappear (often only temporarily) and air pressure increases rapidly (often only temporarily). Only under the influence of high pressure is improvement long term. [See diagram 007.]

AN OCCLUDED FRONT IS ADVANCING This is the result of a cold front over-running a warm front. Ahead of the occlusion, the weather is similar to that ahead of a warm front. When the front has passed, the weather is similar to that behind a cold front. [See diagram 008.]

VERTICAL WIND

Vertical winds (winds that lift and sink the air masses) create and dissolve clouds. When the air is moving upwards, clouds are formed, and the clouds dissolve when the air is moving down.

When the dry air rises, it cools at 1°C per 100 metres up to the level where the water vapour condenses and clouds are formed whereupon the saturated air continues to cool at 0.6°C per 100 metres. There are three major ways in which vapour rises and produces precipitation.

Orographic lifting Air that moves horizontally towards a mountain chain is forced to rise in order to pass the obstacle. The greater part of the precipitation in the mountains during the winter is due to orographic lifting. [See diagram 009.]

Frontal lifting The warmer air will always rise on top of the colder air, because the colder air has a higher density (as shown above).

Cyclonic lifting As described before, large air masses are lifted due to complicated patterns in the atmosphere (as shown above).

ISOTHERMS (LINES OF EQUAL TEMPERATURE)

The altitude of the 0°C isotherm is where the temperature is 0°C, free of any influence from the ground (this is established with balloons). For a skier, it is more important to know at what altitude freezing occurs. This varies with weather conditions, ground conditions and time of day. During the day the freezing level will be located at a higher altitude than the 0°C isotherm because of the sun, but it will be at a lower altitude on a clear night.

Knowing at what altitude the 0°C isotherm is located is very important information for us, especially when we're skiing on spring snow and the run ends at low altitude. It is easy to make the mistake of starting a run in perfect spring snow at high altitude only to ski into a trap at low altitude of rotten (wet snow that doesn't carry a skier) snow that may avalanche.

In a weather forecast, the only information that will tell you anything about this is the 0°C isotherm. You have to use this information as a basis for your own forecast of what the temperature on the ground is going to be like at different locations on the mountains and at different times of the day.

SNOWFALL

When vertical winds lift moist air, the water vapour cools and forms ice crystals. These ice crystals will float on the upward vertical wind and continue to grow until they become so large that they fall from the cloud as snow. [See diagram 010.]

The warmer the air the more moisture it can hold, which is why the big dumps often come from the warm oceans. And the faster the air rises the more intense the snowfall (in the mountains).

The limit for snow/rain depends on the altitude at which the 0°C isotherm is located. If it snows for a long time the limit for snow can go down with the 0°C isotherm. Loss of heat from the warmer air in melting the snow that falls through it (below the 0°C isotherm) will eventually lead to the air cooling. This is often the reason why rain changes to snow after a time, and the limit for snow/rain continues to move down in altitude during prolonged snowfalls. The quality of the snow will of course vary with altitude.

FOEHN/CHINOOK

This is a phenomenon in which warm winds blowing down a valley can cause the temperature to rise 10–15°C in a very short time. As a result it will be very windy at higher altitude and very warm at low altitude. The effect on snow at high altitude is either wind pack, or increased avalanche danger due to the formation of wind slabs. At low altitude all the snow will evaporate or melt and the avalanche danger will increase.

Foehn can arise when great differences in air pressure occur across a mountain range. It can blow in any direction, but always from the high-pressure side of the mountains to the low-pressure side. [See diagram 011.]

Foehn is formed when a strong wind flows across a mountain range. The air rises, clouds are formed and the air cools (at 0.6°C per 100 metres). As the air cools it can contain less vapour and the result is precipitation on the windward side. The air that has passed the top is much drier and will therefore reheat at (1°C per 100 metres) a higher level. Consequently, the air temperature will be much higher at low altitude on the lee side than at the same altitude on the windward side.

Windward side On the windward side of the ridge it will be foggy, windy and with rain or snow.

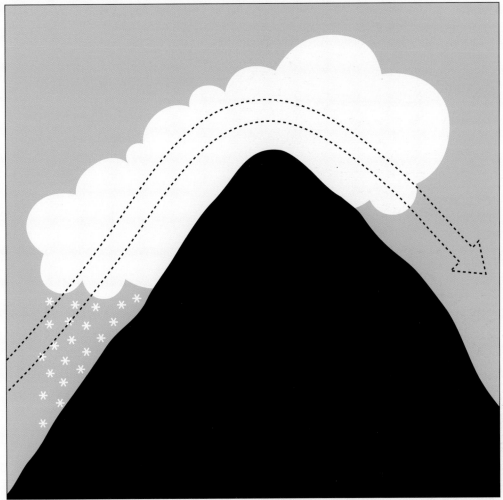

009 Orographic lift.

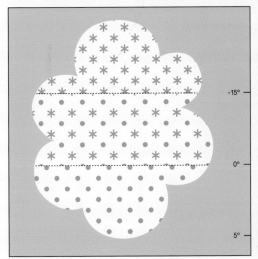

010 Snowfall.

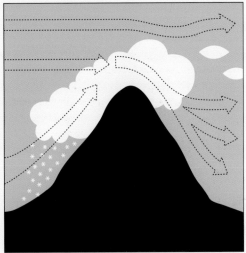

011 Foehn and Chinook.

Lee side On the leeward side it will be sunny and warm. Grey clouds in the shape of lenses can form after the ridge and in the valleys affected by the Foehn; the wind will blow strongly and will strengthen with altitude. This can go on for days.

HIGH PRESSURE

An anticyclone or area of high pressure is associated with stable, fine weather, but a mountain range should ideally be in the centre of the high pressure to ensure this.

The more the barometric pressure has risen, the closer to the centre you are.

INVERSION During the winter, the air in the mountain valleys (often more cold and moist than the air above) falls in a high-pressure system. The warmer air will stay above the cold air, resulting in two completely different climates. In the valley it is foggy, moist and cold, while above it the weather is beautiful and warmer. Note: There will not be a problem for skiers as long as the cloud stays at the same altitude in the valley, or is sinking and the high pressure persists.

WINDS DURING FINE WEATHER In general there is very little wind in the centre of a high-pressure system, but local winds could be produced by the sun. During the winter these winds are almost non-existent, but they become more active towards the spring when the sunshine gets stronger. The strength of this wind varies a lot from place to place, but in general it is stronger in the morning than in the evening. Note: As long as the winds are regular it is a sign that the weather is stable.
In the morning The sun warms up the slopes at high altitude while the valley is still in the shade. The warm air rises and clouds are formed above the ridges. This results in a breeze blowing up from the valley to replace the rising air.
In the evening The air cools, becomes more dense and sinks into the valley, producing a breeze blowing downhill, and the cold air accumulates in the valley bottom. The wind reaches maximum activity just after sunset.

METEOROLOGICAL RULES

It's easier to predict what the weather will be like in the near future if you know a few simple rules. To be of any value, observations on visibility and wind must be combined with observation of the air pressure. It is extremely difficult to estimate how long it will take for the bad weather to arrive, so make your decisions in good time.

AIR PRESSURE If, when you wake up in a hut, the altimeter has gone down a lot during the night (more than 100 metres) this give you a signal that better weather is developing. So even if it is still cloudy you could start your tour with some white-out navigation, as the weather will probably clear up during the next few hours.

Suppose you are out ski touring and clouds form. You compare your actual altitude (by locating your exact position on the map) with what your altimeter is telling you. You realise that your altimeter has gone up 100 metres, and there-

fore the pressure has fallen approximately 10mb, indicating that the weat
getting worse and it's time to hurry up or think of alternative plans.

A simple rule is to go up when the altimeter goes down, and to go down
the altimeter goes up. Minor changes can be ignored (30—40m or 3—4mb).

VISIBILITY An improvement in visibility in the mountains is normally due to the
air in a high-pressure system falling, so it's a sign that the weather is improving.

As long as the clouds in the valley stay at the same altitude or are falling,
the high pressure will persist.

WIND

Non-existent or weak winds during fine weather are a sign of stable weather. An
almost certain indication that the weather will change is if the wind changes
direction. Strong wind that increases with altitude (you can see the snow blowing off the ridges) indicates that bad weather is approaching.

003

SNOW- AND AVALANCHE KNOWLEDGE

The guy with the film camera is asking me to be careful. He's pointing towards the bowl, telling me that the whole side might give way. I nod my head, but I'm not sure I'm really listening.

It was my first season in Verbier, on a beautiful powder day. We had skied down into Creblet, traversed west, and just stepped over the ridge into the Col des Mines bowl when we ran into some older ski bums who were filming for a ski movie. And, after only a few minutes of conversation, I had volunteered to ski the line down from the ridge for their camera.

I don't know what went through my head. I had been skiing full time for three seasons, but as the camera started to roll, what little knowledge and experience I had collected just disappeared. Thinking back, all the signs were there and it was as good as certain that the side would slide. When I made the second turn, I could see the snow starting to move around me. It looked like waves. And I didn't fully realize what was going on until someone behind me on the ridge started yelling "Avalanche!"

My first emotion was a sense of calm, since I was convinced that I would be able to ski out of the slide quite easily. The second was surprise, as I all of a sudden found myself on my back. This wasn't how I'd envisioned it. When I was dragged down under the snow, I started to swim and fight to get to the surface. I desperately tried to turn around, to get the skis pointing downhill again before going over the small rocks I knew were in the fall line. Suddenly, I got a hard blow over my upper right arm. And then I stopped. I'd come to a full stop just after going over the rocks, while the slide had continued another 50 metres before slowing to a halt. A sharp rock had cut right through my jacket, my fleece sweater and my thermal. But still, I had been very lucky not to get my face crushed against those rocks. So except for the shame of being incredibly stupid, I came away with only a scar on my right arm.

Apart from this incident, I have on two other occasions been carried about 20 metres in small slides. What these incidents all have in common is that the signs have been there, but that I, for various reasons, haven't responded correctly and have had to – at least once – rely on luck to save the day.

Now, three small slides in 15 years might not be all that bad. But one thing is for certain: On the mountain, you can't afford to put your trust in luck.

Just because someone is a good skier doesn't automatically mean that they have the knowledge and experience to judge how stable a snow pack is. Having the theoretical knowledge of snow crystal formation doesn't do much to help you when you're standing on a slope asking yourself the eternal question: Do I ski it or not?

There is no single test or piece of information that can give you the answer to decide whether to ski or not. It's essential to see the whole picture and consider the many variables. This is not an easy task due to the vast amount of information and the complex and poorly understood inter-relationships between different factors. You have to learn which information is important and when. Therefore the skill of judging avalanche hazard should be regarded as an art rather than a technique. It's an intuitive process that is sometimes referred to as 'snow sense' and must be learned through practise and experience.

Hazard evaluation is an ongoing process; information must be gathered continuously and the evaluation has to be upgraded with every new clue.

To be able to do that you have to know the mountain environment and its processes.

This chapter is based on the northern hemisphere but it can be applied anywhere in the world. For the southern hemisphere it would be the exact opposite; the conditions on north faces in the northern hemisphere would be the same as on south faces in the southern hemisphere.

LOOSE SNOW AVALANCHES

Dry, loose snow avalanches (aka point release) start at a single point in the top layer of the snow pack and, through a chain reaction, more snow is pulled in from both across the snow pack's width and its depth. The snow cover is characterised by very poor bonding between the snow crystals, whether it's dry or wet snow. The release starts with a small wedge of snow breaking away, due either to a weakening between the snow crystals (for example through heat radiation from the sun) or to an external force such as a skier or a falling rock. Imagine a pile of dry, unboiled rice grains which, when poked in one place, cause the whole top layer to slide. [See diagram 001.]

Loose snow avalanches can be both wet or dry snow avalanches. Only a bare minimum of avalanche accidents are caused by loose snow avalanches, possibly because they are fairly easy to predict and so can be avoided.

SLOUGHS Dry loose snow avalanches mainly occur during, or in the days after, big snowfalls or after a spell of cold temperatures where the snow has dried out mainly on the north-facing slopes. The terrain has to be steep for these avalanches to occur, 40—60°. In contrast to the slab avalanche it's relatively harmless for a skier to trigger a loose snow avalanche. The top layer slides away below the skis (aka a slough). However, even if most of the time the sloughs are small and shallow, it could be enough to throw you off balance and drag you over a cliff. For this to happen the avalanche has to be released from above by either someone or something. If you release a slough when you're descending steep terrain at high speed and continue down the fall line, or worse stop in the fall line after a couple of turns, there's a risk of getting caught. If you ski past the slough you must continue to ski sideways away from the fall line.

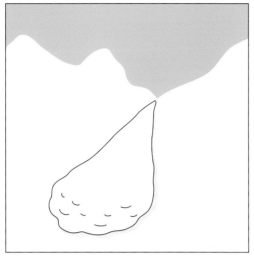

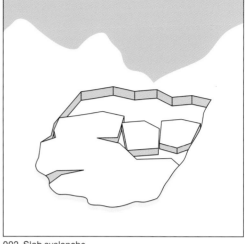

001 Loose snow avalanche (point release).   002 Slab avalanche.

WET SNOW AVALANCHES

Wet snow avalanches occur mainly in the spring when the sun heats the snow pack. They can sometimes occur even earlier in the season e.g. on coastal mountains when the temperature rises or when it's raining. Wet snow avalanches can be loose snow or slab avalanches. Slab avalanches are generally full depth (all the way down to the ground), the whole snow cover slides away on grass or smooth rock. Wet snow avalanches can occur on less steep terrain than the dry snow avalanches (on slopes as low as 20°). Remember that even if you're on flat terrain you can still be exposed to avalanches starting above you. Wet snow avalanches have enormous powers of destruction and they can travel a long distance on flat ground, especially if they are released by rain. However, as both the avalanches themselves and the paths they follow are quite easy to predict, they normally don't present as much danger to skiers.

SLAB AVALANCHES

A slab avalanche is characterised by a large area of snow (a slab) breaking away initially as one piece. The slab starts to break up into smaller blocks as it slides downhill. This process is very fast and immediately after being triggered it reaches its full power and speed. When a slab has been triggered it leaves a well-defined crown wall and a flat surface bed behind. [See diagram 002.]

The majority (90%) of all the fatal avalanche accidents are dry slabs triggered by the victim. Unfortunately 30—45° is the perfect angle for both skiers and slab avalanches, 38° being the most critical angle. They also occur less frequently on steeper terrain of up to 50°.

Often the slab breaks away higher up than from the point where the skier triggers the avalanche. This creates a trap where the ground is pulled away from under the skis and, once the skier looses his balance he will be sucked in by the chaotic waves of snow. [See diagram 003.] If the skier is travelling at great speed

Top layer sloughing on a steep descent, Alaska Photo Myriam Lang-Willar

Slab avalanche Photo Eidg. Institut für Schnee- und Lawinenforschung, Davos

003:1 The skier enters a slope.

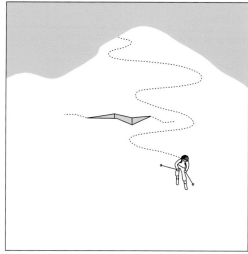

003:2 The slab is triggered by the added weight of the skier.

003:3 A large area breaks off simultaneously.

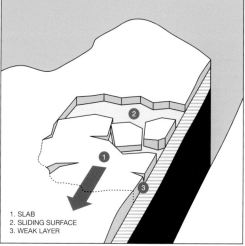

1. SLAB
2. SLIDING SURFACE
3. WEAK LAYER

004 Basic criteria for a slab avalanche.

when he triggers the avalanche he may be lucky enough to be outside the slab when it releases.

This is often seen in ski movies and photos where incredibly strong and good skiers have enough speed to ski out of the avalanche before it sets off and breaks up. Right or wrong, it's all up to how much risk you're willing to accept but I've never met anyone who with full understanding and knowledge of the mountains does this on purpose. Most often they have misjudged the conditions. Don't make the mistake of thinking that it's harmless or that you can control it. It's impossible in the long run to estimate how big an area is going to break off, how deep it will be and how much speed you will need to cross the slab before it slides away.

Don't confuse this with a technique used by very skilled and experienced mountain guides and pisteurs where they secure an area or a couloir before skiing it, by setting off the slab on purpose. This is done by cutting the snow pack or by adding extra weight above the slab and releasing it from higher up. The slab releases while you're standing safe above the fracture line. It takes an incredible snow sense to judge where and when this is possible. Only a minority of skiers and professionals have this skill and this can't be learnt from a book.

There are a few criteria that need to be fulfilled in order for a slab avalanche to occur.

A slab This is a relatively strong layer in the snow pack where the snow crystals bond well.

A weak layer A weak layer — such as facets, depth hoar, buried surface hoar or graupels. When it collapses it causes the slab to break off from the snow pack and then it reduces friction by creating a weak interface between the slab and the sliding surface.

A sliding surface Under the weak layer you need a surface that offers little friction and therefore can provide the sliding surface for an avalanche, such as ice crust, old hard snow, grass or smooth rock. [See diagram 004.]

A critical balance between strength and stress A slope section is unstable if stresses in the snow pack almost equal its strength. Then all that is needed is a trigger.

Trigger (failure of the snow slab) Avalanches occur when the weight of the snow pack and the forces from a trigger exceed the strength of the snow. A slab avalanche can be triggered by an increase in load or a decrease in strength. Both can occur together.

Angle When all of the criteria above have been fulfilled and the avalanche has been triggered it's only the angle of the slope that decides if the slab is going to slide off as an avalanche or not. [See diagram 005.]

LAYERS IN THE SNOW PACK

Snow is a material in constant evolution. Snowflakes change while still in the air; the snow crystals change in both shape and character. This continues when the snowflakes are on the surface and in the snow pack. A snow pack contains layers from different occasions of precipitation — each layer has been affected by different weather and then buried under new layers of snow. This creates layers with different characteristics, some weaker and others stronger. [See diagram 006.]

THE METAMORPHISM OF SNOW

This is the term used to describe the change of form that snow grains undergo after becoming a part of the snow pack. These changes will either strengthen the snow pack or weaken it. These two processes can occur simultaneously within the snow pack but it is quite common for one of them to predominate. The temperature gradient within the snow pack is the determining factor as to which metamorphic process becomes the most dominant, strengthening or weakening.

If the temperature gradient within the snow pack is less than 1°C per 10 cm a process called rounding dominates. This breaks down the snow crystals and stabilises the snow pack. If the temperature gradient is greater than 1°C per 10 cm a process called faceting dominates. This builds up the snow crystals and destabilises the snow pack.

Since snow offers very good insulation the temperature at ground level is always 0°C. This means that the lower the temperature and the thinner the snow pack, the greater the temperature gradient per 10 cm.

Note: The depth and stability of the snow pack varies with season, altitude, aspect and terrain features.

ROUNDING OF SNOW CRYSTALS The name refers to the result of the process where the snow crystal is transformed from its original star shape to a rounded grain. The snow becomes more firmly packed and the contact surfaces increase.

Rounding of snow crystals is the result of water vapour being deposited on concave parts of the changing crystal. The vapour moves from convexities to concavities. That's why the crystals rapidly lose their points. Eventually the rounding process produces grains of uniform size that form a solid and stable snow pack. This process occurs faster with snow temperatures close to 0°C. [See diagram 007.]

Conditions that favour the rounding of snow crystals:
A temperature gradient of less than 1°C per 10 cm.
A snow temperature warmer than −10°C.
Dense snow.
Small grains.

FACETING OF SNOW CRYSTALS This is the process where rounded snow crystals are transformed into angular shaped crystals or facets. These crystals don't bond well to each other and therefore form weak layers.

The water vapour moves from warm surfaces to cold surfaces and since the snow pack is usually warmer near the ground and colder towards the surface, the vapour moves from crystals in the lower layers to crystals in the layers above. If this process continues, the crystals will develop into a cup shaped crystal called depth hoar (sugar snow). [See diagram 008.] They form very unstable layers with no bonding between the crystals. These layers normally form deep down in the snow pack and it almost seems as if the whole snow pack is resting on ball bearings. This happens where the snow is loosely packed and the air is warmer, as it is around boulders, scree, bushes and on moraine ridges.

Conditions that favour the faceting of snow crystals:
A temperature gradient higher than 1°C per 10 cm.
Cold snow temperatures.
Loose or low density snow (around rocks and bushes).
Depth hoar/sugar snow forms rapidly in thin snow cover during cold conditions. Thin snow packs at the beginning of the winter (November—January), in combination with low temperatures and clear weather, will create a lot of depth hoar. These crystals are very persistent and can stay in the snow pack for the whole winter, especially where the temperature is low such as in shady places. Slopes with depth hoar in the snow pack become extra avalanche hazardous after every new snowfall and may release spontaneously. The reason we could ski these slopes before the snowfall was that we didn't put as much weight on the snow pack as the additional snow. That is why we always have to consider what the additional weight of fresh snow means to the snow pack on different slopes.

During dry and cold spells the top 10—20 cm of the snow pack dries out on the north faces and other shady slopes. The ski conditions become incredibly good with dry, cold snow. This is a result of faceting due to big temperature gradients close to the surface. However if the faceting goes on for a long period of time the result will be a snow pack with top to bottom sugar snow that is impossible to

These bricks are subject to the same stress as the layers within the snowpack.

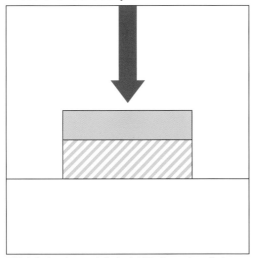

005:1 On level ground, their stability depends on their resistance to pressure.

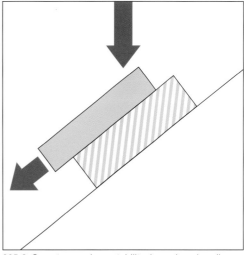

005:2 On a steeper slope, stability depends on bonding between layers.

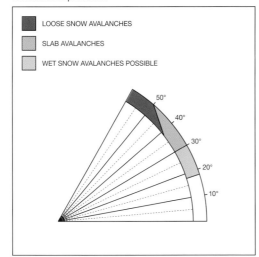

005:3 Angles for different types of avalanches.

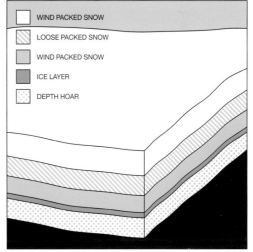

006 Example of layers in the snow.

ski because it doesn't carry the skis, no matter how wide they are. This snow forms a very weak layer when buried under a new snowfall.

MELT-FREEZE METAMORPHISM At a temperature of 0°C the snow begins to melt. Thawing increases avalanche hazard in the short term, while subsequent re-freezing solidifies and strengthens the snow pack. [See diagram 009.]

If the thawing process is strong, the high water content and melting between individual grains turn the snow into a soft and soggy slush (aka rotten snow). This creates a situation of high avalanche danger.

When the melted snow refreezes on cold nights it forms a melt-freeze crust. During the first days of this cycle this layer is going to form the worst type of skiing conditions, breakable crust. However, repeated cycles of melt and freeze

007 Rounding of snow crystals.

008 Faceting of snow crystals.

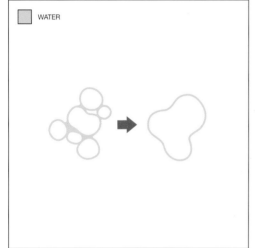

009 Melt-freeze metamorphism.

010 Greenhouse effect.

over several days lead to the development of a solid layer which carries a skier on top when frozen. From a skier's point of view this snow is not a pleasant snow to ski on when frozen (it's like a washboard) but from an avalanche hazard point of view it's very safe (like concrete). When the frozen top layer softens during the day and turns into spring snow the ski conditions become excellent for a short period of time (it could be as short as 30 minutes). Further melting (and increased water saturation) softens the entire snow pack and transforms spring snow into rotten snow that has no strength. This is a sign of very high avalanche danger!

This cycle of thawing and refreezing is typical of spring conditions but could occur at any time of the year due to warm winds (Foehn or Chinook), rain or intense solar heating on south-facing slopes.

While clouded skies reduce the intensity of the solar radiation and prevent softening of the snow pack, a thin veil of clouds results in the opposite. Almost all the energy from the sun shines through a thin veil of clouds and reaches the snow. The snow surface reflects this energy, and if the sky was clear, the reflected heat would disappear into space. But under a thin cloud cover the radiation is reflected back to the snow.

Note: The result of this greenhouse effect is that the snow pack rapidly heats up in all aspects. In the short term this will result in increased avalanche danger, but in the long term the result will be that the snow pack transforms faster into spring conditions (as long as it refreezes overnight). [See diagram 010.]

A cloud cover overnight will also reflect the earth's radiation back to the snow and may prevent the snow pack from refreezing.

MELT-FREEZE CONDITIONS FROM A SKIER'S POINT OF VIEW Plan to start the ascents early in the morning/night when the snow is frozen. Time the descent to start shortly after the snow surface has started to melt and soften.

Make sure that the snow pack is frozen all the way when you're descending from high altitude in the mountains to low altitude and warmer temperatures of the valley. It is easy to ski into a trap with very high avalanche danger due to rotten snow. When the spring snow is perfect at altitude the snow is, in general, already rotten down in the valley.

Keep track of how cold it was during the night and for how long, so you know at what altitude the snow really froze. If just the top layer froze it will fast become dangerous with the first sunlight. This is especially important if you're descending down to a lower altitude than where you spent the night.

Be careful if you're descending into a different valley that could have had a cloud cover overnight (higher temperatures and the altitude of the frozen snow limit are higher than the valley you're coming from).

WHY, WHEN & WHERE SLABS ARE FORMED

Wind is the single most important modifier of the snow pack and therefore very important for the development of hazardous avalanche conditions. The wind will pick up the snow crystals and, while being transported by the wind, the crystals will break into smaller particles from colliding with each other and the terrain. The small particles are deposited in accumulation zones such as lee slopes and depressions where they get packed close together by the wind, forming a very dense layer which rapidly bonds to form a solid and rigid layer. It can be a hard slab (which bears the weight of a person on foot) or a soft slab (which does not, but tends to break up in blocks between the skis).

LEE SLOPES It's important to remember that the aspect of a lee slope can vary around a mountain. Depending on local air currents both lee and windward sides can form on the same side of a mountain due to cross loading over ridges or wind running down the fall line. [See diagram 011.]

WINDWARD SLOPES Slopes exposed to the wind tend to receive less snow deposition. The scoured, shallow snow pack may result in the formation of depth hoar but normally the snow is firmly compacted by the wind action. [See diagram 012.]

DETERMINING WIND DIRECTION Since the wind can very rapidly increase the ava-

THE WIND TRANSPORTS
THE SNOW FROM THE
WINDWARD SIDE

AND DEPOSITS IT
ON THE LEE SIDE

011:1 Snow transport. The wind transports the snow from the windward side and deposits it on the lee side.

lanche danger even long after a snowfall, it's important to keep track of how the wind is affecting the snow pack. Wind direction is best evaluated locally by observing natural features of the terrain that are either the result of erosion or of deposition. The most important features to look for are:

BLOWING SNOW Snow plumes streaming off ridge tops in clear weather indicate strong winds at altitude. The length of the plume gives you a good idea of how much snow is being deposited on the lee slopes. Note: Just because the plume disappears doesn't necessarily mean that the wind has stopped blowing. It could just mean that there is no more snow to move from this specific ridge.

RELIABLE INDICATORS OF PAST WIND DIRECTION These show you that snow has been transported. You need to ask yourself where all the snow has been deposited. Remember that the present wind direction can be completely different.

011:2 Snow transport. The wind transports the snow from the windward side and deposits it on the lee side.

Cornices Cornices are deposits of wind-drifted snow overhanging the lee side of a ridge. They indicate past wind direction. [See diagram 013.]

Sastrugi This is the term used to describe the erosion of snow that forms a surface pattern that looks like waves. They are often very hard and unpleasant to ski on. The steep side of the sastrugi is always on the windward side. [See diagram 014.]

Snow ripples & dunes These surface ripples and dunes run perpendicular to the direction of the wind. The steep side of the dune is its leeside, the opposite of sastrugi. [See diagram 015.]

Old ski tracks Sometimes you can also see old ski tracks sticking up 30 cm above the rest of the snow. The snow in the tracks has been compressed by skiers and the surrounding snow has been transported by the wind.

Drifting Blowholes often form around trees and rocks where a long tail forms on the leeward side.

Rime Rime can be observed on any object standing above the snow surface. Rime deposits always grow into the wind. The longer the rime branches, the higher the wind speed and the heavier the deposit.

Scoured ridges When you can see the bare ground or glacier ice on a ridge you can tell that the wind has been blowing hard.

WHY, WHEN & WHERE WEAK LAYERS ARE FORMED

In addition to the conditions discussed in "faceting of snow crystals" which form very weak and unstable layers in the snow pack, we also have to consider the formation of snow crystals on the surface, known as surface hoar.

<u>SURFACE HOAR</u> This is a flaky, feathery shaped crystal that forms when the vapour in the air comes into contact with the cold surface snow.

Certain criteria are required in order for them to form:

___ Moist air.
___ Surface temperature lower than the dew point of the air.
___ Very calm and still conditions.

These conditions occur most frequently on cold, clear, frosty nights. When the first rays of the sun come over the ridge in the morning and hit the snow, the surface hoar will sparkle like diamonds in the sunlight.

During the day the sun burns off much of the surface hoar and some is destroyed by the wind. However, in shady depressions and lee slopes it keeps developing, protected from the sun and the wind. Due to the shade and subsequent low temperatures this layer persists for a long time. It forms a very weak layer when buried under new snow and this tends to occur where the formation of wind slabs is most likely.

<u>GRAUPELS</u> Graupels are rimed snow crystals with a similar appearance to hail; they also form a weak layer when buried so keep that in mind for the next snowfall if you see them on the surface.

WHY, WHEN & WHERE SLIDING SURFACES ARE FORMED
& THE ROLE OF THE ROUGHNESS OF THE GROUND

A sliding surface is one that offers little friction to anchor the snow slab. Generally, the rougher the ground surface, the more snow depth is required before avalanching will take place. Scree, rocks and boulders won't become avalanche slopes until the snow has filled and covered the irregularities. Once covered, the irregularities will help to anchor the lower levels but layers above the anchors will not be affected. [See diagram 016.]

Smooth rock or grass surfaces don't need much covering before avalanches can occur. When buried, ice crust from sun or rain forms a very good layer for the slab to slide on. A surface scoured by the wind can also provide a good sliding surface when buried. It's important to remember what the surface conditions were in different aspects and altitudes before the new snow was deposited. Also, be careful even if irregularities are showing through the snow surface. Faceted snow crystals may be present and the obstacles may provide a weakness and a starting point for slab avalanches.

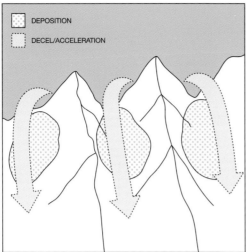

012:1 The snow is picked up in acceleration areas and deposited in deceleration areas.

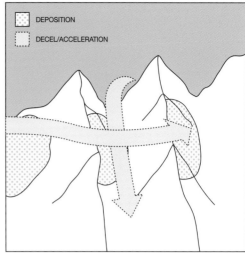

012:2 Cross loading over ridges.

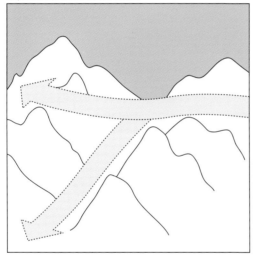

012:3 Wind direction at ground level is modified by terrain features and is therefore not necessarily the same as at altitude. Determine the wind direction by observing snow surface clues.

Note: Just because the plume disappears doesn't necessarily mean that the wind has stopped blowing. It could just mean that there is no more snow to move from this specific ridge.

WHY, WHEN & WHERE A CRITICAL BALANCE BETWEEN STRENGTH & STRESS IS FORMED

In the snow pack there is a slow downhill movement called creep. The layers in the snow pack move at different speeds. The top layers creep at a faster rate than the lower layers which move more slowly with increasing depth, friction and ground surface. The difference in the rate at which the different layers creep creates a shear stress between the layers in the snow pack. [See diagram 017.]

Static friction between snow layers opposes the shear stresses that occur in the snow pack. [See diagram 018.]

Rime on a telecommunication mast, indicating past wind direction, Åre/Sweden Photo Marcus Lindahl

Slab avalanches triggered by the person walking on the ridge Verbier/Switzerland Photo Jansci Hadik

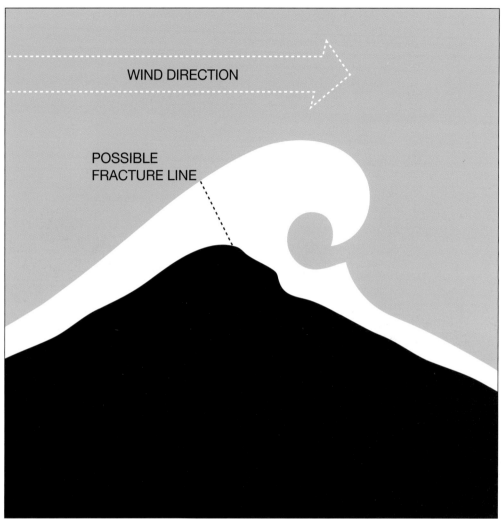

WIND DIRECTION

POSSIBLE
FRACTURE LINE

013 Cornice.

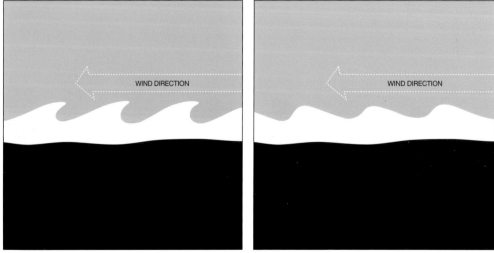

WIND DIRECTION

014 Sastrugi.

WIND DIRECTION

015 Snow dunes.

016:1 Surface roughness. Thick snow cover; buried anchoring.

016:2 Thin snow cover; visible anchoring.

016:3 Smooth surface; no anchoring.

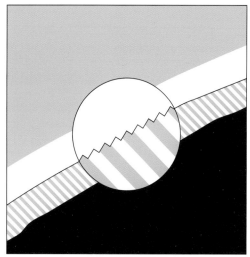

017:1 Static friction between layers.

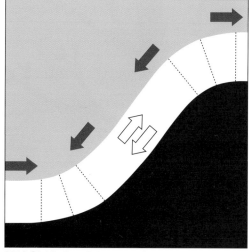

017:2 Distribution of stress on a slope.

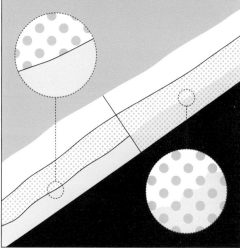

018 Varying friction within the snow pack.

Note: Sometimes you will be able to hear the pack collapse with a hollow 'whumpf', a very scary sound caused by the weak layers collapsing. It's one of the strongest warning signals you will get. If the terrain is steep enough to avalanche you're in a life-threatening situation where you must quickly evaluate your options.

HOT SPOTS The "hot spot" idea is quite theoretical but the implication is that the hitting of a hot spot may release the whole slope. The problem with hot spots is that they are hidden in the snow pack and therefore you can't see them. So this theoretical knowledge won't help you to make direct decisions in the terrain, but it will help you to understand that if you dig a snow pit to check the layers, it doesn't tell you anything else other than the snow structure of that particular point due to the irregularity of the snow pack.

Earlier in this chapter you learnt that the snow pack is not homogenous, it varies in thickness, density, layering and bonding. To complicate things further, the stresses vary greatly between different sections in a given slope depending on where there is static friction and where there are weak, layers reducing the friction. In all slopes that don't get skied regularly you will find these complicated patterns of stable and unstable zones next to each other. In areas where the bonding is weak the surrounding areas have to compensate and that creates tensions in the snow pack.

Imagine a glass plate on which there's a thin layer of flour. Then blow away the flour from parts of the plate. Take another plate and put a thin layer of glue on it and put them together. The glue will stick on the areas where there is no flour. It's the same in the mountains when for example surface hoar is buried. You will find stable areas (where the snow slab is bonding well with the layer underneath) next to weak areas with weak bonding (hot spots). [See diagram 019.]

When you ski down a slope you may cause the weak layer to collapse but since the slab is still strong enough it will stay in place. However, the tensions make the collapse spread through the snow pack and the weak layer grows. But since the strength exceeded the weight, the slab remained in place. When you have triggered enough weak spots the slab will have just enough support at the top, bottom or the flanks to support its own weight and remain in place. Now it's a trap just waiting to be triggered by the next skier. That is why it's still possible to trigger an avalanche even though there are already ski tracks on the slope. I've even seen a slope with roughly 100 ski tracks avalanche and create a fatal accident.

Sometimes you will be able to hear the pack collapse with a hollow 'whumpf', a very scary sound caused by the weak layers collapsing. It's one of the strongest warning signals you will get. If the terrain is steep enough to avalanche you're in a life-threatening situation where you must quickly evaluate your options. Normally turning back, trying to create as little force on the snow pack (think light) as possible, is the best option.

WHY, WHEN & WHERE A FAILURE OF THE SNOW SLAB OCCURS & WHAT TRIGGERS IT

In a stable snow pack, the strength of the snow is greater than the stress exerted on it.

For an avalanche to occur, something must tip the balance so that the stress on, or within, the snow pack becomes equal to, or greater than, its strength.

During a deposition of snow (snowfall, wind or both) the extra weight of the new snow causes stresses that exceed the strength of the slab. An avalanche will release naturally when a slab is unable to support its own weight but often the slab will get just enough support at the top, bottom or the flanks to remain in place waiting to be triggered by either:

An increase in load; a skier moving onto the slab, the weight of a new snowfall, a cornice collapse from above.

A decrease in strength; the collapse of a fragile layer, a ski track cutting the snow, a rise in temperature, melt water at ground level weakening anchors. An increase in load and a decrease in strength can of course appear together.

Nobody knows exactly how much extra weight you can add to a given slab before the weak layer (if there is one) underneath collapses and the slab breaks away. If you take the risk of guessing several times every day, sooner or later you will guess wrong. Instead you should try to recognise the slabs and where and how they are formed, so you can avoid them. This can be very difficult and sometimes impossible, especially after a new snowfall when the old slabs have been buried.

A lot of skiers are afraid of huge mountainsides avalanching. In general this is not difficult to avoid, as this tends to happen if the conditions are known to be very dangerous. More problematic and complex are the days when the ava-

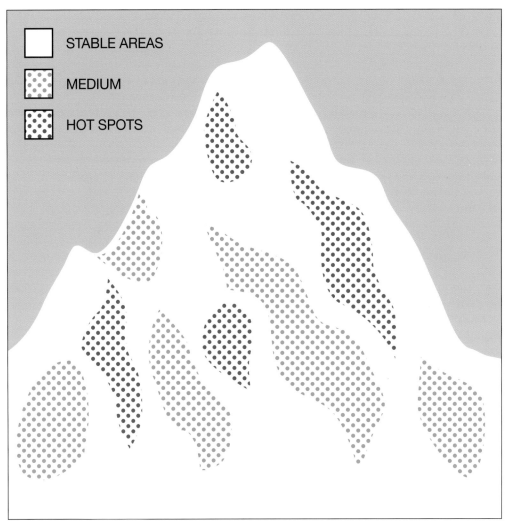

STABLE AREAS

MEDIUM

HOT SPOTS

019:1 Varying stability on a slope.

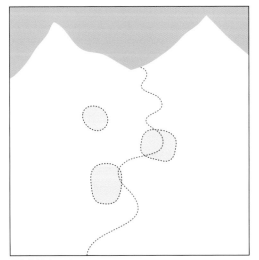

019:2 Hot spots.

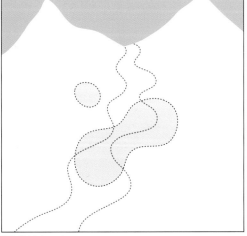

019:3 Hot spots.

019:4 Hot spots.

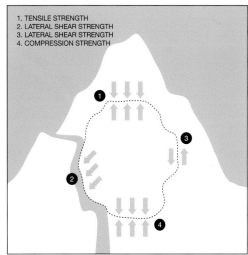

1. TENSILE STRENGTH
2. LATERAL SHEAR STRENGTH
3. LATERAL SHEAR STRENGTH
4. COMPRESSION STRENGTH

019:5 Forces that hold the snow slab.

lanche danger is known to be moderate or considerable (see the avalanche scale) and skiers start to ski steeper slopes. After a snowfall it's not enough to merely gauge how the new snow is bonding to the old, you must also consider the consequences of the added weight to the snow pack.

Suffice it to say that a group of experienced skiers making careful route choices and maintaining good group discipline is taking a much lower risk than a group of beginners who rush down the slope at the same time. Also, remember that the first person or group of persons entering the slope triggers 90% of all fatal avalanches.

TERRAIN FEATURES

Since terrain features help to build and spread stress, certain features are by their shape more exposed to avalanche hazard than others.

CONVEX SLOPES This formation favours a stress within the snow pack. Most tension usually occurs at the top of the convex slope and it is probably the most dangerous terrain feature for skiers. To be able to read the terrain when descending you often tend to ski out on to the steepest section and either stop or make a big turn to reduce the speed enough to get time to pick a line. The stop or the turn puts an extra load on the snow pack where it's already weak, causing the slab to break off behind the skier. [See diagram 020.]

CONCAVE SLOPES Concave slopes are generally considered to be safer than convex slopes. However, it favours the deposition of windblown snow. You have to be especially careful with hard slabs on small slopes. They are supported from below so cutting this support by traversing the slope while skiing or ascending on skins can cause avalanching.

GULLIES Shallow gullies on an open slope are an ideal location for slabs to form. [See diagram 021.]

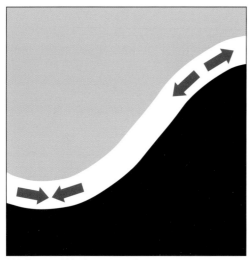

020 Stress within the snow pack on convex and concave slopes.

021 Gullies.

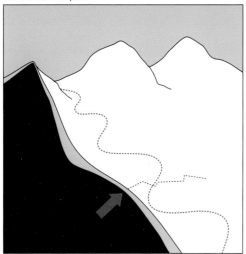

022:1 Steep, straight slopes.

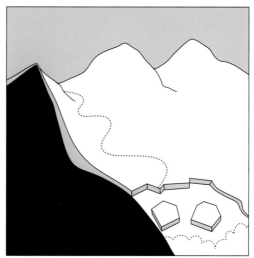

022:2 The avalanche is likely to occur where the snow pack is thin.

STEEP STRAIGHT SLOPES Uniform slopes are often the best shaped slopes to descend. However, if the slope is avalanche hazardous, it's often difficult to predict where a fracture may occur. Avalanches will often start at some discontinuity in the slope, such as exposed rocks. [See diagram 022.]

TERRAIN-TRAPS

Terrain-traps are features that make the consequences of an otherwise relatively small avalanche severe. With some common sense they are fairly easy to detect. Ask yourself: What would happen if an avalanche occurred here? [See diagram 023.]

A couple of years ago I was digging out a young skier who triggered a 10x5 metre wide and 40 cm deep soft slab avalanche on a 15 metre high slope next to a flat groomed piste. He landed on the piste with all of the snow on top of him. Luckily enough we happened to ski by and could dig him out in 3—4 minutes. I was surprised to see that such a small slope next to the piste could produce such an avalanche. The seriousness of the situation even with such a small amount of snow was due to the presence of a terrain-trap, in this case flat ground. It resulted in a fairly deep burial.

LIKELY TRIGGER POINTS

Some features of the terrain concentrate stresses in the snow pack and are therefore often the starting point for avalanches. [See diagram 024.]

SLOPE ANGLES

Most slab avalanches occur on 30—45° slopes with 38° as the most common angle.

Note: In order to assess avalanche terrain it's important to be able to estimate the angle of a slope's steepest section.

If you feel that conditions are not very stable and decide to ski a lower angled slope (under 30°), even a few degrees more or less can be important. In these conditions you don't want to ski down to the steepest section of the slope and start to measure the angle with an inclinometer or different, dubious ski pole techniques. If you're not experienced enough to estimate the angle you can check from the top of the slope with the inclinometer on your compass. [See diagram 025.] But the most efficient way in the long term is to develop a feeling for the steepness, so you can, by just looking at the slope, estimate the angle. With this experience you can make safe route choices and avoid critical terrain while skiing.

The best way to develop this skill is to ski in stable conditions and periodically have a guess at how steep the slope is and then check the answer with an inclinometer. The basic rule is to be able to tell if a certain slope is steeper or flatter than 30°.

There are a few tips when it comes to estimating the steepness: 25° is the approximate point at which you start making switchbacks to save energy when skinning uphill. 30° is the angle at which slopes become fun to ski in deep powder.

Note: Keep it simple; estimate only the angle of the steepest section that is relevant to the line you want to ski.

In very unstable conditions you can ski in low-angled terrain and from there still trigger avalanches on steeper terrain above you. Remember that even avalanches on small, steep sections can have serious consequences. If you're skiing a couloir, note that the sides in a couloir are steeper than the fall line in the middle.

SLOPE USE

This is a very important term that changes a lot of the factors we have been discussing. When a slope is frequently skied, skiers are constantly cutting up the layers and compressing the snow pack to a homogenous, almost groomed slope. This happens on all the standard runs of all aspects in all the major ski resorts.

023:1 Terrain-traps. Dense forest.

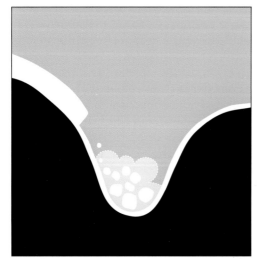

023:2 Steep-sided valleys.

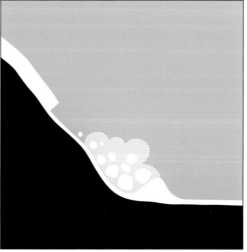

023:3 Plateaus and benches.

023:4 Crevasses.

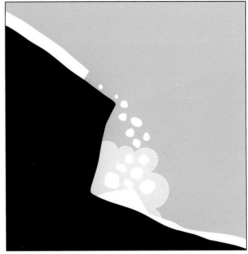

023:5 Cliffs.

This means that you only have to worry about how the additional snow sticks to the old and not what the extra weight does to the layers farther down in the snow pack. However, this only applies where the slope has been regularly skied, as soon as you go outside that area by even a few metres you're back to all the problems of different layers, hot spots and so on.

Note: Don't apply your knowledge of snow pack stability in proximity to a ski resort (where the runs get skied after every snowfall) to the mountains when ski touring, or even when you're skiing runs that are less frequented.

Be careful after storms or strong winds, even if a slope gets skied frequently, as it can still produce a large avalanche in the top layers.

NEW SNOW & AVALANCHE HAZARD

In the section about snow slabs you learnt how wind affects the snow and creates an increased avalanche danger due to the formation of slabs. Another important factor is the temperature during the snowfall. 10 cm of snow that falls during high temperatures weighs more (due to the higher content of water) than 10 cm of snow that falls in cold temperatures, and the extra weight affects the snow pack differently.

Even after a snowfall with no wind and cold temperatures the avalanche danger increases, not only from the added weight to the snow pack but also due to the bonding of the new snow to the old surface. Avalanche danger has to be considered when new snow accumulation reaches 20—30 cm or more. The danger normally lasts for two or three days before the fresh snow bonds to the surface.

The amount of fresh snow needed to affect the avalanche danger is much higher during favourable conditions than unfavourable conditions.

Favourable conditions are low winds or little wind loading. The temperature should be around freezing when snowfall starts (and decreasing). A stable snow pack at base, such as frequently skied slopes. In these conditions, you will find powder snow which bonds well with a stable snow pack. The critical amount of fresh snow is 30—60 cm.

024:1 Likely trigger points. Convex slopes.

024:2 Trees.

024:3 Rock outcrops.

024:4 Corniche.

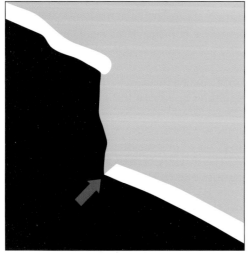

024:5 Base of a cliff.

Note. In order to assess avalanche terrain it's important to be able to estimate the angle of a slope's steepest section. [See diagram 025.]

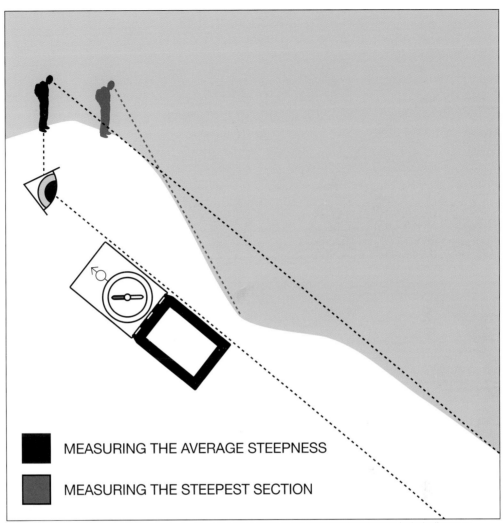

MEASURING THE AVERAGE STEEPNESS

MEASURING THE STEEPEST SECTION

025 Measuring steepness; one person looks along the edge of the compass while the other reads the inclinometer.

Unfavourable conditions are high winds more than 10 m/sec, with temperatures below −8°C (increasing during the snow fall). Surface hoar on top of a layer of icy crust or hard snow, such as on rarely skied slopes. In these conditions, you will find heavy snow slabs on top of a perfect sliding surface with a weak layer of surface hoar and dry snow in between. The critical amount of new snow is 10–20 cm.

Deposition rate The general rule during a snowfall is, the faster the snow is deposited, the higher the hazard. During an intense snowfall the snow pack has less time to adjust to the extra weight than when the same weight is added over a much longer time. That is why the risk factor of triggering avalanches during an intense snowfall is much more important. An intense snowfall is 3–5 cm per hour and in extreme situations more than 10 cm. The intensity has no relevance a couple of days after the snowfall. Big dumps (100–150 cm) will drastically increase the level of avalanche danger in the short term and the more snow, the greater the danger. However the weight of the snow consolidates the snow pack rapidly after the snowfall.

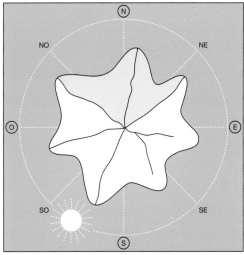

026 The sun's effect on the aspect of the slope.

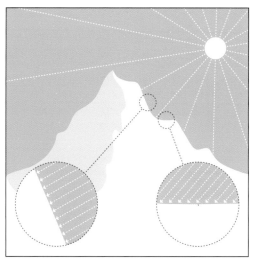

027 Orientation to the sun.

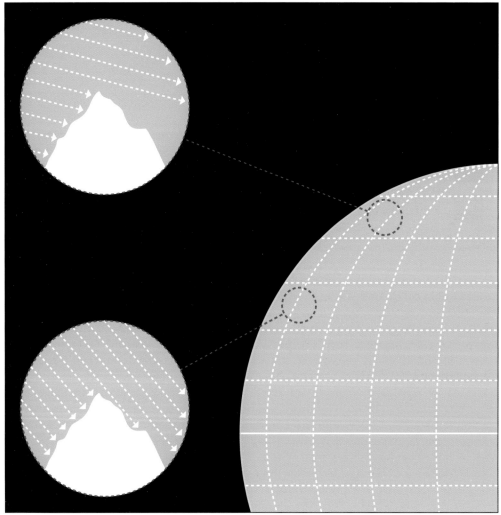

028 The importance of latitude.

Note: New snow increases the avalanche hazard and that the amount of fresh snow can vary with altitude and aspect.

Be careful on a powder day when you start to ski runs of different aspects and altitudes. Not only does the layering in the old snow pack change but you may have skied all day at low altitude where the snow wasn't affected by the wind.

The added weight from a snowfall affects the snow pack. 10 cm of fresh snow falling during high temperatures can be the same weight as 50 cm of snow falling during low temperatures.

ASPECT (SLOPE ORIENTATION)

Snow conditions are greatly influenced by the aspect of the slope. The aspect is the compass direction of the slope's face when you're standing on the top and looking down its fall line. If you're standing on the top of a south-facing slope at midday you will have the sun in your face. [See diagram 026.]

Orientation to the sun The sun moves lower across the sky in the winter than in the summer. On 21 December, the sun reaches its lowest point. After that date the days become longer as the sun rises higher over the horizon. 21 June is the longest day of the year; the sun has reached its highest position and now it begins to sink again.

How much heat a snow surface gains from the sun is dependent on the direction it faces, the angle of the slope, its latitude and season. Since how the snow settles and changes depends on temperature, it's important to know a slope's aspect. Even in mid-winter when the sun is low in the sky and air temperatures are below 0°C, a steep south-facing slope receives strong radiation because it faces the sun at almost a right angle. During the same period a north-facing slope receives no radiation. [See diagram 027.]

South-facing slopes These receive the most solar radiation and therefore rounding of the snow crystals occurs faster than on other slopes. Stabilization and settlement is more rapid and for these reasons (not taking into account other factors such as wind and terrain), south-facing slopes tend to be the safest during mid-winter. As spring approaches with warmer days, the previously safe slopes now become very dangerous and melting can result in wet snow avalanches.

North-facing slopes These receive little or no sunlight in mid-winter and are therefore subject to maximum cooling that favours the formation of faceted snow crystals and surface hoar. Stabilization and settlement is slow and avalanche danger due to layering lasts for long periods (the greater part of the season). By spring the conditions are reversed, north-facing slopes generally provide a safe route from wet snow avalanches when south faces are dangerous (as long as you ski at an altitude higher than that at which freezing took place).

East- and west-facing slopes These slopes will exhibit characteristics somewhere between south- and north-facing aspects.

Especially from early winter until midwinter when the sun is very low on the horizon, these aspects will have different snow conditions in localised areas due to the long shadows cast by even small features of the terrain. You can have well settled south-facing conditions on one side of a ridge and unsettled north-facing on the other side. Later in the winter, west-facing slopes tend to be a bit safer than east due to the heat in the afternoon. East-facing slopes are also subject to the sun but at the coldest time of the day.

Latitude While it is always important to consider slope aspect in the lower latitudes (30–55°) it is not as important farther north during mid-winter when the sun is low or under the horizon. [See diagram 028.]

By spring and early summer the days are much longer at higher latitudes and the snow pack receives more radiation than farther south.

Particularly dangerous aspects Around 75% of fatal avalanche accidents occur on slopes facing northwest, north or east. 60% of all those fatalities occur in the north sector (northwest to northeast). [See diagram 029.]

Note: A slope's orientation to the sun and wind (see formation of slabs) is very important when considering avalanche hazard and trying to find good skiing conditions.

If there is enough radiation for melting, sun crust will form during the night when the melted layer freezes. On steep south-facing slopes the snow will transform faster providing excellent skiing conditions (spring snow), while slopes less angled or east- or west-facing still offer breakable crust.

Due to different features of the terrain, you can ski different orientations to the general aspect of the slope. Make sure that this is from choice and not because you have been forced to by poor route choice.

REGIONAL CHARACTERISTICS OF THE SNOW PACK & AVALANCHE DANGER

The general climate of a region plays a major role in snow pack stability and its general characteristics. You can roughly distinguish between two major types of snow pack; the continental and the maritime. These are the two extremes at each end of the scale but nature is of course never that simple and predictable. So keep in mind that any mixed form of climatic conditions and snow pack can occur. Therefore instead of learning too many general rules, develop and use your snow sense/knowledge of what triggers and controls the different processes in the snow. With greater understanding you can adapt to conditions anywhere in the world.

CONTINENTAL SNOW PACK Areas with cold, sunny and relatively dry winters are usually characterised by shallow and unstable snow packs. These conditions are found far from the oceans in the continental zone and here you will find the dry and light snow (Champagne powder) that most skiers dream about. The shallow snow pack in combination with the cold temperatures give a complex snow pack with a multitude of hidden weak layers. Depth hoar and surface hoar is very common here and weak layers are long-lasting. Avalanches may occur many days after the last snowfall. Early and mid-winter are the most dangerous seasons. Avalanches in February/March may slide on weak layers that formed in November/December. Spring is safer due to warmer temperatures and deeper snow pack. The general avalanche hazard can vary greatly from winter to winter depending on temperatures and snow depth in early winter. Continental areas such as the Central Alps and the Colorado Rockies lead the statistics in avalanche deaths.

Note: In a continental zone, you should remember to judge how the new snow is bonding to the old, and consider what the consequences are of the added weight to the snow pack.

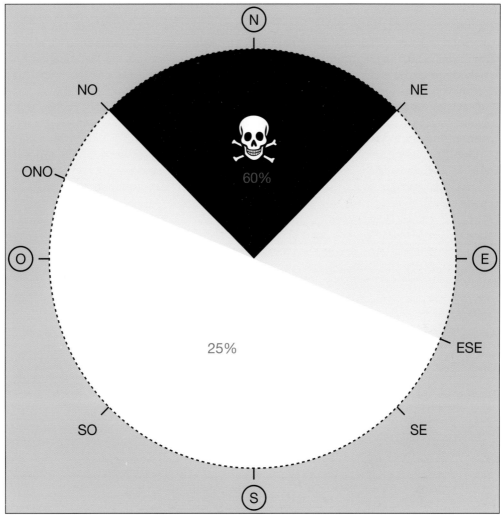

029 Distribution of fatal accidents according to slope aspect.

MARITIME SNOW PACK Areas with relatively mild winter temperatures that receive high amounts of precipitation are usually characterised by deep and stable snow packs. These conditions are found in coastal mountain ranges. Avalanches generally release naturally during or after storms. In general, avalanche hazard is not persistent over extended periods of time. At mild temperatures the moist and heavy snow normally bonds well with the old, rather homogenous snow pack (that's why most of the steep ski descents in the Alps are made late in the season, often as late as May and June).

Rain is common and wet snow avalanches occur throughout the ski season. Weak layers often occur in new snow and are caused by temperature changes during a storm. The avalanches most often slide on ice crust caused by sun or rain.

In good conditions it is possible to ski very steep slopes that it wouldn't be possible to ski in the shallow and less stable continental snow pack.

Note: Even in a maritime snow pack the general rules apply; cold temperatures and shallow snow packs favour the formation of depth hoar. The more new snow the higher the avalanche danger (especially if it falls on icy crust).

THE SKIER'S CONCLUSION Remember that depth and stability of the snow pack vary with season, altitude, aspect and terrain. Winters and regions with thin snow cover and cold temperatures are more dangerous to skiers. Rocks, bushes and trees are weak points in the snow cover since loose packed snow favours the formation of facets.

The snow is weak when water is present but very strong when frozen. New snow increases avalanche danger.

When you doubt snow stability, stay on ridges and on fairly flat ground (less than 30°) to play safe. Different terrain features on any given slope mean that there is a variety of different orientations available to ski on.

Last but certainly not least: A slope is not safe just because there are ski tracks on it.

004

AVALANCHE HAZARD EVALUATION

For the last two days, I had been monitoring and analysing the weather forecasts to decide if it would be possible to bring my clients on a run down to a small village called Fionnay.

I knew that under the right circumstances the spring snow would be excellent. But I was also worried that it wouldn't freeze sufficiently overnight, or that we wouldn't be fast enough while it was still frozen.

From the top of Mont-Fort, you ski some way down the backside before putting on skins and hiking for roughly an hour to reach the top of a vertical 1500 metre descent. From here you can choose aspects from east to west, and that's what makes it such an excellent run in spring conditions. However, the last bit down is a south-west facing couloir, and for the very last 200 vertical metres, you have to ski through lots of old avalanche debris. Above that, on one side, there's a south-east facing slope from which everything that falls – snow, ice or rocks – will end up in the couloir. On the other side, there are icefalls that collapse in the springtime, sending down huge blocks of ice. And to top it off, in the couloir – in which you have to spend a considerable period of time – there's no quick escape. So, timing is everything.

Early that morning, I checked my thermometer for the lowest temperature reading of the night. I noticed that the snow outside the house – which is at the same altitude and aspect as the end of the run – was frozen solid. So I decided to give it a go.

I knew we had no time to lose, because the temperature rises quickly in the springtime. But this would not be a big issue, as the two women I was supposed to ski with were my fittest clients, as regards both skinning uphill and skiing down.

While we were going up with the first cable, I met two ski bum acquaintances. They told me they had planned to do exactly the same run, and I *reminded them that they should do it quickly. Which they said they would.*

Anyway, my clients and I kept up very good speed, both when skiing down the back of Mont-Fort and skinning up. As soon as we got up there, we took off the skins and had a little sip of water and a quick snack, before skiing all the way down to the valley in one go. By 11.20, we had already passed the couloir. The spring snow was close to perfect all the way, with no rotten snow, even at the bottom. We did see some big chunks of ice in the couloir, and a lot more was sure to come later as it was getting warmer very quickly. But for us, the timing was excellent.

Happy about this accomplishment, we had a drink in the sun and waited around for the taxi to arrive. After more than an hour, there was still no sign of my ski bum friends. I figured they had changed their plans.

Later that afternoon in Verbier, I ran into one of the "lost ski bums". To my surprise, and rising anger, she told me that they had indeed done the same run as us – after having had a long picnic at the top before doing it!

I could not believe my ears. This girl, with all her years of skiing experience – had she not put two and two together when she saw the ice chunks in the couloir and the icefalls on the side?

It struck me how differently things can be evaluated, and how time is such a decisive factor. I had been hesitating nervously for more than 24 hours, and when we finally did the run, we did it quickly. My friends on the other hand, had been totally relaxed about the whole thing, and – I had to confess – had had just as good skiing as us. So was I being paranoid? Or had they taken a much bigger risk? There are of course no black or white answers, but in my opinion it was the latter. Of course, usually you get away with it. But the day you don't, all your problems are bound to come at the same time. That's why you should always make sure to have the odds – and if possible the timing – in your favour.

Statistics show that 90% of fatal avalanche accidents are triggered by the victims, or someone in the same group as the victims. So we have to assume responsibility for our actions and acknowledge that avalanche accidents are directly related to our decisions, and are not a random coincidence. The problem is that because of complex and poorly understood inter-relationships between different factors, it's impossible to tell with 100% accuracy whether an avalanche is going to occur or not.

When we acknowledge that it's impossible to be certain whether a slope is safe or not, we can either choose to stop skiing on terrain that could produce an avalanche (off-piste slopes steeper than 20°) or we have to accept that skiing in the mountains involves a certain risk. By analysing the information we try to judge the avalanche hazard as accurately as possible, and then make decisions according to our risk acceptance.

SNOW PITS

Snow pits provide a very good way of learning more about snow and its processes. It's a useful method for developing your snow sense. I recommend everyone to hire a mountain guide or attend a course to do this, but I've never actually dug a snow pit to judge avalanche hazard myself. As discussed in 'hot spots', a snow pit doesn't tell you anything other than the condition of the snow pack where you're digging. You would have to dig 12 snow pits in different places, aspects and altitudes and then analyse the results to judge effectively, and by then the day would be over. It's common sense that if you're worried about a slope then you don't ski down to the most critical point on the slope, take off your skis and start to dig a snow pit to decide whether to ski it or not. If you are so uncertain about the stability of the slope that you feel the need to dig a snow pit, then you already have your answer — don't ski!

THE AIM

As mentioned before, hazard evaluation is an ongoing process in which information must be gathered continuously and any evaluation or forecast upgraded with every new clue. To be able to do that you have to understand the mountain environment and its processes, as discussed in the previous chapter. Without understanding this, there's no way you can adapt to the mountains, make an evaluation of the avalanche hazard, or base your decisions on anything other than luck.

The art is to observe and put together as many pieces of the puzzle as possible to see the whole picture in detail. Gather information before you leave home.

When on the mountain, look for recent avalanche activity, rapid settling of the snow pack, or cracks on the surface. Observe weather and wind. Feel the snow with your skis to detect any changes to hardness or texture. Keep your eyes open and senses alert. Collect as much information as you can.

The experienced skier depends largely on "feel". This is the "feel" of the snow beneath the skis and a "sense" of the terrain. Experience enables you to anticipate potential problems. This is not the same thing as having a good feeling about everything all the time; never querying conditions and decisions is a sign of lack of experience.

When you start to learn something new, you may experience information over-load. Then you need to find a structure and system to make sense of it. Here is a framework that you can follow to make hazard evaluation and problem avoidance easier to understand. If you spend enough time on the mountains, this process will become second nature. The framework shouldn't be followed blindly, but if used with an understanding of the information in the snow and avalanche chap-ter, it will help with decision-making and in developing your snow sense.

The framework is designed to work both for ski touring (backcountry skiing) and off-piste skiing. This can be especially demanding in a large ski resort where you may ski between six and ten runs on different aspects and at different altitudes during a single day. Conditions change all the time, and to get as much good, safe skiing as possible out of your day, you have to be able to make quick decisions and assess the whole picture.

This framework is based on a series of questions that need answering for both high and low altitudes, and the four general aspects. For every question there is an answer box, the colours of which range from green to red.

If all the factors are coloured green to yellow, then the conditions are stable and there is no need to have a limit for the steepness of the slope you choose to ski. You should have a map that gives you a reasonable idea as to where it is safe to ski and where it is not. Next, add the human factor to the equation, and choose the appropriate terrain to ski.

The same questions are asked three times; prior to a trip or ski day, out on the mountain, and before you ski. Remember that in each geographical snow area some information is of greater importance than other information, and this will vary as the season progresses. Inspiration for this framework has come from the work of mountain guides, Werner Munter and Marcus Landrö.

PRIOR TO A TRIP OR A SKI DAY This is homework. This is where you collect informa-tion so you can avoid problems. [See Prior to a trip.]

Explanation of the different categories.
Avalanche bulletin The AB provides information concerning current avalanche dan-ger and expected conditions. The level for an area is based on information col-lected at various locations by experts and at weather stations. A national or local avalanche centre deciphers all the information and publishes an avalanche bul-letin. The avalanche bulletin is available on the Internet and by phone. It is often also posted near the lifts and in mountain huts. A five level danger rating sys-tem is used in Europe and in the US and Canada. This is based on the stability of the snow pack and the degree of probability of triggering a slide.

The AB is a very important source of information, especially for planning a trip or ski day, but bear in mind that it is a forecast of expected conditions and not a one hundred per cent guarantee. There is always a risk that it might be wrong locally, especially if the area covered by the forecast is large. The fore-cast can give you a general picture and be a rough guideline, but it will never give you the answer as to whether or not to ski a certain slope. It is just one of the clues to help you. The decision has to be made by you. Bear in mind that this is not an exact science, and because of the human factor, a level 3 in your local

PRIOR TO A TRIP! – General information/expectations

AVALANCHE BULLETIN

FRESH SNOW
- [ ] Total amount of fresh snow?
- [ ] Is the fresh snow bonding with the old?
- [ ] Time after last snowfall?
- [ ] Has the snow settled?
- [ ] Is the snow deposited by wind?
- [ ] Can the weight of the new snow create a critical balance?
- [ ] Forecast for more snow?

THE SNOW PACK – *The seasonal history of the snow pack*
- [ ] Old, unstable layers?
- [ ] Slope use?

THE WIND – *Has/is or will snow be deposited*
- [ ] Recent activity?
- [ ] Current?
- [ ] Forecast?

TEMPERATURE
- [ ] Temperature at snowfall/snow deposition
- [ ] Temperature history after snowfall
- [ ] Current/general temperature
- [ ] General/forecast temperature
- [ ] Forecast for aspect, is there a time factor?

SNOW SURFACE
- [ ] Has old surface hoar been burried?
- [ ] Does the old snow surface provide a good sliding layer?
- [ ] Is the surface frozen?

Ask the questions in the framework for east, south, west and north in both high and low altitude. Then continue to the human factor and let the experience and ability of the group decide which terrain to choose. Remember to always choose an alternative, thus providing yourself with a back up plan.

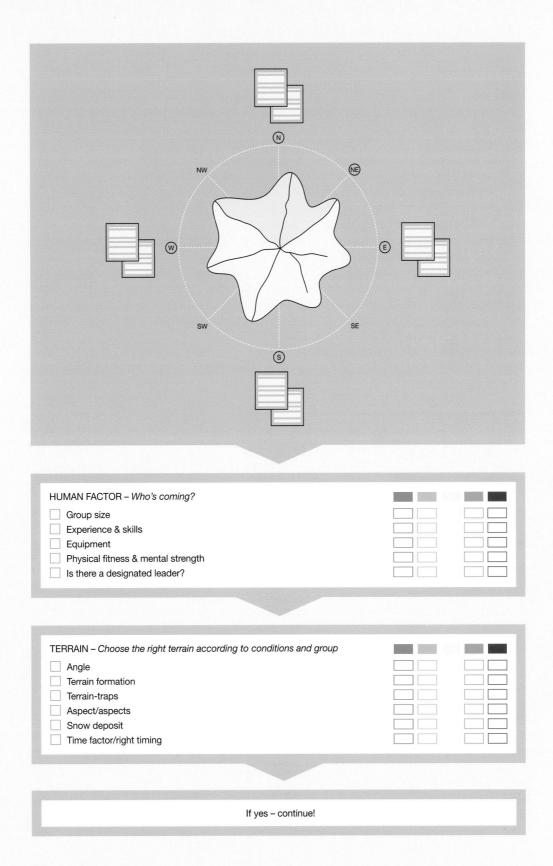

HUMAN FACTOR – *Who's coming?*

- ☐ Group size
- ☐ Experience & skills
- ☐ Equipment
- ☐ Physical fitness & mental strength
- ☐ Is there a designated leader?

TERRAIN – *Choose the right terrain according to conditions and group*

- ☐ Angle
- ☐ Terrain formation
- ☐ Terrain-traps
- ☐ Aspect/aspects
- ☐ Snow deposit
- ☐ Time factor/right timing

If yes – continue!

area could be slightly different to a level 3 in other areas. Therefore, when you are skiing in a new area start out carefully and get a "feel" for the local rating system. [See Avalanche hazard scale.]

Fresh snow Get the details from the AB and the weather forecast. Information on the amount of fresh snow that has fallen is a pay-service that you can obtain in many places. You can receive the information via the Internet or over the telephone.

Ask local experts (mountain guides, pisteurs, etc.) for information, but remember you are getting personal opinions. Conditions change quickly in the mountains and information about stability can become out of date quickly.

The snow pack Try to discover the seasonal history of the snow pack by reading the detailed information in the AB. Ask local experts.

Wind Find out about recent weather changes and weather forecasts. Check whether snow has been deposited, or will be.

Temperature Check recent weather changes and weather forecasts. Is there a certain time during the day when the temperature factor moves from green to red?

Snow surface By thinking about information you have about the snow pack and weather history, you should be able to answer these questions. If not, go back to the same sources as before.

Human factor Who are you skiing with?

Terrain Choose the right terrain according to conditions and the group. Have alternatives ready.

<u>**PERSONAL OBSERVATIONS ON SITE**</u> Collecting information begins in the morning with the latest available weather forecast and AB, then what you have observed on your way to the lift, then when you're up the mountain, and what you feel under your skis. Talk to people you meet and collect more information from their experiences. This continues all day until you're home again, then you have a lot of first-hand information to use the next day. [See Personal observations on site.]

Explanation of the different categories.

Avalanche bulletin Is the AB correct? Be very careful before downgrading the AB yourself. Play safe.

Fresh snow Make your own observations, using all your senses.

The snow pack Keep observing all day, in all directions, both when skiing and when on the lifts.

Visibility This is very important! If you are unable to see or choose your line you must stick to the most stable conditions. Apart from the avalanche danger it's easy to get injured when you can't see the features of the terrain, and it may be impossible to mount a rescue.

Wind Look for all the signs of recent and present wind activity (see when, where and how snow slabs are formed).

Temperature Check for temperature change continuously. Why is snow starting to fall off the trees? Why are sloughs starting to come down from the steep faces? Are your skis starting to sink through wet snow? Notice the warmth of the sun on your face, etc.

Snow surface Information through observation and the "feel" under your skis.

Human factor Did anyone extra team up along the way? Did everyone really remember to bring the equipment and is it working? Don't ski with people who don't have the right equipment. If someone forgot their transceiver then they can't

AVALANCHE HAZARD SCALE

DEGREE OF HAZARD	SNOW PACK STABILITY	AVALANCHE PROBABILITY	STATISTICS
1. LOW	The snow pack is generally well bonded and stable.	Triggering is possible only with high additional loads on a few very steep slopes. Only a few small natural avalanches (sloughs) possible.	Statistically 1/5 of the winter season. Approximately 7% of the off-piste and ski touring victims.
2. MODERATE	The snow pack is moderately well bonded on some steep slopes, otherwise generally well bonded.	Triggering is possible with high additional loads, particularly on the steep slopes indicated in the bulletin. Large natural avalanches not likely.	A bit less than half of the days during the winter. Approximately 34% of the off-piste and ski touring victims.
3. CONSIDERABLE	The snow pack is moderately to weakly bonded on many steep slopes.	Triggering is possible, sometimes even with low additional loads. The bulletin may indicate many slopes which are particularly affected. In certain conditions, medium and occasionally large sized natural avalanches may occur.	Around 1/3 of the days during the winter. Approximately 47% of the off-piste and ski touring victims.
4. HIGH	The snow pack is weakly bonded in most places.	Triggering is probable even with low additional loads on many steep slopes. In some conditions, frequent medium or large sized natural avalanches are likely.	Just a few days per winter, roughly one day per month. Approximately 12% of the off-piste and ski touring victims.
5. VERY HIGH	The snow pack is generally weakly bonded and largely unstable.	Numerous large natural avalanches are likely, even on moderately steep terrain.	Very rare, on an average basis one day per winter. No victims during off-piste or ski touring.

– A low additional load would typically be a single skier or walker.
– High additional load might include a group of skiers.
– Steep slopes – slopes with an incline of more than 30°.
– Natural – without human assistance.

PERSONAL OBSERVATIONS ON SITE – Continuous evaluation of information

AVALANCHE BULLETIN

☐ Is it correct?

FRESH SNOW

☐ Total amount of fresh snow?
☐ Is the fresh snow bonding with the old?
☐ Time after last snowfall?
☐ Has the snow settled?
☐ Is the snow deposited by wind?
☐ Can the weight of the new snow create a critical balance in the snow pack?
☐ Forecast for more snow?

THE SNOW PACK – *The seasonal history of the snow pack*

☐ Old, unstable layers?
☐ Slope use?
☐ Past avalanche activity
☐ Recent avalanche activity

VISIBILITY

☐ Current
☐ Forecast

THE WIND – *Has/is or will snow be deposited*

☐ Recent activity?
☐ Current?
☐ Forecast?

TEMPERATURE

☐ Current temperature
☐ General forecast for the day
☐ Aspect forecast for the day
☐ Is there a time factor?

SNOW SURFACE

☐ Formation of slabs
☐ Cracks in the snow
☐ Is the surface frozen?

Ask the questions in the framework for east, south, west and north in both high and low altitude. Then continue to the human factor and let the experience and ability of the group decide which terrain to choose. Remember to always choose an alternative, thus providing yourself with a back up plan.

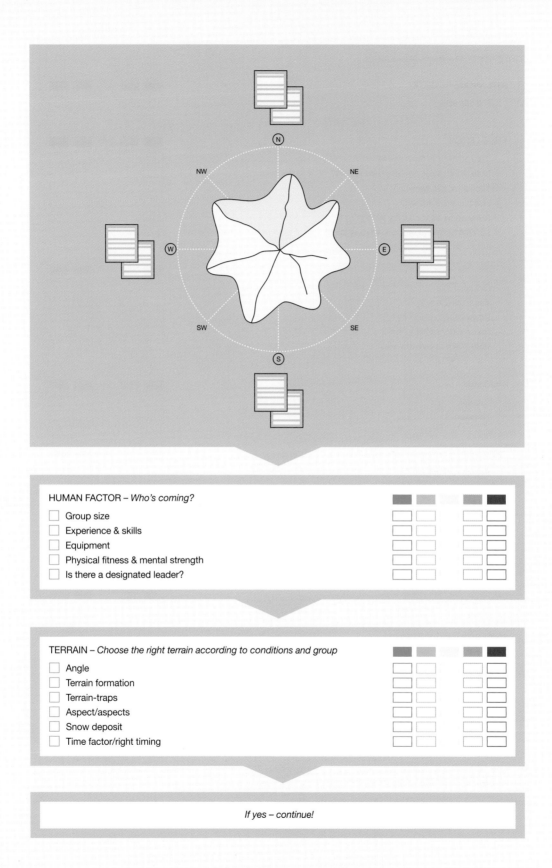

HUMAN FACTOR – *Who's coming?*

- [ ] Group size
- [ ] Experience & skills
- [ ] Equipment
- [ ] Physical fitness & mental strength
- [ ] Is there a designated leader?

TERRAIN – *Choose the right terrain according to conditions and group*

- [ ] Angle
- [ ] Terrain formation
- [ ] Terrain-traps
- [ ] Aspect/aspects
- [ ] Snow deposit
- [ ] Time factor/right timing

If yes – continue!

LAST CHECK! – Decision! – PART 1

AVALANCHE BULLETIN

- [ ] Is it correct?

FRESH SNOW

- [ ] Total amount of fresh snow?
- [ ] Is the fresh snow bonding with the old?
- [ ] Time after last snowfall?
- [ ] Has the snow settled?
- [ ] Is the snow deposited by wind?
- [ ] Can the weight of the new snow create a critical balance?

THE SNOW PACK

- [ ] Old, unstable layers?
- [ ] Slope use?
- [ ] Past avalanche activity?
- [ ] Recent avalanche activity?
- [ ] Rapid settling of snow pack

VISIBILITY

- [ ] Current
- [ ] Forecast

THE WIND

- [ ] Past/recent activity?
- [ ] Current?

TEMPERATURE

- [ ] Current temperature
- [ ] Correct timing for the whole run. Altitude/aspect

SNOW SURFACE

- [ ] Tracks
- [ ] Slabs
- [ ] Cracks in the snow
- [ ] Is the surface frozen?

Continue with the Human factor and Terrain!

HUMAN FACTOR

People above or below	☐	☐	☐	☐
Group size	☐	☐	☐	☐
Experience & skills	☐	☐	☐	☐
Equipment	☐	☐	☐	☐
Physical fitness & mental strength	☐	☐	☐	☐
Is there a designated leader?	☐	☐	☐	☐

TERRAIN

Angle	☐	☐	☐	☐
Terrain formation	☐	☐	☐	☐
Terrain-traps	☐	☐	☐	☐
Aspect/aspects	☐	☐	☐	☐
Snow deposit	☐	☐	☐	☐
Time factor/right timing	☐	☐	☐	☐

If you have a positive feeling after the questions have been answered, ski with group discipline and expose only one team member at a time.

come, or the whole group skis the piste instead.

Terrain Is the choice of terrain still correct according to local observations and the human factor? What are the alternatives?

LAST CHECK & DECISION When you are standing at the top of the slope, go carefully through the various factors one last time. [See Last check.]

If you have a positive feeling after you have answered all the questions, expose only one team member at a time when you ski.

005

SKIING

As long as you keep using your common sense and follow the rules, it's always a good idea not to follow the herd. Just like one day not too long ago, in my hometown Verbier.

It had been snowing heavily for two days. The weather was very cold, with thick clouds and almost zero visibility. In spite of that, most people still took the lifts up to the higher altitudes and were fighting each other for the powder. We didn't. And that turned out to be the first of two great decisions we made that day.

In the morning, we were almost alone among the trees. In waist-deep powder. And perfect visibility. In other words; the skiing conditions were epic.

Then, when it cleared up in the afternoon, other skiers started to follow our lead. But again, we avoided the crowds and stress by going in the opposite direction; we got on the lifts to the higher altitudes, above the tree line. And once again, we were all alone with indescribable skiing. We started with a nice, long descent, put on our skins and hiked for less than an hour – giving us another long, untracked run all the way down to the valley. The smiles stayed on our faces until we went to bed that night.

In short, the conveniences of a ski resort in combination with ski touring equipment. We got so much great skiing out of that day, thanks to the regular lifts and just a little bit of skinning. Sometimes you find that a bit of unconventional thinking will get you a lot further than following everybody else.

And that what you're looking for might just be under your nose.

This chapter assesses gear and tactics used when skiing off-piste from lifts in a ski resort.

EQUIPMENT

CLOTHES Your clothes are supposed to keep you warm and dry. The most efficient way of doing this is to dress in layers, adding a layer when you are cold and stripping off a layer when you are warm. Avoid overheating and sweating too much, it will make you wet from the inside.

All major ski-clothing brands have their own named fabrics. Choice is personal, but cotton should be avoided. Cotton is comfortable, but it absorbs sweat and does not dry quickly, so it does not keep you warm.

Base layer Your body regulates its temperature during exercise by sweating. If you do not get rid of this moisture, the body will over-cool once you stop working.

There are two different approaches for choosing the fabric for the base layer. Either choose a man-made fabric that prevents the body from over-cooling by wicking the moisture away from the skin. Or choose some form of wool that will still keep you warm when wet. Wool can be itchy, but as a bonus it tends not to become smelly. This is of extra benefit if you intend to spend a few nights in a tent or a mountain hut.

Socks should be fairly thin, to give better control when you're skiing. One tip is to pull up the legs of your long johns to just below the knee and then pull your socks up. You then avoid the seam rubbing your shin under pressure from the ski boot.

Middle layer This layer has to cope with the moisture from the base layer, and therefore it has to keep you warm. Choice of fabric is personal but its thickness depends on how cold it will be, and how intense the exercise will be. In this layer, a wind-stopper is best avoided if you want it to breath efficiently (let out the moisture). Especially during intense work, when you take off your shell layer and the middle layer becomes your top layer. If it's windy, just take off the middle layer and wear the shell over the base layer.

When it's cold it is a good idea to wear a pair of knee length fleece shorts (over the long johns). They will keep your ski muscles warm between runs, and help you relax in those chair lifts.

Shells The shell should be both waterproof and breathable. Therefore it should contain a membrane that allows sweat to pass out but prevents larger raindrops from entering. There are several brands, Gore-Tex is the most well known. That's why items of shell clothing are often referred to as Gore-Tex jacket or trousers.

The jacket should be lightweight and have a sturdy hood. Make sure that the jacket is not too short at the back when you are wearing low-waist trousers, or you will get snow between it and the trousers. It should not restrict your movements – try waving your arms around, but it should not be too baggy either.

Trousers Make sure the trousers are long enough to go over the ski boots. They should have a snow stopper on the inside (that you pull over the ski boots to prevent snow and wind from entering). And reinforcement on the inside leg to protect them from sharp edges and crampons. If they are too floppy around the boots, they will get in the way.

Zippers down the sides are handy on warm days as this allows ventilation.

Soft shells These tend to be jackets, but you can find trousers too. The idea is to have a breathable garment during exercise, when no or little precipitation is expected. A soft shell will resist wind and moisture without being waterproof (often a wind-stopper membrane is used). Choose a fairly thin one, as you are most likely to wear it during intense exercise. In any case, remember never to go into the mountains without a Gore-Tex jacket in your backpack.

Outer layer for warmth It is good (sometimes critical) to have an extra layer to put on top of the shell to prevent the body from over-cooling when you are standing still or taking a break in cold weather, after intense exercise or between bouts of intense exercise. Or in case of an accident. There are two options; a down jacket has the smallest pack size and gives the greatest warmth-to-weight ratio, as long as it is dry. Once moist it does not keep you warm at all (the air between the feathers provides the insulation).

A puffball is a lightweight jacket with synthetic insulation. It is not as compact, and not as warm compared to its weight, but it will keep you warm in a moist environment.

Hat/bandana The most efficient place on which to control your body temperature is your head. Never go into the mountains without a hat, at least in your backpack. If your ears get cold from the wind on a warm day, or during exercise on a cold day, wear a bandana to cover the forehead and ears.

Gloves/mittens You feel the ski poles, etc., better when wearing gloves. A pair of mittens will be warmer if it is very cold, or if you have very cold hands. It can be worth getting a waterproof pair if you are learning to ski off-piste, as you will have a lot of contact with the snow.

Facemask This protects your face from the wind-chill effect on very cold days, and is made of neoprene. It is great to wear while skiing. It is essential in really cold, windy conditions because it prevents you making dangerous, rash decisions, just to get out of the wind and cold.

Skis The type of ski to choose depends on what the snow conditions are like where you ski. The wider the skis the more they float in the powder, but it becomes harder to get the edge in when the snow is hard. Some of the techniques for making snow anchors with skis (explained in the chapters Ski related mountaineering skills and Glacier skiing) are impossible with twin tips.

A typical all-round ski would be an alpine ski that is not too heavy or too carved in shape, with a width of between 80–100 mm under foot.

Bindings These should be some form of robust ski-touring binding, such as the Diamir Freeride. It allows you to ski everything, and if there is an injury or avalanche accident back in the group (higher up) you can get back easily within a reasonable time. As a bonus it becomes easier to break trail when traversing, and you already have the equipment to hike and find better snow and access more interesting runs.

Skins Skins are glued under the skis and enable you to walk uphill. There are many models on the market, just make sure they fit your skis. If they are too narrow, the skis will slip when the snow becomes hard. If they are too wide you will not get the edge in on hard snow. The best skins are those that are cut to fit your skis.

Ski boots A normal Alpine boot is best for this type of skiing. Visit an expert who can help you to find the right shell and liner for your foot shape.

Poles Normal ski poles that are thin enough to be held in one hand and have slim handles (so you can turn the pole upside down and shove it into the snow).

Goggles/sunglasses What you wear and with which lenses, is of course a personal choice. However, you do need to protect your eyes from the sun and glare. Most of the time I wear a pair of sunglasses. But I always keep a pair of goggles with orange lenses in my backpack for days with bad visibility and extreme powder days. Orange or yellow lenses will help you to see contours better in bad visibility and flat light, but they won't protect your eyes on a sunny day.

Basic repair kit & tools It's good to carry a basic kit adapted for fixing small problems that might arise with the type of equipment you and the rest of your group use.

Backpack When you are wearing a good backpack you will hardly notice it. Try different backpacks to find one that is good for you. A 25—35 litre backpack is enough for day trips, but if you start doing more advanced skiing get a 40—50 litre pack. It should have a system for carrying skis (or it should be easy to add one). Avoid zippers where possible, because if a zipper breaks on the mountains you are in trouble.

BASIC PERSONAL EQUIPMENT
Avalanche transceiver
Shovel
Probe
Skins
Goggles or sunglasses
Energy (something to eat and drink)

GROUP EQUIPMENT
First aid kit
Bivouac sack
Communication
Altimeter
Basic repair kit and tools
Map and compass

ADDITIONAL PERSONAL EQUIPMENT Helmet; choose an approved helmet that is lightweight but enables you to hear clearly. Back protection; not necessary if you are already carrying a fully loaded backpack. Boot warmer; if your feet often get cold, you can buy a special insole with a small battery pack to keep your feet warm all day.

THE GROUP

A group should consist of 2—5 people, depending on what you do. I personally think the optimal number is 3—4 people. There are enough of you to solve any situation, yet flexibility, speed and group discipline are easy to maintain.

CHOOSING SKI PARTNERS Make sure to choose ski partners who have the same attitudes and risk acceptance as you. You can, and should, demand that everyone you ski with carries safety equipment, and knows how to use it. Your aim is to be independent (as a group), and everybody is responsible for each other. Because you can never choose when an accident will happen, always be prepared. If you tolerate exceptions it is your own life you gamble with.

TRANSCEIVER CHECK & RESCUE NUMBER Find out what the local rescue number is and put it on speed dial on your mobile phone. You can always call the police emergency number, but in certain areas the direct number for the mountain rescue is available. By using this number you will definitely save time.

It is very important to check your transceiver on a regular basis. Over the years, when working as a guide, I have found approximately five transceivers that had no signal from a distance of more than one metre. In each case the light was blinking and the owner had skied off-piste believing that the transceiver worked.
Analogue transceiver Put it in search mode and on the lowest volume. If you have a

signal at approximately one to 1.5 metres distance, the tested transceiver works. [See diagram 001.]

Digital transceiver At least one brand model has a special check mode. If your transceiver has this feature, consult your owner manual and learn how to use it properly. If not, you need to do the full range check. Note: If you put your transceiver on search and test another transceiver too close to it (0—30 cm distance), you will only learn that the transceiver is switched on and that the batteries are working. You need to find out if the transceiver has a signal with a full range.

Full range check One person skis or walks away and keeps his transceiver in receive mode and on maximum volume (range). Each group member then skis slowly past. The person being tested skis out of receiving range on the other side before the next person starts. [See diagram 002.]

Note: You can't check the distance if you ski past too quickly, as then the transceiver does not have time to react. Don't choose a place where a lot of people with transceivers are skiing or walking past, or it will be difficult to separate the signals.

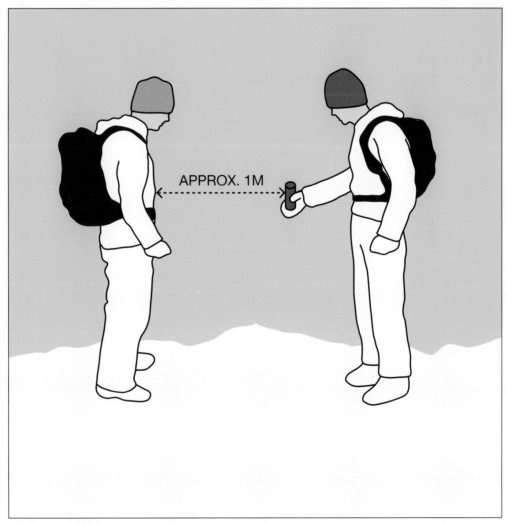

001 Transceiver check.

002:1 Full range check. Put the transceiver in receiving mode.

002:2 Raise your hand when your transceiver picks up the signal.

002:3 Make sure the previous skier is out of range before checking the next skier.

Note: You can't check the distance if you ski past too quickly, as then the transceiver does not have time to react. Don't choose a place where a lot of people with transceivers are skiing or walking past, or it will be difficult to separate the signals.

FINDING GOOD SKIING

Good skiing almost always exists; it's just a matter of knowing what to look for. You can narrow your aim to two major snow types: Powder and spring snow (corn).

After a storm, you could start skiing south-facing slopes where the powder may only last for a day before it starts being transformed into spring snow. The problem is that for a number of days (depending on how much sun or heat the slope gets before it re-freezes) the snow will have breakable crust before it supports the weight of a skier. Meanwhile you are still skiing powder in other aspects, working your way towards north-facing aspects. The last places to search for powder are the steep north-facing slopes at high altitude that will hold the powder the longest, but they also need the longest time to settle. When the powder cycle is over, it is time to look for spring snow, starting with the steep south-facing slopes that transform and become supportable the fastest. Over the next days you start skiing east and west depending on the time of the day. On a cloudy, cold day during a spring snow cycle (east, south and west will stay hard and icy due to the lack of solar heating), try north faces where conditions should normally be stable enough for some steeper skiing. Where the last days' clear weather has dried out the snow, leaving 10—20 cm of dry, cold snow.

When it snows again the powder cycle starts all over again. The nearer summer is, the shorter the powder cycle and the faster the transformation into spring snow.

So go with the flow — don't search for powder in the middle of a spring snow cycle or vice versa.

THE KEY ELEMENTS

The three key elements for finding good skiing are ASPECT, ANGLE and ELEVATION. Knowledge of them enables you to ski powder or spring snow when other skiers are skiing breakable crust. Use the avalanche hazard structure as a base for avoiding dangerous slopes, and consider the three key elements to find the good snow.

Aspect North-facing slopes will hold the powder (and avalanche hazards) longer, whereas south faces will receive the most sun and the powder day may just last for a day. On south-facing slopes you will also find the first spring snow. East faces will receive the morning sun and therefore hold the powder longer than south-facing slopes, and on them it also takes longer for the snow to transform into spring snow. In a spring snow cycle, east will be the first aspect (during the day) to be in condition but also the first aspect to be avalanche hazardous. West-facing slopes will receive the afternoon sun and therefore hold the powder longer than south-facing slopes, but on them it takes longer for the snow to transform into spring snow. In the mornings during a spring snow cycle, it will be very icy and a fall can easily result in long slides. However, in the afternoon when east-facing and south-facing slopes are avalanche hazardous, you will find excellent spring snow conditions on the western slopes.

Angle In deep snow, it can be a fine line between finding a slope that is steep enough to turn on, yet shallow enough to be safe. Lower angled slopes can be better in crusty, breakable conditions because you can stay on top of the crust. Steeper slopes can make 20 cm of fresh snow feel as if it's knee-deep. In a spring snow cycle the steeper slopes transform and become supportable faster, while you still have breakable crust on lower angled slopes.

Elevation High altitudes get more wind and can often be blown out, leaving you with the choice of skiing either tip-wrecking frozen sastrugis or breakable crust. However, high altitudes are also colder, so without wind they will hold the powder longer. Lower altitudes are generally warmer, so they transform and become supportable faster in a spring snow cycle.

BREAKABLE CRUST

If you hit a crusty layer when skiing, check the altitude and the aspect. Try to determine what caused the crust and, if possible, finish the descent on another aspect. Then avoid that altitude or aspect for the following runs. Ice crust is water in the snow that has refrozen over night. On the first clear day after a storm you normally won't find any ice crust above the fresh snow level, but when skiing that day make a mental note of the altitude at which the snow became wet and the aspect. This will probably be the altitude of the ice crust layer the next day (as long as it freezes over night, otherwise it will be avalanche hazardous).

Crust can be basically caused by four different factors; sun, rain, isotherm and wind. These factors can work together of course.

Sun If the crust is caused by sun, the altitude of the crust will be higher on the south faces than on the north faces, and east- and west-facing slopes will tend to be somewhere in between.

Rain If the crust is caused by rain, the altitude will be the same in all aspects in a smaller area. It could be different in a larger area if the rain is due to the Foehn or the Chinook.

Isotherm If the crust is caused by isotherm, the altitude of the isotherm will be the same on all aspects, although if it was sunny the day before, see 'sun' above.

Wind Even a gentle breeze that you wouldn't notice in the valley can turn perfect powder into breakable crust overnight. This is hard to forecast and normally you find out the hard way by going there. Affected slopes are those which face the wind direction. Try to ski other aspects or, if necessary, try to read the snow texture and either avoid all the islands with smooth surfaces (breakable) or ski on them (if they support your weight). If the wind is strong, all the snow will be transported and instead you find a hard, blown-out snow pack and, on the opposite aspect, there will be slabs. This type of wind action should be forecast or locally observable.

Note: You can often avoid a lot of poor skiing by poking the snow with your ski pole next to the lifts at different altitudes. By poking different sides of small terrain features next to the lift you can normally get samples from all aspects. This will give you a lot of answers without having to find out the hard way.

TACTICS & SAFE SKIING

In Alpine terrain there are many factors that you can't control. You have to be open-minded and flexible to determine what and where the real hazard is and choose an appropriate technique or approach to manage the risk.

Primary hazard & exposure time Try to figure out what the primary hazard is; a fall, an avalanche, rock falls, etc. Does the time required to carry out one-at-a-time procedures actually increase overall exposure to a hazard? Use techniques that minimise exposure time.

The time factor If you know your run is ending with a traverse under a south-facing slope at low altitude, you can't spend too much time beforehand using overly safe techniques and thereby arriving too late and exposing yourself to a great avalanche danger. Speed is safety.

Realistic risk analysis If, for example, the risk of an avalanche is low and the consequences are minimal, increased exposure may be acceptable. That's not the same as accepting and exposing yourself to risks that you know exist just because you don't have the time or patience to wait until conditions become acceptable. There are so many hidden dangers that if you accept the ones you know about, sooner or later everything will escalate and lead to an accident.

POWDER CONDITIONS In major ski resorts everything moves fast after a snow-fall. Many people seem to develop powder fever when the race starts in the morning. People will step right out of the cable car and first thing in the morning push down a 45° couloir filled with 50 cm of fresh powder. Surprisingly, more often than not, nothing happens. However, don't think that they know something you don't — they are just taking a huge risk and are depending on luck.

You will see tracks everywhere, in every direction but you still have to make up your own mind. It's you who have to face the consequences of your decisions.

Skiing like this, changing aspect and altitude over a fairly large area with people stressing all around you, requires skills that far exceed the ability to simply pick a good line and ski it well. You need to keep your emotions under control in order not to catch powder fever.

You must base your decisions on what you actually see and not what you expect or want to see. You have to master the terrain by being very flexible and taking intuitive decisions as you ski. You have to manage your group and at the same time be aware of what everyone else is doing around and above you. While fully concentrating on what you're doing, you still need to check out the terrain farther away to get more information about which runs are in condition for later in the day or the next few days.

When someone asks me in the lift on the morning of a powder day "where are you going to ski?" I always answer, "we'll see where the skis take me," meaning that I have no exact ideas. I try to keep my mind as blank as possible so that I can take in all the information in an objective way, without already setting my mind on a specific goal or run. The later I make the decision, the more information I'll have. For every metre I move on the terrain I get new information and see the terrain from a different perspective. That is why I often "change my mind" several times from the top of the run to the bottom.

Several days after a snowfall when the conditions are more stable is when you should make plans to get the most out of you ski day. By then the conditions should be predictable and you know what to expect from different runs.

Tactics to test the terrain after a snowfall If you've done your homework correctly you already have a good idea of which aspect and altitude you want to start with skiing in the morning. If there's been no wind, the natural plan for the first clear day after a storm would be to start on a lower angled south-facing slope at low altitude, or a lower angled slope of any aspect or altitude that gets skied a lot. Then you just have to consider how the fresh snow is bonding with the old snow; you don't have to worry about the stability within the snow pack. By provoking the snow at small steep slopes along the way you will get an idea of stability. Try to jump on top or ski them off. As your confidence in snow stability increases, more aggressive lines can be chosen. Over the next clear days or weeks you will work your way toward the steeper north-facing slopes at higher altitude.

PICKING A LINE

___ If possible, enter the slope from the top, so you don't trigger anything above. But look out for slabs when entering close to a ridge or a summit.

___ Start skiing a slope at the sides, working your way towards the centre on successive runs.

___ Spines, ridges and other such formations are good places to start skiing on.

___ Avoid entering a slope from below a corniche or jumping from it. Watch out for terrain-traps.

GROUP DISCIPLINE Never expose more than one skier at a time to avalanche danger. This rule is applied to steeper terrain in powder conditions. Otherwise we try to move together with a 30 metre distance between each person, to move as efficiently as possible. [See opposite page.]

___ Ski one at a time and watch each skier for the entire run. If the entire run is not visible you should divide the run into shorter pitches.

___ Regroup (to the side) at any changes in steepness or direction so you can watch each other while skiing. Stop and regroup at safe spots such as ridges, knolls or behind large rocks. Don't stop on the steep sections, ski through them. If the safest possible place is not practical, regroup with skis pointed in the direction of greatest safety. Don't make any strict plans from the top as where to regroup, let the first person have the freedom to improvise.

___ If you ski very short pitches, it's time consuming and you may be taking a higher risk by being exposed for a longer time. If you ski very long pitches, it's very time consuming to get back up if anything should happen to anyone in the group.

___ Never cut the snow above each other or someone else, regardless of whether you're skiing, traversing or regrouping.

___ Pair up in twos and stay within sight or sound of each other when skiing among the trees.

___ When skiing at the same time, the second to last person has to make sure that the last one is with the group. Always wait for each other, don't assume that someone skied home or to the pub. For that matter, don't ski home without telling the others. Be patient if there is a group below you, don't stress them and respect the way they are doing things.

TRAVERSING The first thing to do if traversing a suspect section (most often a shallow gully), is to look for an alternative in order to avoid the section. If it's the whole slope you shouldn't even be there and if you have a bad feeling turn around! Ask yourself what would happen if an avalanche occurred.

If you're satisfied with the answer, cross the section on a slanting traverse (to maintain speed if anything should happen). Close jackets and wear hats and gloves. Ski one at a time and watch each other.

SPRING SNOW CONDITIONS In spring, timing snow conditions is everything. Too early and the snow is rock hard, and a fall would mean sliding to the bottom if it's steep enough. The German mountain guide organisation has published a paper stating that the theoretical speed of a person sliding on a slope of only a 30° angle, reaches 97% of the theoretical speed at freefall. So be careful, even if you're only doing a short traverse over a steep south-facing slope early in the morning to ski powder on a north face.

Too late and it's very dangerous due to avalanche danger. Be careful with wide skis, which prevent you from sinking in to rotten/slushy snow and therefore allowing you to ski the slope when it's dangerous. The window of perfect timing varies from day to day depending on the temperature, so don't make up any fixed rules. Static thinking will not only make you more danger-prone but you will also miss out on a lot of good skiing.

Note: Don't ski spring snow too late! This is not only dangerous but it ruins the slope for days or weeks ahead. If spring snow is skied too late, ski tracks are left in the snow which then freeze overnight. On the next day there won't be any smooth surface for spring skiing, just a slope of bumps and holes, so be responsible.

Group discipline general rules apply, but the need for skiing one at a time is not as great because we don't need to worry about the weight we add to the snow pack. However, in certain situations it's still good to ski one by one as long as you don't forget about overall exposure. I.e., on steep sections if there's a fall it could result in crashing into group members skiing below, causing the whole group to slide. Note: It's not the place that's dangerous. It's your timing and the techniques you apply.

006

COMPANION
AVALANCHE RESCUE

Luckily, I don't have a story for this topic.

After 15 years of full-time skiing, I still have the privilege of not knowing how it would feel to have to dig a member of my group out after an avalanche incident. You might think that means that I have not needed to practise how to do it very much over the last few years.

But the opposite is closer to the truth.

If there is one thing my years in the mountains have taught me, it is that you can not control the environment there. No matter who you are and how much experience you have had, accidents can and will occur. And because you don't get to choose when or where they might happen, you always have to be prepared. Always. Just because nothing has happened to you for a couple of years (and hopefully never will), you cannot relax. You have a huge responsibility – towards your friends and yourself. To ensure that you carry the right equipment, and know how to use it. To look for the warning signals.

To adapt to the mountains. Anyone ignoring all this should not be allowed to ski in a group.

At the beginning of every winter season – and every once in a while during it – I think through the actions that will be needed in the event of an avalanche accident. I also practise with my transceiver. If the worst comes to the worst, there cannot be any question about what to do, and in what sequence to do it.

Companion avalanche rescue is not a skill you can develop automatically just because you ski a lot. It has to be practised frequently to reach an acceptable level.

However, this somewhat time-consuming preparation is a small price to pay if you want to continue to enjoy the pleasures of skiing off-piste.

I would like to thank Manuel Genswein; the majority of the diagrams in this chapter are based on his work and publications. What chances do you have? Of course you don't know that, but the best information we have is to be found in statistics.

15-MINUTE WINDOW

Phase 1 0–15 minutes. Over 90% of victims are still alive when excavated within the first 15 minutes. However, that does not mean that they will survive. The victim could still die within a short time from multiple trauma.

Phase 2 15–35 minutes. There is a huge drop in the calculated chance of survival, from 91% at 15 minutes to 34% at 35 minutes (acute asphyxiation of victims without an air pocket).

Phase 3 35–120 minutes. A victim who is completely buried cannot survive for more than 35 minutes without open airways, and the existence of an air pocket (it can be as small as a few centimetres). Great care must be taken by a rescuer to avoid destroying any possible air pocket.

Phase 4 120–130 minutes. There is a second drop, to 7% at 130 minutes. Death is from slow asphyxia (due to "closed" air pocket), and hypothermia. [See diagram 001.]

<u>CONCLUSIONS</u> It takes time for an organised rescue team to arrive. Survival of victims who are completely buried depends mainly on rapid action by those individuals remaining on the surface (companion rescue). Safety equipment and its proper use are important to cut down burial time,

First of all, in order to avoid time-consuming mistakes, you have to know how to organise a companion rescue. Well-practised use of an avalanche transceiver is essential, as is the use of a probe, for locating the victim once the transceiver search has identified the target area. A good quality shovel is necessary for removing hard snow.

AVALANCHE SAFETY EQUIPMENT

The lives of all of you depend on the quality and function of your equipment, and your skill in using it effectively. Don't go out in the mountains without taking correct, fully functional equipment, and knowing how to use it.

<u>BASIC PERSONAL EQUIPMENT</u> Basic personal equipment consists of an avalanche transceiver, a shovel and a probe.

Avalanche transceiver The transceiver is both a transmitter and a receiver. It allows you to locate, or be located, by anyone carrying a similar device who knows how to use it! In the mountains, both you and everyone in your group should always wear the transceiver close to the body, under the jacket (never in the backpack). Switch it on in the morning and have it turned on all day while skiing. It transmits a signal that the human ear can't hear. If a member of the group should be buried in a slide, then switch the transceiver over to search mode (thereby receiving the signal from the buried group member's transceiver, which is still transmitting) and locate him. To do that you need to learn and understand how to conduct a rescue, and you have to practise often!

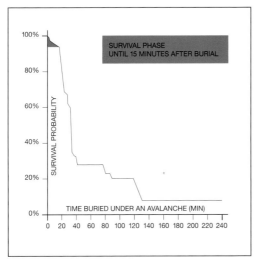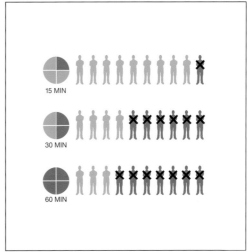

001 Statistics on fully buried victims in open areas. Swiss data, 1981–1991, calculated by Falk et al, 1994. Reprinted from Brugger et al, 2001.

There are both digital and analogue transceivers on the market, and you can locate a victim equally quickly with either. With a digital-only transceiver you can cut down training time a lot. However, digital-only transceivers have disadvantages as regards range and multiple burials. They can be fast to use after much less practise (although you still need to practise).

Every morning you should carry out a group check to make sure that everyone has switched on their transceiver, and that all the transceivers are working properly. Then leave each transceiver on all day. Don't try to save the battery in the lifts or during lunch! Sooner or later you will forget to switch the transceiver on again.

Note: Every three years, send your transceiver to the manufacturer to be inspected.

Shovel Everyone in the group has to carry a shovel in their backpack. You can't move snow effectively with your hands or skis. It is essential that everyone in the group carry a shovel. You never know who's going to get buried! The shovel should be lightweight and sturdy with a large, unbreakable blade (scoop). The blade should be removable, the handle collapsible, and the whole thing should fit inside your backpack so you actually have it when you need it.

There are different models with blades either of plastic or metal. Both materials are fine for most avalanche rescues, but the metal blade has the advantage that it will work much better for digging an emergency snow cave in hard snow, if you ever need to do that. In general, metal blades tend to have bigger scoops and move snow much faster. This advantage outweighs the slightly lighter weight of the plastic blade. Also, plastic shovels are more likely to break in very cold conditions.

Probe The probe is a long, collapsible rod that fits in your backpack. When assembled it should be roughly 2.4 metres long. It's a time saving tool, which can save lives by confirming the precise location of a victim. And it's the only way to find a victim without a transceiver before a rescue team with dogs arrives. A study made by Dominique Stumtert, TRACE 02 Chamonix, showed that three persons looking for a victim completely buried under one metre of snow took an average of 26 minutes to find him using transceivers and shovels. That figure went down to 15 minutes when they used probes as well. So don't underestimate the value of the probe.

Various materials are available, but choose one that is sturdy, lightweight, approximately 2.4 metres long, and fits inside your backpack when folded.

GROUP EQUIPMENT Think through different scenarios to be able to decide strategically where in the group people with certain pieces of equipment should ski. What happens if a person with a particular piece of equipment gets buried? Maybe the group should carry more than one piece?

Adapt to the situation and destination, whilst trying to be as lightweight as possible without taking unnecessary risks.

First aid kit Most 'ready-made' first aid kits go for quantity instead of quality. They are filled with things that you don't need, and thus take up unnecessary space in your backpack. Pack your own kit and adapt it to your requirements and destination. Carry a back-up kit in the group and know how to use it.

Bivouac sack The bivy sack should be carried for an emergency. It can keep an injured person warm and protected, to avoid hypothermia. It offers an emergency shelter if caught in bad weather. It should be lightweight, solid and take up minimal backpack space.

Communication If possible make sure that you can be in contact with the outside world. It could be by mobile phone, satellite phone or radio. Just make sure that everyone in the group knows where you are and how to contact the rescue service.

Bear in mind that a mobile phone is good for making an emergency call, but compared to a radio it is pretty useless for organising a rescue operation.

If you use a mobile phone in Europe, the local rescue numbers will often put you in direct contact with the mountain rescue service. This will be the fastest way of getting assistance. However, the number 112 will connect you to an emergency operator, and with the phone you will be able to use any available network, giving you the best possible coverage.

ADDITIONAL PERSONAL EQUIPMENT Here is a selection of avalanche equipment that is available on the market. Equipment you may consider using together with the basic kit, never instead of it.

ABS – Avalanche Airbag System This consists of a normal backpack, available in sizes ranging from 10 to 50 litres (600 to 3000 cubic inches), with a built in airbag system. If you are caught in an avalanche, you pull a handle. Within two seconds this inflates two airbags, of a total volume of 150 litres (9000 cubic inches). To use it again, you only need to change the gas container. The system is designed to keep you afloat, so as to prevent you being buried and injured in the flow. Tests and experience in real life situations give very positive results. Of course, it is not a guarantee for survival, but it is the only system that actively tries to prevent you from being buried. And it could save your life.

On the down side there is the price, but your life is worth more than that. The only really negative point is the weight. But if you are only carrying a daypack containing basic equipment, the weight is not too much of a problem.

Avalung The avalung is a vest or a roll with a mouthpiece connected to a filter system at the front that allows you to breathe in air when you are under snow, and expel the warm, low-oxygenated air through a valve at the back. It reduces the risk of snow icing up around your face (thus causing carbon dioxide poisoning), and the mouthpiece prevents snow from blocking your airways. The avalung can give you extra time, and so increase the chance of a successful rescue.

Experience from tests and real life situations shows that an avalung can save lives, but there are limitations. With an avalanche, you have to be able to put the mouthpiece in your mouth. Another limitation is that you may not be able to breathe for mechanical reasons; pressure on chest and stomach for example.

Recco system This is a small reflector that is sewn in to clothing or attached to ski boots. The reflector is passive, which means that the professional rescue team has to be equipped with a special recco detector to be able to find the victim. Many ski resorts in Europe and North America are equipped with this system. The limitation of the system is the crucial time factor. You have to wait for the rescue team to arrive before you can locate the victim, but it is an inexpensive addition that could save life.

AVALANCHE SCENARIO

There is much said about what to do if you are caught in an avalanche. I think you need to refresh the following items sufficiently often to be able to act on instinct if you ever do get caught in one. The items are in the logical order in which they should be carried out.

At the moment of triggering The victim should shout loudly for attention. This alerts the others so that they can start observing what is happening. At the same time, try to escape to one side. This will give a greater chance of not being completely buried and injured. If you have any additional equipment, now is the time to use it.

Observing what other team members do, shout loudly to warn the rest of the group. You have to get everyone's attention so they can carry out the following two actions simultaneously: Personal safety and observation. You have to think about your own safety first to be able to rescue anyone else later. Three people looking for one is of course much better than two looking for two. You also have to assess whether there is a risk of more avalanches.

Gleaning information from careful observation can save time. Observe the victim(s) the whole way and if they disappear behind a terrain feature, follow (if safe). Where is/are the last point(s) seen, are there any other people below, if so, how many are caught?

When caught Toss your poles away and release the skis. If you can't ski out of the avalanche and you fall over, try to get rid of your equipment as soon as possible. Otherwise it will act as an anchor and pull you down. This is a problem regarding gear that does not have a self-releasing system, or for anyone with safety straps connected to his or her gear. Mainly telemark and snowboard gear have this disadvantage, and also certain types of ski touring bindings.

Try to remain on the surface in any way you can; swimming, rolling, kicking, running — try anything. Try to grab anything on the way, trees, rocks, etc. You will have to be quite strong physically and coordinated to do this, so if it does not work, close your mouth, cover your face with your arms to create an air pocket. By holding your elbows in front of your chest you will hopefully create some space for your chest to expand, so you will be able to breath mechanically. Stay in this position, or otherwise continue.

When the avalanche slows down and is about to come to a complete stop: Try to kick or swim or push an arm or leg to the surface. If you still know which way is up and which way is down, that could save you from being buried completely.

Close your mouth, cover your face with your arms to create an air pocket. Hopefully, by holding your elbows in front of your chest you will create some space for your chest to expand, thus allowing you to breath mechanically.

When the avalanche comes to a stop, try to push with your arms. If you manage to keep your airways free and create a small air pocket, you can get enough air to survive for up to two hours.

Relax as much as possible. This is easier said than done, but if you panic you will use up much more oxygen.

COMPANION RESCUE

A couple of friends of mine skied in a small resort during a big dump of snow. At one stage they skied under a three-man chair lift where they saw a person being completely buried in a small slide. At first this scenario doesn't seem very complex. However, on every chair lift there were three skiers with transceivers, and there were people skiing past among the surrounding trees who had no idea what had happened. This meant that my friends had to separate and ignore up to six or eight signals moving around in the search area. An almost impossible task, even if you have trained a lot. My friends managed to rescue the victim through thinking flexibly; they stopped the chair lift and had the people on it switch off their transceivers.

Companion rescue is much more than just a transceiver search; it's a chain of different decisions and actions that should be taken and carried out in the correct order. If any of the links fail, you will probably miss your 15-minute window. That's why it is important to realise that you won't have the time to make the correct decisions within 15 minutes by thinking logically. You have to know the routine by heart and practise a lot. From when the avalanche starts the observers have to:

1. Get an overview.
2. Overcome shock.
3. Organise everyone.
4. Develop a strategy.
5. Search with transceiver, eyes and ears.
6. Pinpoint the victim with the probe.
7. Excavate the victim.
8. Clear the victim's airways.

All this within 15 minutes! There may even be more than one victim buried, with signals that are interfering with each other, and you have more people to dig for. Still within 15 minutes!

There's no end to how complex a rescue situation can become, and there are so many variables involved. For these reasons there can be no tick list to follow blindly. However, there are basic rules and actions that you should know by heart, so that you are able to improvise in the case of an accident.

LEADER In this next stage a leader has to take charge. Without a leader and organisation, the 15 minutes will be long gone. That leader could be you! The designated leader could, for example, be the victim and the second most experienced in the group is in a state of shock. Everyone skiing off-piste has a responsibility towards the group. You must be prepared to take charge in a companion rescue.

If you have to take the lead roll, remember to make fast decisions but without rushing them. It's better to lose a few seconds and do it correctly from the beginning. Don't stress, stay calm — you can only do your best.

Information Meet up at a safe place, collect information from everyone in the group and only take pertinent information into account. For example, where the victim was last seen. Note the time, as that can be useful information when it comes to making priorities.

Check up Make sure that everyone in the search team is okay and 100% up to the job. The area has to be searched in one go! Time is an issue!

If you are uncertain whether a particular person is able to do the job, then you cannot let him or her be part of the search team. Bring them along for the digging.

Strategy Make up a rescue plan according to the situation and how many people there are left. The area should be covered completely, as fast as possible, in one go.

Make sure all the transceivers are in search mode! It is easy to forget, and if someone is walking around sending an extra signal without knowing it, this could be very confusing and waste a lot of time. Note: Everybody who is not actively searching must switch their transceivers off.

Call for help (know your location). When the search team has started to look for the victim, it's time to call for help.

During the first two hours don't send anyone away for help if you need them in the rescue team. Time is an issue! Don't let anyone ski away for help alone, always go in pairs. You are still in avalanche terrain that has already produced a slide!

HOW THE TRANSCEIVER WORKS

In the transceiver there is an antenna that emits an electromagnetic signal at an international standardised frequency of 457kHz. There is no back or front to the antenna. This means that the transceiver receives the signals equally well at "the front" as from "the back". [See diagram 002.] Due to the curved shaped field lines, the signal usually leads you to the buried person in a curve. [See diagram 003.]

In user manuals, transceivers can have a range of between 20 to 80 metres. However, in my experience, in an average ski group where people are carrying different models both of analogue and digital transceivers (and not always with fresh batteries), a realistic receiving range would be between 10–25 metres. The effective range of the transceiver depends on many factors, but as users we can only affect two of them; the battery strength and the orientation between the antenna in the receiving transceiver and the antenna in the transceiver sending a signal.

The first of the factors we can change is simple; range usually decreases with battery power. The second is harder since we don't know the orientation of the buried transceiver (antenna). To receive the optimal signal (and have the longest possible range), the antenna has to be in an optimal orientation (in line with the field line). Theoretically there is no signal when the antenna is oriented 90° to the field line. That's not a problem in real life though, because we are constantly moving. You will receive a weaker signal and the receiving range will be shorter. [See diagram 004.]

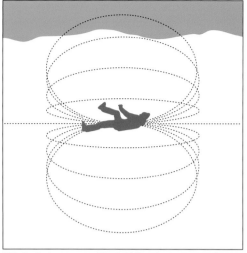

002 Buried person and the field lines from a transceiver.

003 Field lines seen from above in a simplified two-dimensional mode.

COMPANION AVALANCHE RESCUE

The rescue is divided into two phases. The first phase is everything up to the moment when the first signal has been picked up from the victim's transceiver. The second phase is the field line search. Pinpoint is the part of the second phase in which we locate the exact position of the victim using gridsearch and probes. It continues until the victim has been uncovered. [See diagram 005.]

PRIMARY SEARCH PHASE

The area should be completely covered as quickly as possible at one go. You don't have time to stand at the bottom of the debris not having found the signal because you've been sloppy. If you don't get it right the first time you will miss the 15-minute window. You have to improvise and make up a rescue plan to fit the situation. Calling for help at this stage is not high on the list of priorities. Get everybody searching before you start to think about the call. Don't forget that the clock is ticking.

Strategy Don't be too technical! Use eyes and ears when searching. Search all the surface debris, looking for anything sticking up. Pull up poles or skis to see if they are still attached to the victim. If not, put them back in the snow exactly where you found them and leave them until you've searched the entire debris for a signal. If you don't find a signal, go back and probe around the gear. [See diagram 006.] Note: Don't waste time by searching the sliding surface, only search the debris.

Mark the last-seen point. If you cannot find the victim, this is valuable information for the professional rescue team. Only do it if it doesn't take any time (i.e. if it's below you).

If you have a last-seen point you should be able to narrow down the likely burial areas by following the flow lines of the avalanche down the hill. [See diagram 007.]

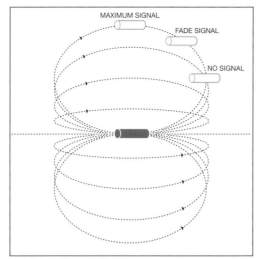

004 Orientation to the field line.

Note: Everybody who is not actively searching must switch their transceivers off.

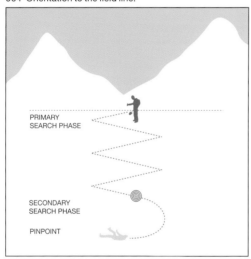

005:1 The two phases of companion avalanche rescue.

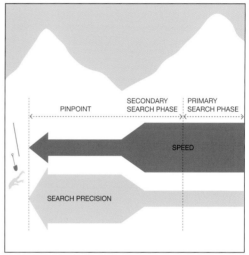

005:2 At the beginning of the rescue, speed is of greater importance than search precision. As you get closer the need for precision increases and speed has to be reduced.

If there is a last-seen point you can concentrate your efforts on the likely area. However, be very careful to ignore the other areas, working with a receiving range that is recommended by the manufacturer. In most cases you can keep a greater distance if you rotate your transceiver slowly (to find the optimal orientation). If you don't know the effective receiving range of your transceiver you must assume the worst — that the transceiver only has an effective receiving range of 10 metres in each direction and so adapt the search patterns accordingly. [See diagram 008.]

If you don't have a last-seen point you have to search the whole avalanche debris. [See diagram 009.]

If there are only two people to cover a wide area then draw an imaginary line down the middle and each person covers one sector. [See diagram 010.]

Don't get it wrong by not joining up in the middle. [See diagram 011.]

Figure out whether you should go on foot or on skis? Try to find a balance be-

006 Objects from a buried victim sticking up.

tween speed and safety. You don't want a person in the group breaking a leg whilst trying to ski too fast in the debris, and by skiing too fast there is also the risk of missing the signal.

Equally you don't want anyone to spend too much time wading around in the snow because they are being overly careful.

If there is no signal If you are unable to find a signal, you have to consider the flow lines of the avalanche, and spot–probe likely areas such as compression and deposition zones, around equipment, in front of trees, rocks or obstacles. [See diagram 012.]

If this doesn't work you have to form a probe line and probe downhill from where the equipment was found, and secondly probe very close to the toe of the deposit. [See diagram 013.] Because the possibility of survival decreases markedly with burial deeper than 1.5 metres, you can speed up the process and cover more ground by marking your probe at 1.5 metres and probing no deeper than that. You're trying to save a life! Later on you will have all the time in the world to probe full depth to recover a body.

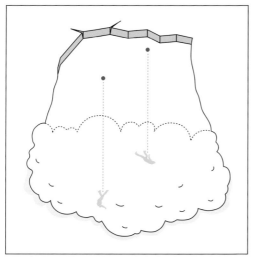

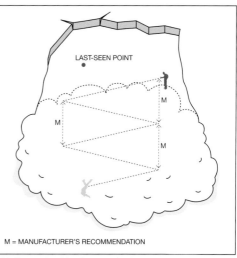

007 The lower down a slope a victim is when the slab is triggered, the more likely he is to end up further downhill in the debris.

008 Scenario with a last-seen point.

M = MANUFACTURER'S RECOMMENDATION

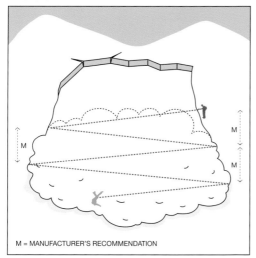

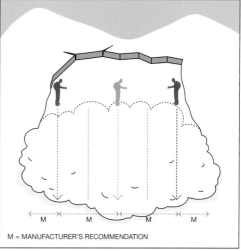

M = MANUFACTURER'S RECOMMENDATION

M = MANUFACTURER'S RECOMMENDATION

009:1 Scenario without a last-seen point, the entire debris has to be searched.

009:2 Scenario without a last-seen point, the entire debris has to be searched.

SECONDARY SEARCH PHASE

The secondary search phase starts as soon as a first signal has been picked up. If you're only searching for one victim, once the signal has been picked up, everyone can stop looking for further signals and assist in the further locating and excavation effort. If there are more victims, everyone should continue to search for signals in accordance with the strategy that has been established.

Mark the point at which you received the first signal. If, for any reason, you lose the signal, in a stressful situation you always have this point to come back to and start over. Preferably mark it with a ski pole — not with your gloves or your backpack or your hat, you can't dig efficiently without gloves, you'll need the gear, and you need to stay warm and dry because you might have to stay on

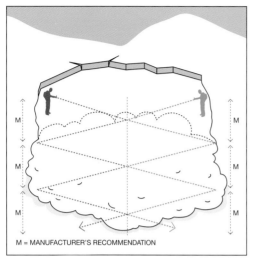

010 Scenario without a last-seen point, the entire debris has to be searched.

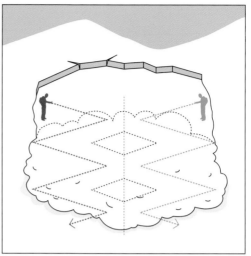

011 If stopping short of the imaginary line, you risk missing a sector in the middle.

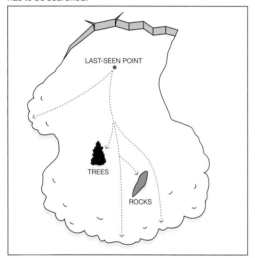

012 Likely burial areas.

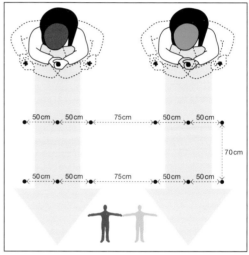

013 Analogue transceiver search.

the spot for hours. Carry out the transceiver search. Let one person do the search to avoid confusion, and the rest of the group should prepare with shovels and probes.

ANALOGUE TRANSCEIVERS Use the grid search method for analogue transceivers without any visual guidance.

The use of an analogue transceiver takes much more practise, as you only follow an acoustic signal to locate the victim. Certain models also offer some visual guidance. However, the advantage is that you get a raw signal to interpret and the receiving range is longer.

To be able to get the maximum from your analogue transceiver, use it with earphones to filter out background noise. Keep the transceiver vertical and still, so the antenna is oriented in the same direction the whole time throughout this phase of the search.

From the point at which you picked up the signal:
1. Continue ahead as long as the signal is getting stronger.
2. As soon as the signal gets weaker, turn around 180° and go back to where you had the strongest signal (you don't have to be exact, speed is more important at this stage).
3. Turn down the volume as much as possible (to shrink the area you're searching).
4. Turn a 90° angle and start again (if the signal becomes weaker, just turn around 180° and go in the other direction).

Repeat the procedure until you are down to the lowest two volumes (normally 3–4 times), and when the signal is loudest at a minimum volume you are close to the victim and the pinpointing phase takes over.

To be successful with the grid search you have to move fast (run) over larger areas to hear the difference in the signal. It's better to run a few metres extra to be certain that the signal is getting weaker. The biggest mistake is to move slowly, stopping to analyse the signal. [See diagram 014.]

SINGLE ANTENNA TRANSCEIVER WITH VISUAL GUIDANCE The tangent search method is for a single antenna transceiver with visual guidance.

Keep the transceiver parallel to the ground in front of you and remember that visual guidance helps locate where the field line is. To know which 180° direction to walk in, you have to pay attention to the volume of the signal – is it getting weaker or stronger? If there is a distance indicator, then consider it as a scale showing you how close you are rather than the distance in metres. As long as the numbers are decreasing you are walking in the right direction.

From the point at which you picked up the signal:
1. Sweep the transceiver slowly in front of you from left to right. By using visual guidance, mark the boundaries (either mentally or in the snow with your foot) where the signal gets weaker to the left or right.
2. Take five large steps ahead exactly in between the two marks (as long as the signal is getting stronger you are on the right path, otherwise turn around 180° and go in the other direction).
3. Turn down the volume as much as possible (to shrink the area you're searching).
4. Repeat the procedure until you are down to the lowest three volumes, then take three steps instead of five (to avoid going past the victim) and get closer to the snow with the transceiver.
5. When the signal is loudest at a minimum volume you are close to the victim and the pinpointing phase takes over. [See diagram 015.]

Getting it wrong: The arrows or visual guidance give you a direction, but the signal is getting weaker and the distance indication is increasing — you've walked past the victim and you are now receiving the signal from behind. Just turn around 180°, and you will be walking in the right direction along the induction line.

MULTIPLE ANTENNA TRANSCEIVERS The field line method is for multiple antenna transceivers, In the modern, user–friendly, multiple antenna transceiver there is at least a second antenna, plus a small processor that interprets the signal and makes the search much easier. The minor disadvantage of the shorter receiving range is compensated by easy use, and therefore it does not take longer to complete a rescue.

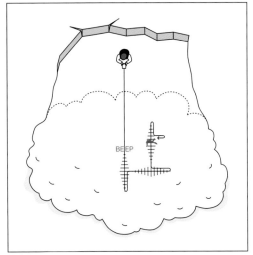

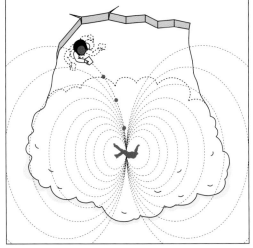

014 How to form a probeline.

015 Search, using a single antenna transceiver with visual guidance.

From the point at which you picked up the signal:

1. Keep the transceiver parallel to the ground in front of you and go in the direction indicated by the arrows or lamps. (Remember that the visual guidance only helps you to follow the field line. To know which 180° direction on the field line to walk in, you have to pay attention to whether the signal is getting weaker or stronger and whether the distance indicator is increasing or decreasing).

2. The closer you get, the slower and lower you need to be. Ultimately, you will be sweeping the transceiver just above the snow level. Continue until you get the lowest distance reading on the field line, then the pinpointing phase takes over. [See diagram 016.]

PINPOINT

Try to be as exact and fast as possible without getting stressed. If you move your transceiver too quickly in this phase it will not have time to react, which will result in you finding nothing when probing. Then you will have to start all over again. Practise and learn how fast your transceiver can be moved and still have time to react and give a correct reading. Use it correctly the first time, and then you should only need to probe once.

AFTER THE GRID SEARCH METHOD Keep the transceiver oriented the same way and sweep it very slowly, as closely as possible to the snow surface, but at the same vertical plane. [See diagrams 017 and 018.]

Mark where the signal disappears or drops off significantly. Probe in the middle. Leave the probe in when you hit the body so you can dig along it.

AFTER THE TANGENT OR THE FIELDLINE SEARCH METHODS Keep the transceiver oriented and facing the same way and sweep it very slowly, as close as possible to the snow surface but at the same vertical plane. If you move your transceiver too fast it will lose the signal and react by increasing the volume (thereby in-

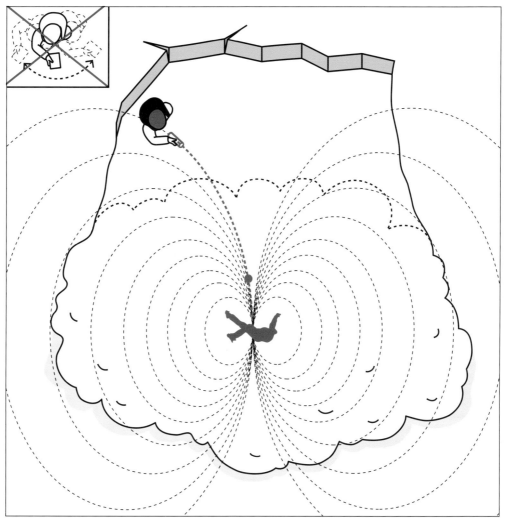

016 Search, using a multiple antenna transceiver.

creasing the search area) to find the lost signal before it can decrease the volume again and you can continue to pinpoint. Learn how quickly you can move your transceiver. Search for the lowest distance reading (it will most likely be along the line you walked in). Probe at the lowest distance. [See diagrams 019 and 020.]

PROBING Always probe at an angle of 90° to the snow surface and leave the probe in the snow when you hit the body. When probing, make sure that you penetrate all the different layers. Don't worry about injuring the victim while probing, if you don't find him quickly he will be dead. [See diagrams 021 and 022.]

EXCAVATION Don't dig along the probe as it will be difficult to move the snow and you will end up standing on top of the victim. [See diagram 022:2.]

If possible try to see if the victim had an air pocket. This is important when the victim has been buried for more than 35 minutes and you have to start making priorities (see chapter on first aid). As soon as the victim's head and chest are exposed, clear his airways and check for breathing. [See diagram 023.]

Due to the three-dimensional shape of the field lines, there can be as many as ten false maximums. This effect causes problems with single and dual antenna transceivers, as they cannot incorporate problems that have field line inclination. Only transceivers with at least three antennas are not affected by problems caused by misleading maximums. If you encounter a low signal and a high distance indication during the pinpoint search, it is probably a deep burial. To solve the problem with high search precision you have to use Manuel Genswein's "pinpoint in a circle" technique.

Definition of terms A maximum is a point where (due to an optimal orientation of the antenna), you have maximum volume (respectively to a low distance indication), that will decrease no matter in which direction you move your transceiver. A misleading maximum doesn't lead to the victim, while the real maximum does. [See diagram 024.]

This doesn't affect the strategy that you choose with an average burial depth, but because the distance between the false maximums and the real one is roughly the same as the burial depth, you could be probing more than two metres away from the real maximum in a deep burial. Probing that deep over a large area is too time consuming. You can also get misleading readings under snow, but this would only affect the search if the debris were lying on an extremely steep slope, which is very unlikely.

Shadow box If it's a vertical burial, you will find a box of false maximums surrounding the actual burial place. [See diagram 025.] There are different ways of avoiding these problems. People with a lot of experience normally just push through all the weak signals to see if there's a true maximum on the other side. This takes a lot of practise. It can't be taught because it is a personal technique that is built on trial and error. It can also be time consuming.

ANALOGUE TRANSCEIVERS By holding the transceiver in a vertical position you only have to deal with two false maximums (unless the terrain is extremely steep). [See diagram 026.]

The victim is always buried under one of these points or somewhere between the two. The more tilted the buried antenna is, the smaller the distance between one of the false maximums and the real one. If there's only one maximum, it's the real one (due to a vertically buried antenna). [See diagram 027.]

Pinpointing in a circle:
1. Hold the transceiver vertically and search for the first maximum.
2. Mark this point.
3. Leave the volume at the same level, walk away from this point until the signal has almost gone and then increase your distance from the marked point by another 50%.
4. Walk around the first maximum in a circle.
5. If you hear a signal again, search for the second maximum (normal fine search).
6. Mark the second maximum.

If there is no signal in the circle (you only have one maximum), it is a vertically buried transceiver and the victim is under the first maximum. But if you have two maximums:

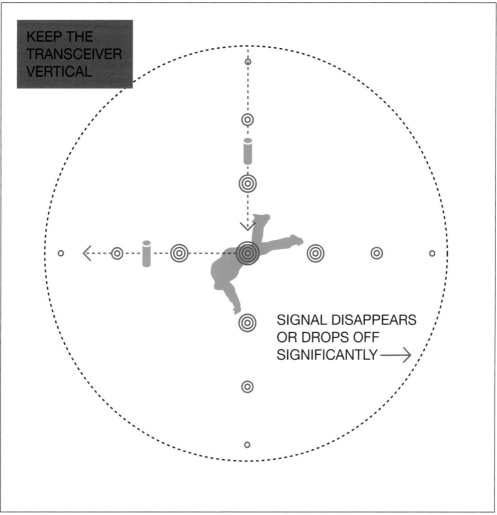

KEEP THE TRANSCEIVER VERTICAL

SIGNAL DISAPPEARS OR DROPS OFF SIGNIFICANTLY →

017 Pinpoint with an analogue transceiver.

1. Hold the transceiver, first horizontally on the snow surface, and in the axis of the two points.
2. Search for the strongest signal between the two maximums.
3. Probe at the strongest signal. [See diagrams 028 and 029.]

DIGITAL-ONLY TRANSCEIVERS If pinpointing in a circle is applied with digital-only transceivers, the following adaptations are necessary:

1. Search the first distance minimum while holding the device horizontally, as is usual with this category of transceivers.
2. Estimate the burial depth based on the distance indication on the screen. If shallow: Proceed to locate the victim with a probe. If deep: Remember the indicated distance, and apply "pinpointing in a circle".
3. Hold the transceiver vertically and search for the first distance minimum, and mark this point.
4. Walk in any direction (the distance in metres noted previously) away from this point.

018 Pinpoint.

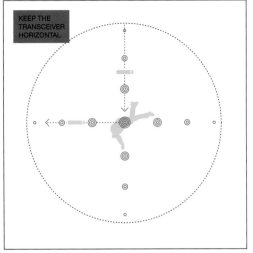

KEEP THE
TRANSCEIVER
HORIZONTAL

019 Pinpoint with a digital dual antenna transceiver.

020 Pinpoint.

025 CM

025 CM

021 Probing pattern.

5. Proceed in a circle in the given radius around the first minimum. If the distance indication drops significantly, search for the second distance minimum, and mark it.
6. Hold the transceiver, first again horizontally on the snow surface and in axis to the two marked minimums. Search for the lowest distance indication between the two vertical minimums.
7. You are now above the victim, check by probing.

MULTIPLE BURIALS

Multiple burials add complexity to the search scenario. If the victims are within close proximity, the situation requires the application of special search techniques. Different transceiver brands and models are designed to be used in dif-

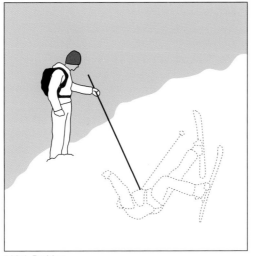

022:1 Probing.

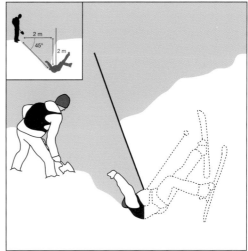

022:2 Digging strategy.

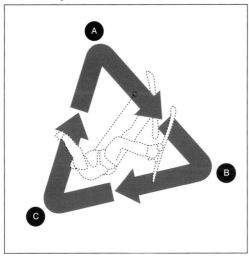

023 First aid.

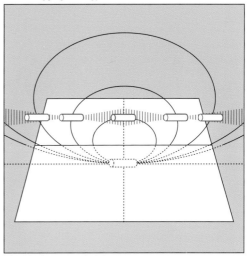

024 Maximums and minimums.

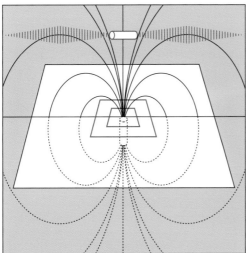

025 Maximums and minimums.

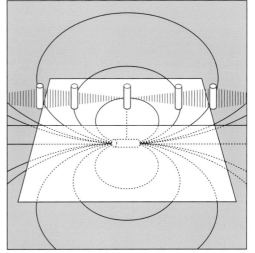

026 Maximums and minimums.

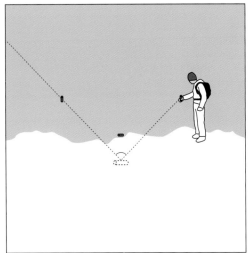

027:1 The effect of horizontal to vertical burials.

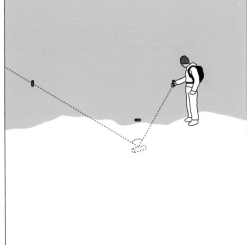

027:2 The effect of horizontal to vertical burials.

027:3 The effect of horizontal to vertical burials.

027:4 The effect of horizontal to vertical burials.

ferent ways. There are too many models on the market to go through them all here. Because most of them suggest different search strategies, you simply have to read the instruction book for your transceiver and follow the recommendations. However, there are some general guidelines that apply to all transceivers. To start with, you should turn off a victim's transceiver as soon as possible, to stop it from interfering with those of the other victims. This reduces the complexity of the remaining search scenario.

Two or more victims: Ask yourself how many victims are buried in the search area in front of you, and how big the area is. In most cases you know how many victims are buried, and this can help save time.

Digital-only transceiver: While moving or standing still, count how many different transceivers you can hear.

Transceiver with digital sound: Stand still, and while slowly rotating the device 180°, count the different distance/direction indications.

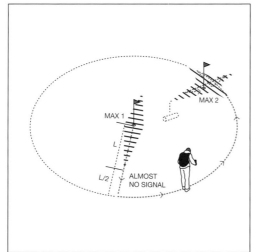

028:1 Pinpointing in a circle.

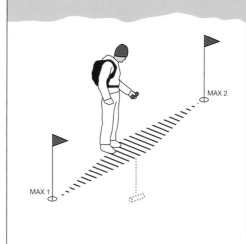

028:2 Pinpointing in a circle.

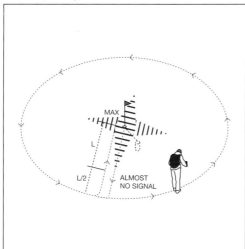

029 Pinpointing in a circle.

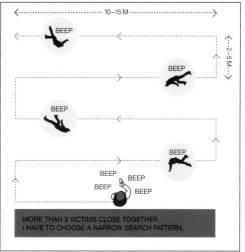

030 Micro search strips.

MICRO SEARCH STRIPS The micro search strip strategy has been designed to solve the problems of multiple burials in close proximity. The micro search strip has to be applied on areas fulfilling the following criteria. A multiple burial within 10–15 metres or less. The more victims there are and the closer together they are, the narrower the search strip. You have to decide on the width of the search strip, usually between 2–5 metres (depending on how many victims and how close together they are). [See diagram 030.]

You have reached the outer border of the area when the distance indication is more than 10–15 metres and the signal volume only gets weaker and/or the distance indicator only increases. Keep the transceiver oriented and facing the same way and sweep it as close as possible to the snow surface, but at the same vertical plane. Ignore direction indications and focus on the increase and decrease of the distance indicator and the analogue signal. Note: To increase the chance of saving lives, always solve multiple burial problems before you solve deep burial problems. Digging takes a lot of time and survival is less likely for a deeply buried victim.

HOW TO PRACTISE

PROBING You can save a lot of time by having learnt how to recognise what a body feels like when probing. Bury a backpack. Try to recognise the different sounds and feeling you get from the probe. The difference between a ski boot and a rock. The rock makes a much more metallic sound when you hit it with the probe. The difference between the ground and the body. The body flexes when you hit it, while the ground is soft (due to insulation by the snow, which keeps it at 0°C). The ground grasps the probe as you pull it up. Learn the difference between bushes and hard or soft snow layers, and push a bit harder to see if you get through.

TRANSCEIVER SEARCH Everyone who skis off-piste should practise with the transceiver regularly. There's no excuse for not practising.

Single search Choose an area with deep snow, and mark the four corners to make a square of approximately 50x50 metres. Put a transceiver in a backpack and make sure that it's switched on and transmitting. Place the backpack at a realistic burial depth of at least one metre. If you are several people, take it in turns to bury the backpack and search for it. Use a probe to locate the backpack. Start timing as you enter the area and record the time when you hit the backpack. Everyone should run around in the snow to disturb the surface layer so you can't see where the transceiver is buried. With a bit of practise everyone should be able to find the backpack within two minutes, unless it's a deep burial.

Multiple burial search When you can accomplish the single search quickly, move over to multiple burial search. Do the same exercise as above, but with two backpacks, each with a transceiver. Locate the first backpack with the probe only because you are unable to switch off the transceiver. When the first backpack is located, leave a ski pole at the spot and go for the second backpack. Stop the watch when the second backpack is located. At first, times will vary between 3–15 minutes depending on how complicated the scenarios are. Try to analyse what you did well and what went wrong.

When you can accomplish this three times in succession (in different scenarios) and in less than five minutes, you are doing well. You are doing really well if you succeed in less than three minutes.

Micro search strip The same size area and exercise as before, but bury an unknown number of backpacks (with transceivers) fairly close together. The same rules as before, but because there is no limit to how complicated this can be, it's impossible to give any time limits. Just compete against one another. Vary the depth of burial and antenna orientation as much as possible.

007

FIRST AID AND RESCUE

When they tried to move him he screamed in agony, at the top of his voice. It took a second shot of morphine from one of the mountain rescue team members to calm him down enough to get him on the stretcher.

Like most amateur skiers, he had always dreamed of riding a helicopter in the Alps, but so far he hadn't been in one. This was certainly not how he'd envisioned his first time. Later, he even said it was a shame that he couldn't remember anything from the helicopter ride down.

He was a friend of a friend in the ski bum community, who had recently come down to Verbier to ski for a few weeks. Back in those days, we were all telemarking, and the rest of us had been doing that every day that winter. So we felt quite strong. This particular day was an amazing powder day, and we had just kept on going and going and going. At the end of the day, we were all completely exhausted. Still, we wanted to squeeze just one more run out of that day; the infamous last run. I remember how tired I was, and I can only imagine how our guest must have felt at that point.

The run ended in the piste, but from the powder you had to jump about a metre down to the groomed slope. And our guest was simply too tired to control his skis. As he landed, one of his skis cut sideways and he dislocated his femur. The whole leg popped out and his thigh muscles cramped up from our hard day of telemarking. There was no way of getting his leg back in the right position – he didn't even let us touch him.

No big mistakes caused that accident. Until it happened, this was just another ski day, and that's the whole point. The run or route doesn't necessarily have to be dramatic for an accident to be dramatic. And you definitely don't get to choose when, where or how. All you can do is stay prepared.

When going on expeditions into very remote areas, a group has to be totally self-reliant. This requires a lot of equipment and extensive knowledge and training. You may even decide to take someone who has proper medical training. On a smaller scale however, you can still save lives with some basic skills and a small, well-planned first aid kit. Everybody in the group should know what to do and what not to do if you ever end up in this extremely stressful situation. That is, having an accident up in the mountains.

The aim of this chapter is to go through the basics of how to treat and stabilise minor injuries, so that the group can get out of the mountains on their own. And also, how to keep an injured person alive until a professional mountain rescue team arrives. The scenario in this chapter covers proximity to civilisation and professional rescue within 24 hours.

EQUIPMENT

Tape A roll of good tape for blisters and wounds, for example Leukoplast 5x5 cm.
Band-Aid To cover wounds and stop bleeding. Snögg is excellent for wet, cold conditions, as it is self-adhesive. Otherwise you can cut off a roll of cling wrap (approximately 5 cm wide) and put it on top of your blood stopper to keep it in place.
Elastic bandage A roll of elastic bandage, for multiple uses.
Steristrips For small cuts.
Painkillers Painkillers containing paracetamol.
Safety pins For multiple use.
A pair of scissors For adjusting Band-Aid, tape, elastic bandage, etc.
Personal medication If you are suffering from any personal complaints, bring your personal medication.
SAM splint For splinting.

THE ACCIDENT

When confronted with an accident, the first thing you must do is assess the whole situation while remaining calm. As always in the mountains, the prime thing to think about is your own safety. Don't complicate the situation by becoming a victim yourself. When you start making decisions about what to do, your aim should always be: Don't leave the injured person worse off than when you began.

Go for help as soon as possible! If you are alone, taking care of one person, I suggest you do the ABC first, but emergencies in the mountains are always complicated, and communications vary, so improvise. There is no golden rule.

To make sure that you deal with urgent matters in the right order, your actions should follow the ABC priorities. This will help you keep priorities straight, for example, to ignore the urge to start with the broken femur sticking out through the ski pants instead of starting with the airway. ABC stands for Airway, Breathing and Circulation. Note: Whenever you have taken action, check the effect according to the ABC priorities. It doesn't matter how well you take care of a broken leg if you fail to keep an airway open. [See diagram 001.]

CPR (cardiopulmonary resuscitation) is not covered in this book. It is a skill that needs to be practised, and cannot be learned from a book. Moreover, it is not likely to be applicable in the mountains (except in the case of a heart attack).

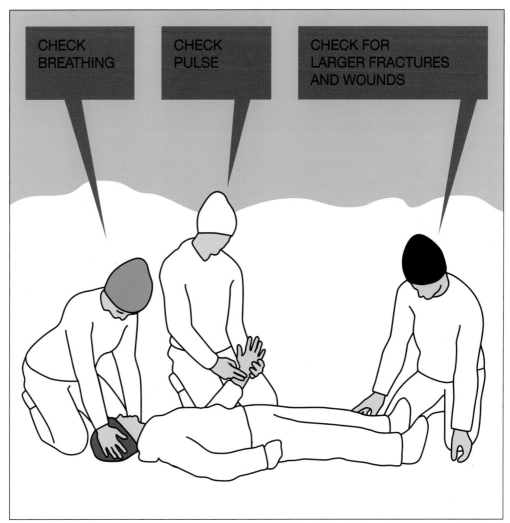

001 Monitoring the situation.

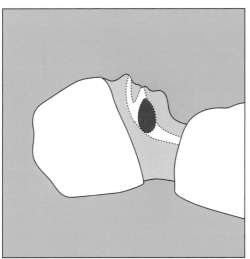

002 Obstructed airway.

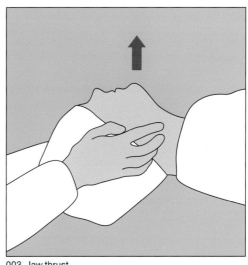

003 Jaw thrust.

If you encounter a cardiac arrest due to blunt trauma, only professional rescue and surgical treatment within minutes can help you. However, you might benefit from it in two circumstances: Asphyxia in avalanche burial (CPR), and apnoea in head trauma (mouth to mouth resuscitation). Remember that the ABC principle applies to all life-threatening conditions, but this chapter focuses on trauma, and not medical problems like asthma or epilepsy.

PRIMARY SURVEY-ABC

The aim of the primary examination is to recognise any condition that would be fatal within seconds or minutes, and to treat it. When you have secured the environment and are about to approach the victim, take a three-second timeout to calm down and recall the ABC in your mind. You can only do what you can do. Nobody expects a miracle.

A: AIRWAY (WITH SPINAL CONTROL) When approaching, first call the victim by name. If there is no answer, shake or poke him gently. The airway is always open if he speaks or screams.

If an unconscious person is lying on his back, his tongue will fall back and block the airway. By lifting his chin or making a jaw thrust, you prevent his tongue from obstructing his airway. [See diagrams 002 and 003.]

If necessary, open his mouth and remove foreign objects. Put him in recovery position to maintain the airway as soon as possible (usually after the ABC, see further down). If there is vomiting or a lot of bleeding in the nose or mouth you'll have to do this at once.

Remember that a blow to the head that makes a person unconscious is always hard enough to sever the cervical spine. If in doubt as to whether to protect the spine or maintain an airway the answer is always: The airway is the most important! You don't know if the spine is severed, but you know for sure that a person without an airway will die. If possible, always immobilise the neck of the unconscious victim with a neck collar or SAM splint.

If the victim is wearing a helmet, and it interferes with your efforts to maintain an airway, take it off very carefully and stabilise the neck with the SAM splint. Taking off a helmet without severing the spine has to be practised and is only recommended to non-professionals if it is a matter of life and death (for example to create an airway). [See diagram 004.]

A neck collar is never perfect and only supports your efforts in keeping the spine protected. When moving an injured person with a neck collar you must always immobilise the neck manually. [See diagram 005.]

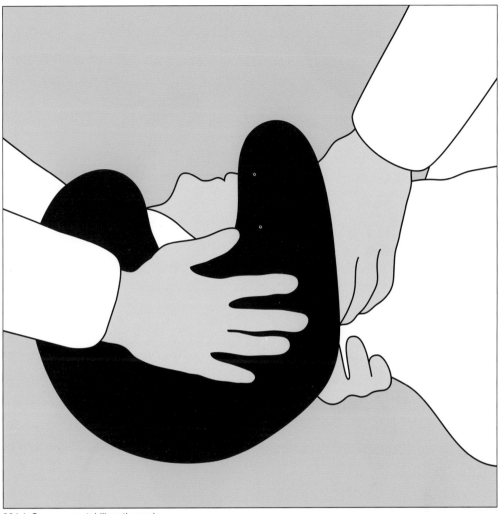

004:1 One person stabilises the neck.

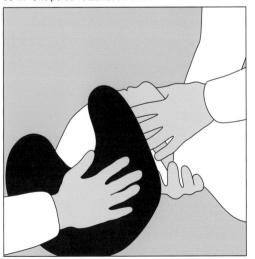

004:2 The other should very gently rock the helmet to remove it.

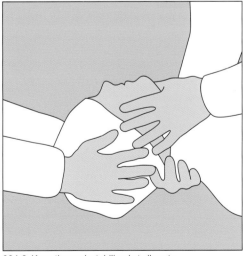

004:3 Keep the neck stabilised at all costs.

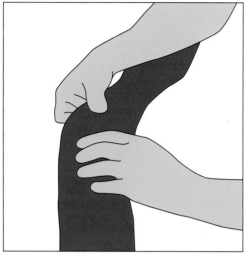

005:1 Measure a hand span's width from the end of the splint.

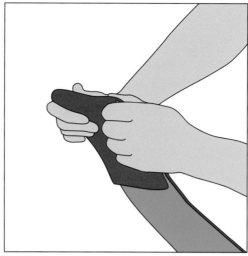

005:2 Fold the splint to make a bend.

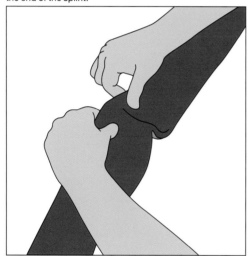

005:3 Flare the edge to create a chin shape.

005:4 Place under the chin.

A. Airway.

CONDITION	OBSERVATION	ACTION
Open airway	Breathing	Maintain an airway
Partially obstructed airway	Snoring sound	Create an open airway, using the jaw thrust/ chinlift
Obstructed airway	No breathing sounds Movements of the chest/ abdomen, but no air going in and out	Create an open airway (see above) Remove foreign objects from the mouth, such as snow, vomit, blood or teeth

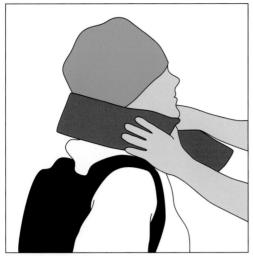

005:5 Bring the splint around the neck loosely to ensure it touches the breastbone and supports the chin.

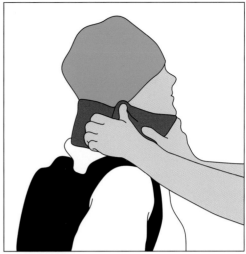

005:6 Pinch the sides of the splint to create stability.

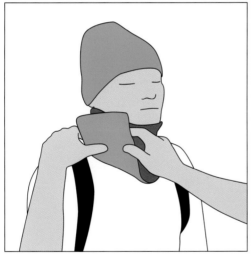

005:7 Fold away any extra splint.

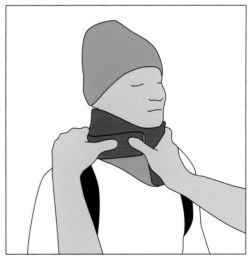

005:8 Tape or bandage over the top.

B: BREATHING Once you have made it possible for air to move in and out of the lungs (A, Airway), you have to make sure it does so! A normal rate of breathing is 12–15 breaths per minute. This varies a lot depending on exercise, stress, pain, fear, etc.

To find out whether a person is breathing, feel with your bare hands or hold a cold, blank object in front of the mouth (such as a watch or cell phone display). Any vapour? Look for chest/abdomen movements.

If you decide to perform mouth to mouth resuscitation:
1. Make sure that the airway is free at all times by lifting the chin with one hand. Do not bend the neck unnecessarily, or at all.
2. Pinch the injured person's nose with the other hand to make sure the air is not leaking out through the nose.

3. Breathe in and slowly blow air into the injured person (for two seconds). Make sure that the chest or abdomen expands, showing that air is actually getting into the lungs. Repeat. [See diagram 006.]

B. Breathing

CONDITION	OBSERVATION	ACTION
Normal breathing	Normal, regular breathing	Maintain an airway
Affected breathing	Pain, unnatural sound when inhaling and exhaling Panic if conscious Blueish skin and lips	Open the airway. Unzip the jacket and shirts around the neck. Sometimes the victim finds it easier to breathe when sitting
No breathing	No sound, air or movement	Check for pulse Pulse — Mouth to mouth No pulse — CPR

C: CIRCULATION It's crucial to have sufficient blood circulating in the body. Vital organs will be damaged if there is excessive loss of blood. In the worst case it will lead to cardiac arrest. Circulation failure due to severe trauma is most likely caused by internal bleeding, and sometimes external (visible) bleeding.

The first thing to do is check the pulse. If it's okay, continue looking for blood. At this stage you have to ignore minor cuts and look for major bleeding. A person can lose up to half a litre of blood (this is what you give when you donate blood) without any major affect on health. That will look like a lot of blood at the scene of an accident, so don't panic. This is especially true of scalp wounds, which can look alarming, but one actually never bleeds to death from such a wound, at least not within the first few hours.

If there's no pulse, consider CPR, but remember that in trauma, only ultra fast professional rescue and evacuation to a hospital can save this person.

Internal bleeding Death from internal bleeding is more common than the obvious external bleeding. For example, a ruptured spleen. Evacuation is urgent. Persistent abdominal pain, especially when moving, should alert you. There is not much you can do, except for internal bleeding associated with femoral and pelvic fractures. See secondary survey. Let the victim assume the most comfortable position.

Heartbeat rate & pulse quality When checking the victim's pulse, the radial artery in the wrist is the most simple. [See diagram 007.]

If you can't find it there, try the carotid artery or the femoral artery.

To find the carotid artery, slide sideways from the Adam's apple with two fingers to the softer tissue surrounding it.

Only with practise can you be sure that you're checking the right spot for the artery, but not even medical professionals can be 100% sure. You could practise to check the femoral pulse, which is usually easier to find, even in harsh conditions.

Normally, the heartbeat rate ranges between 50—80 at rest. At high altitude it could be faster. It is true that you could check for the quality and rate of the pulse. But to be honest, in a stressful situation such as an accident in the mountains, who can interpret the difference in pulse quality and rate on the cold wrist

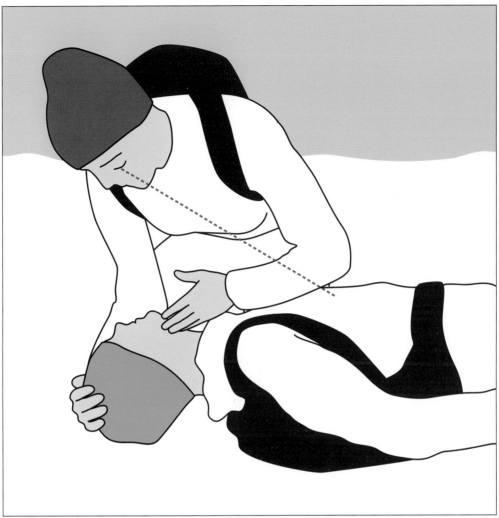

006:1 Mouth to mouth resuscitation.

006:2 Mouth to mouth resuscitation.

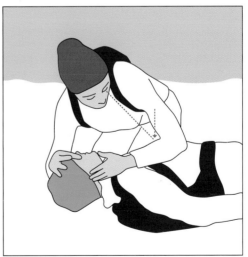

006:3 Mouth to mouth resuscitation.

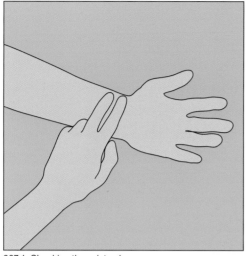

007:1 Checking the wrist pulse.

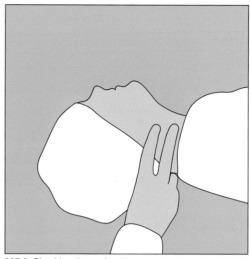

007:2 Checking the neck pulse.

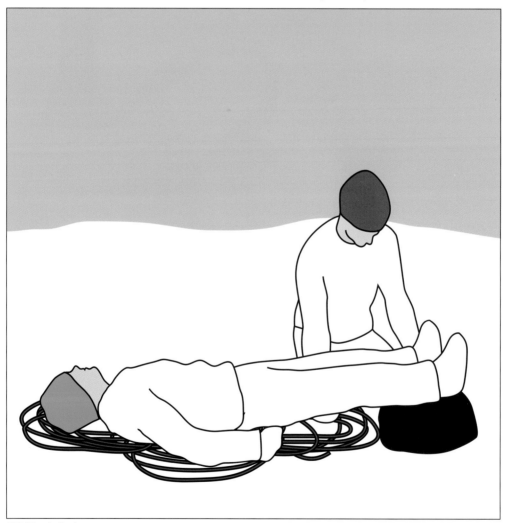

008 Elevate the legs.

of a pain-afflicted, hypothermic, scared, exhausted victim? You should always try to check, but don't waste any time on it if it won't affect your decisions. As stated, you can't fix internal bleeding, only a surgeon at a hospital can. So don't bother with fine-tuning diagnoses you can't treat. However, a fast, thin pulse might be a sign of severe bleeding.

Apart from stopping the bleeding, it is important to place the victim's feet about 30 cm higher than their heart. For example, on a backpack. This will transfer the blood from the legs to the more vital organs. [See diagram 008.]

Severe external bleeding Control severe external bleeding by direct pressure to the site of the wound. Try to elevate the wound, so that it is higher than the heart. Apply padding and firm bandaging. If the wound bleeds through the first bandage, put another bandage on top. [See diagrams 009 and 010.]

Don't hesitate to cut clothes open to inspect the injury, so as to control the bleeding. Cutting is best done with a blunt-pointed pair of scissors that you should have in your first aid pack. Never use strangulating (tie-off) methods to control bleeding, except for extreme cases when ordinary methods have been tried and won't stop the bleeding. For example to stop bleeding if a limb has been traumatically amputated.

C. Circulation

CONDITION	OBSERVATION	ACTION
Normal circulation	Regular, strong pulse	Keep the victim warm and insulated from the cold ground
Affected circulation	Any abnormality in the pulse	Check for internal bleeding, femur and pelvis Keep the legs elevated and head low. Keep warm
Circulation failure	No pulse	CPR

SECONDARY SURVEY

Now you have probably saved the victim from imminent death.

The aim of the secondary examination is to recognise and treat any other injuries that are not immediately life threatening, for example broken bones and minor wounds. If possible, get out of the mountains, otherwise stabilise the situation and keep the victim warm while waiting for rescue.

If a victim's condition deteriorates at any given time, always go back to the ABC and check: A) Is the airway still okay? Vomiting? Recovery position needed? B) Is he breathing? Count the frequency. C) Check the pulse. No sign of bleeding? Is the bandage still doing its job?

Use the following pattern for the secondary survey:
1. Check the level of consciousness. If unconscious put in recovery position, not forgetting possible spinal injuries.
2. Check for large fractures and wounds by systematically looking and feeling

all limbs and skin surface, including the scalp, starting from the head down to the toes. Don't hesitate to cut clothes open if you suspect an injury that needs treatment.

3. Treat fractures and wounds.
4. Comfort the victim. Keep him warm and continue to monitor vital signs (pulse, breaths per minute, mental status). Obtain additional information, such as medication and allergies.

<u>CONSCIOUSNESS</u> Check the consciousness level according to AVPU: Alert, speaks and open eyes spontaneously; Verbal stimuli needed to get a response; Painful stimuli needed to get a response; Unresponsive.

<u>HOW TO TREAT A VICTIM WITH A SUSPECTED BACK OR NECK INJURY</u> First of all, if there is a suspected spinal injury and rescue is coming soon, let the rescuers handle it. Don't move the injured person at all. Only move him if you must in order to perform a life saving manoeuvre, in accordance with the ABC method.

Pain in the back or neck is the cardinal symptom. A total loss of function and sensations below a certain level are grave signs. The fact that a victim has been standing up after the accident is not proof of no injury. Bear in mind that pain from a fractured femur, for example, can override the pain from a broken neck, so that a stressed but conscious victim might not note the neck pain.

When moving victims with potential spinal injuries, for instance when you have to put them on top of ground insulation (if rescue is not coming soon), or put them in the recovery position, the principle is the "log". The whole spine, from head to pelvis, should be kept in the same position as it was when found, no matter how you lift or turn the injured person. Like a stiff log. For a single rescuer this is virtually impossible, but try your hardest. The easiest way to move someone if there are two or more of you, is with the clothing–lift and the log–roll.

It is important to perform a coordinated lift, so the spine does not bend in any direction. The person who holds the head is in charge, and counts to three. Before you lift he says what should be done, and in what order, loudly and clearly, so you all know. When lifting the victim in his own clothes and before lifting, grab his belt and tighten his clothing on other spots by rolling it up in your hands. Count to three before putting him down again, so you stay coordinated. This needs practise. [See diagram 011.]

<u>THE RECOVERY POSITION (NATO POSITION)</u> To do this properly without aggravating a back or neck injury there needs to be two of you, and preferably three or four of you. Always treat an unconscious person as if he has a spinal injury. If the injured person has a chest injury, put him on his side on the ground, if that is comfortable for him. It will increase the chance of the non–injured lung functioning properly. The head should preferably be lower than the feet. This is easily achieved by putting an injured head down a slight downhill slope. [See diagram 012.]

Use the recovery position if the person is unconscious (remember to protect the spine), or if there is vomiting or significant bleeding from the nose and/or mouth.

The recovery position usually maintains the airway without someone needing to lift the chin constantly. It also offers some protection for the airway with vomiting. Vomiting is quite usual with concussion to the brain, or with stress or unconsciousness.

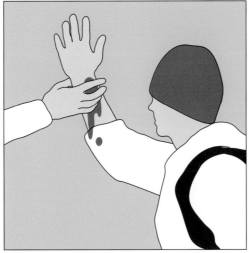

009 Apply pressure and elevate.

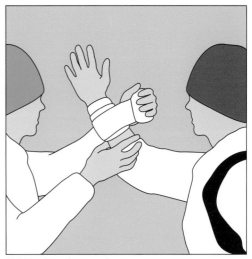

010 Bandage the wound.

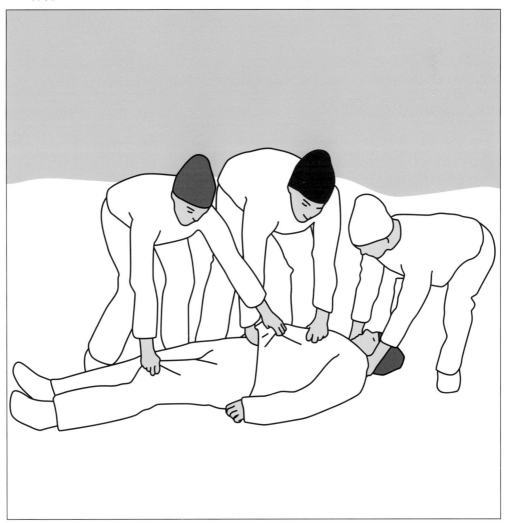

011 The clothing-lift.

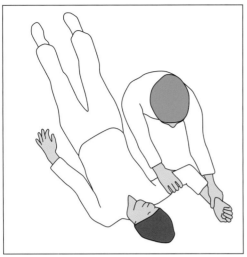

012:1 Place the arm closest to you at a 90° angle to the shoulder.

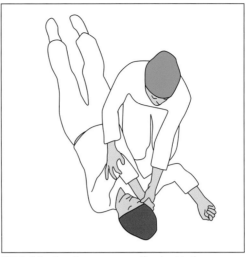

012:2 Bring the other arm across the chest to the ear.

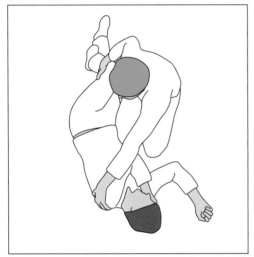

012:3 Lift up the knee, hold the shoulder and knee and roll.

012:4 Ensure the airway is clear.

FRACTURES & DISLOCATIONS A fracture can be open (an open wound in contact with the bone), or closed. [See diagram 013.]

Open fractures should be covered with a sterile (or clean) dressing. Do not try to put the ends back into the wound. Always remove jewellery from the limb, as swelling will occur. Position the fracture 30 cm (1 foot) higher than heart level.

The ends of the fractured bones will harm the tissue (often muscles) around them and cause pain and bleeding. Sometimes big blood vessels get caught and squeezed. This can threaten the viability of the limb. Symptoms of the latter are lack of pulse (compare with the other limb), paleness and coldness. A limb can survive for a couple of hours without circulation. Nerve supply can also be damaged and render the limb useless. If performed correctly, reposition and immobilisation can reverse these injuries. If unsuccessful, urgent surgical treatment is needed to save the limb. Fractures just below the knee and just above the elbow are especially prone to causing these problems. [See diagram 014.]

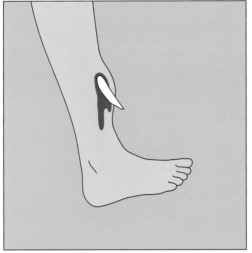

013:1 Open fracture.

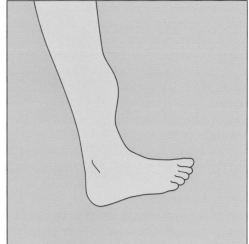

013:2 Closed fracture.

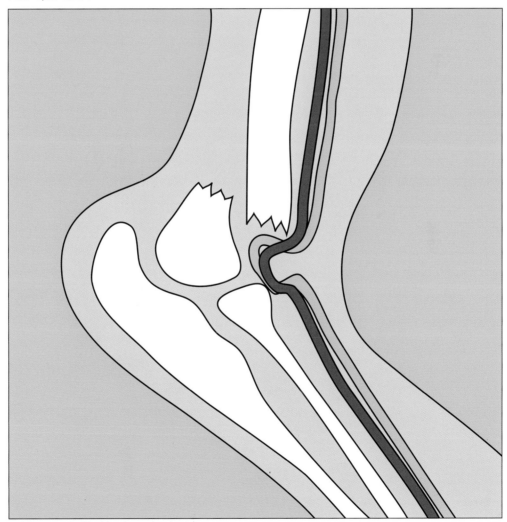

014 Fracture pinching blood vessel and nerve.

In the case of traumatic amputation, save the limb and store it moist and cold, but NOT freezing. For example put the limb in a clean plastic bag and wrap up in wet clothes, and then place the limb in the snow (the limb should not be in direct contact with any object that is colder than 0°C).

If a rescue or medical service is available within hours, do not try repositioning on your own, except with badly dislocated or fractured ankles. These should be corrected immediately. This is also true of limbs without blood or nerve supply. The strategy is fairly straightforward. Gently apply traction along the axis of the bone. The larger the muscles involved, the longer this takes. Never try to straighten a fracture by bending it. When it "snaps" or falls into a more correct position, or the pain fades away, splint and immobilise. [See diagram 015.]

Improvise using ski poles, the SAM splint, tape, slings, elastic bandage, etc. Never fasten the limb to the splint directly over the fracture. To be effective the splint must immobilise both joints on each side of the fracture. Use Snögg for padding hard surfaces on your improved splint

When repositioning and splinting larger fractures, it is often necessary to

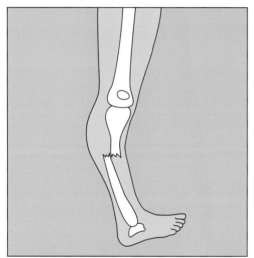

015:1 Repositioning of a lower leg fracture.

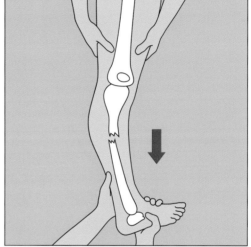

015:2 Repositioning of a lower leg fracture.

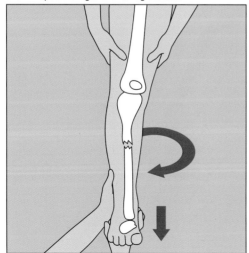

015:3 Repositioning of a lower leg fracture.

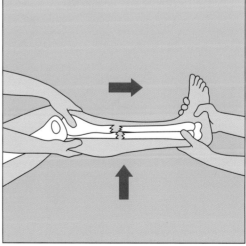

015:4 Repositioning of a lower leg fracture.

keep the traction, or the muscles will pull the bone back again. This is very hard to do in field conditions without the right equipment and proper training. If you try, you will probably end up with no success and a victim who has even more pain and bleeding. But a well-performed repositioning and immobilisation will hurt for a few moments and then afterwards relieve the pain and decrease the bleeding. If the limb is not deformed, splint straight away. [See diagrams 016 and 017.]

A painful fracture of the clavicle can be repositioned by retracting the shoulders with a figure of eight bandage, and thus make it possible to evacuate without calling a rescue team. [See diagram 018.]

Always check the pulse, colour and sensation of the limb before and after repositioning, immobilising or splinting. Note: Do not try repositioning on your own, just splint and immobilise.

COSTAL FRACTURES Pain somewhere in the chest when taking a deep breath or moving. Generally speaking, this only constitutes a threat to you being able to ski for the next four to six weeks, but could mask deeper injuries.

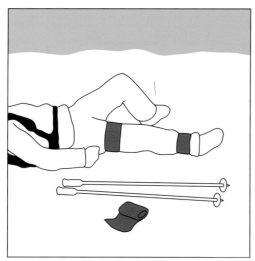

016:1 Splinting a fracture.

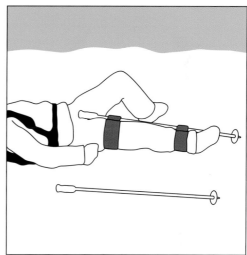

016:2 Splinting a fracture.

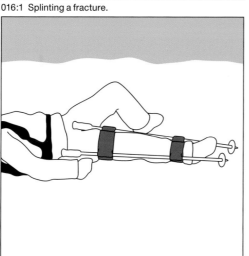

016:3 Splinting a fracture.

Note: Do not try repositioning on your own, just splint and immobilise.

017:1 Different types of sling.

017:2 Different types of sling.

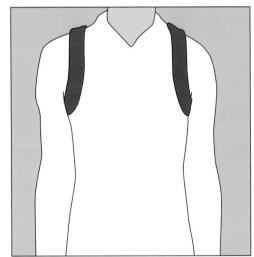

018:1 Figure of eight bandage.

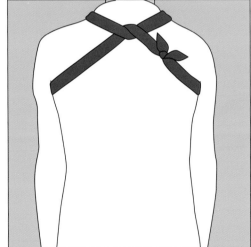

018:2 Figure of eight bandage.

FEMUR & PELVIS Pelvic and femoral fractures are the only bone fractures that can cause life-threatening internal bleeding. Therefore it is critical to immobilise these fractures. Bleeding from them usually takes more than 30 minutes to become critical.

Femur The thigh can be very swollen, and deformity is often obvious. Strapping must go up over the hip and down below the knee. [See diagram 019.]

Pelvis Often no external sign. Pain when trying to move, or when the pelvis is gently squeezed. Do not repeat squeezing, the pelvis may be very unstable and cause even more bleeding. Immobilise by tightening the pants or belt around the pelvis, but not too hard! Treat as cautiously as if it were a spinal injury. Any movement of the pelvis can increase the bleeding.

DISLOCATIONS & DISTORTIONS There is no need to differentiate dislocations from fractures in the field setting. You have to abort the tour anyway. Immobilise the dislocation as if it is a fracture. The injured person should be placed under

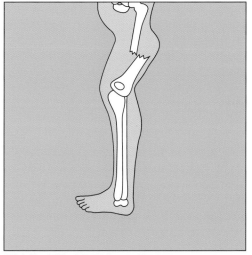

019:1 Repositioning of a femoral fracture.

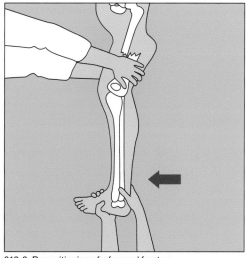

019:2 Repositioning of a femoral fracture.

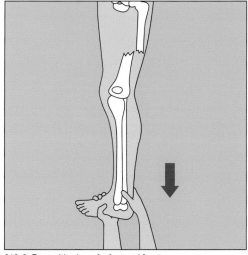

019:3 Repositioning of a femoral fracture.

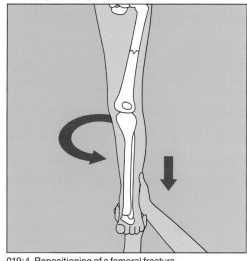

019:4 Repositioning of a femoral fracture.

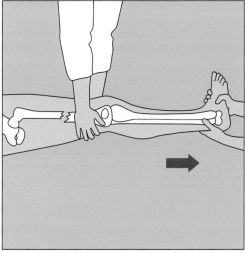

019:5 Repositioning of a femoral fracture.

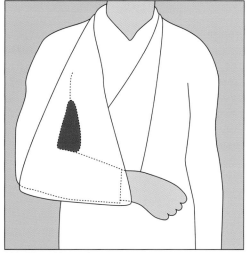

020 Sling with armpit support.

medical care, even if the dislocated part pops back in. To relieve the pain of a shoulder joint dislocation, put a soft supporting cushion (such as a rolled fleece jacket) in the armpit before fixation. [See diagram 020.]

If using an elastic bandage to support a limb, never stretch more than half of the maximum stretch when applying, otherwise the bandage will be too tight and will restrict blood circulation.

If you take a ski boot off a fracture or dislocation, swelling might make it impossible to put the boot back on.

KEEPING WARM Keeping the injured person warm is probably the most likely thing you will need to do. It is very important. Hypothermia develops quickly in the mountains. Whatever it takes to get protection from the wind, use your equipment, dig a shelter or move. Insulate against the ground. Put all the clothes you have on the victim and place his feet in the backpack. Talk to the victim. Comfort him. Get additional information, such as medication and allergies.

OTHER SKIING-RELATED MEDICAL PROBLEMS

FROSTNIP
Symptoms The skin looks white, is numb or lacks feeling. It is more superficial than frostbite, which means that you can slide the skin over the underlying tissue. Common sites are all wind-exposed areas of the skin, especially the face.
Treatment Immediate warming up of the affected area. If you are still in the mountains, apply direct body heat. Simply use the palm of your hand. If sensation hasn't returned after one hour, treat it in the same way as frostbite.
Prevention In extreme conditions, wear a neoprene facemask. Check one another for white spots on exposed skin.

FROSTBITE
Symptoms Looks like frostnip, but the tissue damage is deeper and feels more frozen to the touch. A typical sign is a body part that has felt cold, but is now no longer uncomfortable despite being cold, or can't even be felt. The skin can't be slid over underlying tissue, because the tissue is frozen. Common sites are toes, fingers, feet, ears, nose and hands.
Treatment Treat initially in the same way as frostnip, except that the affected area should not be allowed to refreeze. This means that frostbite is best left as such until you can guarantee keeping it warm continuously. If frozen, re-warm in hand-hot water (39–42°C). Temperatures above 42°C feel burning hot and will damage the tissue. This is very painful, so it's preferably done under medical supervision. Give ibuprofen 600 mg if no contraindications. You could use armpits and the groin to re-warm. Never warm up in front of direct heat.
Prevention Wear the correct clothes for the conditions, unbuckle your ski boots every now and then to allow circulation to your feet, wiggle your toes and fingers continuously. Make a stop in good time in order to warm up your fingers in an armpit, for example.

HYPOTHERMIA
Symptoms Hard to recognise in the early stages, and literally impossible to detect in oneself because decision-making and rationale are affected early on.

Measuring body core temperature in field conditions is impossible in reality. You have to trust other signs. Abnormal behaviour such as disorientation and sudden bursts of energy should be treated with suspicion. Involuntary shivering (can't be consciously controlled) occurs when the body temperature is between 36–32°C. Below 32°C, the body loses the ability to shiver and you will be in a state of mental disorientation (if you are not already). If totally buried in snow (avalanche) the insulating properties of the snow mean that hypothermia is never the reason for unconsciousness in the first 30 minutes, and probably not even in the first hour.

Treatment Find shelter as soon as possible. Take off wet clothes. Insulate against the ground. Use your imagination! If you lack sleeping bags in winter conditions, you must get to a hut. All other solutions, such as digging a snow cave, will merely delay hypothermia, and will seldom lead to actual re-warming. If the victim is conscious and shivering (>32°C), give hot, sweet drinks and re-warm at room temperature.

Check for frostbite. If this is successful, hospital care is not needed. In all other cases, or in doubt, call the rescue service immediately. If the victim is unconscious (generally <28°C) or dizzy, treat him very carefully, as you would treat a spinal injury, because heart arrhythmia can be easily triggered. A person with a body temperature of <25°C appears dead. In this state it is impossible to detect pulse and breathing without advanced medical equipment. Never start CPR. This can make the situation worse for the reason given above. "A person is never dead until warm and dead."

Prevention Wear correct clothes for the conditions and have a regular intake of high-energy foods. Avoid exhaustion.

SPECIAL CONSIDERATIONS FOR AVALANCHE VICTIMS
ABC is still the golden principle! See also the chapter on avalanche rescue.

If a victim is not breathing, has no pulse, and has been buried for less than 35 minutes, start CPR.

If the burial time has exceeded 35 minutes and there is no air pocket (i.e. the mouth and nose are stuffed with snow, ice or debris), and the victim has no pulse and is not breathing, he is dead. Don't waste your time on CPR. Concentrate on searching for other victims. The reason for this is that the absence of an air pocket tells you that the victim has not been breathing for 35 minutes. Nobody can survive that.

If the victim is not breathing but has a pulse, mouth to mouth resuscitation is required urgently. The victim could be suffering from carbon dioxide poisoning (slow asphyxia), and might wake up after as little as a few breaths.

If the victim was totally covered with snow, hypothermia is never an issue in the first 30 minutes. This excludes the possibility of hypothermia being the cause of unconsciousness in this case.

When digging, remember that it is important to note the presence of any air pocket in front of the victim's face. It can be the smallest ice-lined cavity or space. This has a major effect on how to proceed. If the airway is totally obstructed by snow, ice or debris, it's easy; then there is no air pocket. If in doubt, act as if there is an air pocket.

HIGH-ALTITUDE RELATED PROBLEMS
There are three basic, possible problems: Acute Mountain Sickness (AMS), High Altitude Cerebral Edema (HACE), and High

Altitude Pulmonary Edema (HAPE). Generally they don't occur below 3000 metres (9000 feet). The only definite treatment for them all is to descend, which is often easy to do when skiing. Susceptibility has nothing to do with fitness; it's probably in your genes, and generally gets better with age. If you have had it once, be prepared to encounter it again! The key to success is slow acclimatisation. If you have suffered from AMS on earlier ascents, you can try preventing it with acetazolamid (Diamox) 125–250 mg twice daily, starting one day before the ascent. Anyone allergic to sulpha compounds should not use acetazolamid.

Symptoms Headache, nausea and sleeping problems dominate AMS. If symptoms include ataxia (try to walk toe-to-heel in a straight line), altered level of consciousness, wheezing breathing sounds, bloody cough or extreme fatigue you may have encountered the more serious conditions of HACE or HAPE. Your life depends on making a fast descent.

SNOW BLINDNESS
Symptoms Pain (can start 6–12 hours after exposure to the sun), and it feels as if you have sand in your eyes. Can even cause temporary blindness.
Treatment Rest the eyes in the dark (in bad cases 24–48 hours).
Prevention Wear good quality sunglasses or goggles.

DEHYDRATION
Symptoms Loss of strength and coordination, cramps, headache. Disorientation and coma if severe.
Treatment Fluids. If dehydration is due to excessive sweating, salt should also be administered (ordinary food is salty enough, such as sandwiches).
Prevention Drink enough in the morning and regularly throughout the day (before you become thirsty). A late warning sign is if your pee is going a dark yellow colour, or you notice that you haven't peed for the whole day. Then you are most likely already dehydrated.

BROKEN TEETH Try to find the teeth and transport them in the mouth of the injured, if he is fully conscious.

THINGS TO REMEMBER DURING TREATMENT
___ Don't do anything if you don't know what to do. Call the rescue service, they'll know what to do.
___ Don't ever rub frostbite (nips) with snow! Don't rub it at all!
___ Don't give a person who has an altered level of consciousness anything to eat or drink, and avoid any eating and drinking when the injured person needs transport to a medical centre (except for painkillers, if awake).
___ Don't slap unconscious victims to wake them up.
___ Don't ignore vomiting. If a victim throws up, especially if unconscious, this is a threat to A in the ABC priorities. Treat it accordingly (rinse, recovery position).
___ Don't use reflective foil to keep warm. It will give shelter from wind and precipitation, but it is useless for retaining heat. A bivi sack is a much better option.

WHAT TO PRACTISE Practise pulse-counting, chinlift, CPR, splinting, using the SAM splint, logrolling and lifting someone with a back injury. Go on a course.

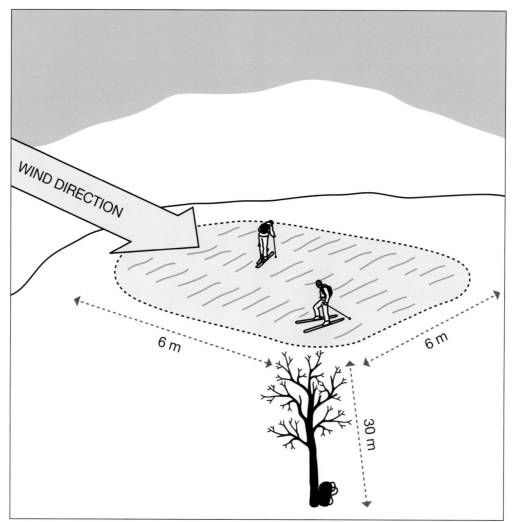

021 Flatten the snow in the landing zone.

022 Signal the helicopter.

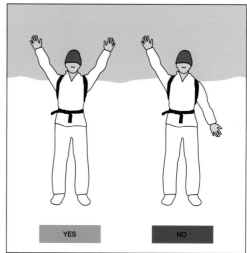

023 Signals to the pilot.

EVACUATION

If an injured person can't get off the mountain with a bit of help, but needs to be transported, it's better to stay put, even if it means waiting for twenty four hours in a snow cave for the mountain rescue team to arrive. Improvised sledges of skis and bivy sacks will definitely worsen the condition of the injured person. The techniques described here are more as emergency techniques for skiing expeditions in remote areas, where a serious accident is life-threatening no matter what you do. Then it doesn't matter if you worsen the status of the injured person while trying to evacuate, since there's no help available.

HELICOPTER PICK UP PREPARATIONS When waiting for helicopter rescue you need to choose a good spot for the helicopter to land. Pick a flat area of 6x6 metres, compress powder snow by side stepping with skis on. The total landing zone should be 30x30 metres without any obstacles sticking up such as trees, pylons, power lines, etc. Make sure that the zone is protected from avalanches, falling rocks and seracs. The helicopter should be able to approach the landing zone against the wind without any obstacles in the way. Make sure you hold on to all loose objects, such as skis, poles, gloves, etc. [See diagrams 021 and 022.]

Signals to the pilot: YES, "We need help", "Landing is possible".

NO, "We don't need help", "Landing is not possible". [See diagram 023.]

Stand in front of the flat landing spot with your arms raised and the wind behind you.

Kneel and stay still (to give the pilot a reference point in the whirling powder snow). Establish eye contact with the pilot and wait for instructions. Do not approach until the crew tell you to. Never approach the helicopter from the rear!

Remember:
1. Make sure the scene is safe for you and the victim. Call the rescue service.
2. Airway with spinal control. Chinlift. Remove any loose objects in the mouth.
3. Breathing. Check breathing. If no breathing, do mouth to mouth resuscitation and check pulse.
4. Circulation. Check the pulse. Stop any obvious bleeding. CPR if no pulse.
5. Recovery position if applicable. Immobilise fractures. Keep the patient warm!

008

It's five o'clock in the morning. We're in Cabane Bertol, in Switzerland, and roughly 30–40 cm of snow has fallen during the night. And it's still snowing. I am supposed to take my clients on the last stretch of the Haute-Route between Chamonix and Zermatt. However, even though I have carefully plotted the waypoints on my GPS device, and even though I feel confident when it comes to traditional navigation techniques, I hesitate. I start reasoning with myself.

Has it been windy during the night? Without visibility, evaluating the avalanche hazard will be difficult, or even impossible.

Will we be able to keep to a flat enough route and, equally important, avoid exposure from above? It's late in the season, and the snow is warming up fast.

Last but not least: Will we make it down within reasonable time, considering the snow conditions? Having to navigate in the white-out, through the maze of huge crevasses, will certainly slow us down. And skiing roped up with less than expert skiers will also be very time consuming.

With quite a few questions still unanswered, I have breakfast and put off making the big decision a little longer, hoping for a change.

An hour passes. We're still in the hut, on a ridge. On the east side, towards Zermatt, it's still snowing, but on the west side, towards Arolla, it's clearing up. Three other guided groups leave the hut, heading for Zermatt. I figure that at least one of the guides did the Haute-Route last week and took the exact waypoints down the glacier. Another colleague, who saw me programming my GPS from the map last night, is trying to convince me to go to Zermatt, as it would be easier for him to have me and the GPS as backup when crossing the glacier plateau.

As the weather clears up towards Arolla, we would get a long untracked run in perfect visibility, all the way down in the valley – but we would not finish the Haute-Route. On the other hand, what would we achieve other than our pre-set goal if we were to try for Zermatt instead? And would it be worth the risk, compared to the other option?

Towards Zermatt, we'll be skiing roped up in the white-out (as opposed to not being roped up in perfect visibility). No one will enjoy that. Also, the snow condition is always a potential risk factor that is difficult to evaluate with zero visibility. Further on, navigating between the crevasses with only waypoints taken from a map will be complicated. Losing time would be easy, and time is also a risk factor here. And on top of everything, it would be difficult in this weather to get assistance quickly if someone snapped a knee ligament – that is always a risk with fairly inexperienced skiers in these circumstances.

I decide to say "no" to my colleague and wait until 7.30. If it doesn't clear up towards the east by then, my choice will be that nice, smooth run down to Arolla. And if it clears up at 7.30, well it won't matter, as it will probably be too late to go for Zermatt by then.

At 7.28, as I step into my bindings, it clears in the east and the sun comes out. In a split second, I make the decision to go for Zermatt anyway. Ten minutes earlier I had told my clients that it would be Arolla, so they're pleasantly surprised.

9 am. The clouds come back so we rope up. The wind has picked up, so there are no old tracks to follow. I have decided to continue the last bit over Tête Blanche and ski down to Zermatt, and have ended up with my group exactly where I didn't want to be, skiing roped up, navigating the white-out, trying to avoid the crevasses. Every time it darkens under the ski tips, we have to back up and turn 90° before we carry on.

Later, on the Zmutt glacier, we get below the clouds and the visibility is perfect. Free at last, with the rope in my backpack, we all enjoy the run down in big cruising turns. Everyone in the group is very satisfied. Still – as we push over the flat sections towards the groomed ski slopes of Zermatt, I can't help asking myself whether or not I made the right choice. Getting to Zermatt in one piece doesn't necessarily mean that the decision I made this morning was right. At least, not if you want to learn something for future use.

The importance of being able to navigate accurately in the mountains is obvious. It is a basic skill. Not only will it make your outings safer, but it will also help you to find better snow and new, exciting runs. Like most mountaineering skills, navigation is an art rather than a technique. The art of collecting available information, and making accurate assessments. This is especially true when navigating in bad weather, which is never as black or white as most inexperienced mountaineers seem to think (that you either know exactly where you are at all times or, if you don't, you are lost).

What makes winter navigation special is that the snow cover disguises all the small objects in the terrain. You won't be able to follow trails, streams, etc. However, there is an advantage — the snow forms a more or less uniform cover on which to travel. This makes timing pretty straightforward, as conditions under foot are fairly predictable and don't change that much. However, the skill of simply navigating from point A to point B during the winter is not enough. When planning a route, remember to consider avalanche danger and other objective dangers as well. It is easy to navigate yourself into problems, just because you know how to navigate in bad visibility. Having this skill doesn't automatically mean that you should always go irrespective of visibility. Take everything into account. For example, on steeper terrain it is difficult to evaluate the avalanche hazard in poor visibility, and the consequences of an accident become more serious.

When planning a route, it is possible to avoid a lot of mistakes by studying the map carefully and considering what the conditions are likely to be; taking into account aspect, altitude and time of day.

EQUIPMENT

Basic equipment for navigating in the mountains consists of: A map, a compass, an altimeter and a map inclinometer. An addition to the basic equipment — but never a replacement — is a GPS (Global Positioning System).

THE MAP

Map reading is the foundation of navigation. Using an altimeter together with the ability to look at the map and picture exactly what the terrain looks like, and vice versa terrain to map, will probably be the only skill you will use for navigating in good visibility.

Make sure that your map is up to date and therefore accurate. You must be careful when navigating on glaciers with a map that is a few years old. A crevasse can open where there is none marked, seracs can form in new places and, as most glaciers are retreating, the end of the glacier may be further back than indicated on the map. Talk to locals and get recent information.

SCALE The scale is the relationship of the distance on the map to the distance on the ground. For example on a 1:50000 map, 1 cm on the map is 50000 cm (500 metres) on the ground.

A 1:50000 map is generally accurate enough for ski mountaineering, and you get a better overview when the map is not too detailed. However, a larger scale, such as 1:25000, is better for navigating on more complex terrain and for navigating in bad visibility. When switching between using both scales, it can be difficult to get the feeling of the relationship between the spacing of the contour lines and the steepness of the ground. If you are used to the spacing between the contour lines on the 1:50000 map it can be easy to underestimate the steepness of the slope when using a 25000 scale.

<u>CONTOUR LINES</u> The contour lines join points of equal elevation. The shape and steepness of the ground can be interpreted from their form. The further apart the contours are, the flatter the terrain is, and vice versa. The altitude of the contours is given at certain places so the altitude of any point on the map can be worked out. These figures appear the right way up when you are "facing uphill". Where the terrain is too steep to show all the contour lines on the map, a steeper cliff symbol is often used. On glaciers, the contour lines are marked in blue. The vertical distance between them is shown in the key. [See diagrams 001 and 002.]

Study the map carefully so that you know what the terrain will actually look like when you get there, so that as features appear you know that you are on the

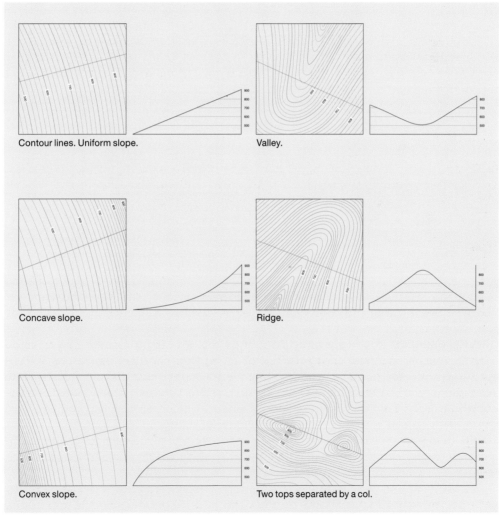

Contour lines. Uniform slope.

Valley.

Concave slope.

Ridge.

Convex slope.

Two tops separated by a col.

001

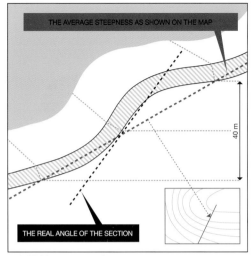

002 Hidden steep sections.

Note: Study the map carefully so that you know what the terrain will actually look like when you get there, so that as features appear you know that you are on the right track.

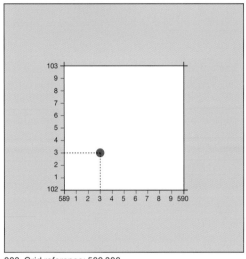

003 Grid reference; 589 300
102 300

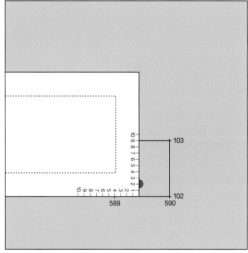

004 Grid reference measured with a compass.

right track. If they don't appear, you must stop, look at the map, and work out where you went wrong and where you are.

GRID REFERENCES Most maps have a set of grid lines running north to south and east to west. These grid lines are numbered, so that coordinates can be worked out for exact positions. These figures are the waypoints that you put into the GPS. But even if you're not using a GPS it is worthwhile learning how to work out the coordinates. As long as you know your precise location on the map you can give the coordinates of your exact location, should you have an accident.

The grid system varies from one country to another, so learn how to measure the grid on the map you are using. But the waypoint is always measured from west to east, and from south to north. [See diagrams 003 and 004.]

SETTING THE MAP BY LANDMARKS Setting the map means getting the top of the map pointing north so that it lays the same way as the ground it represents. By

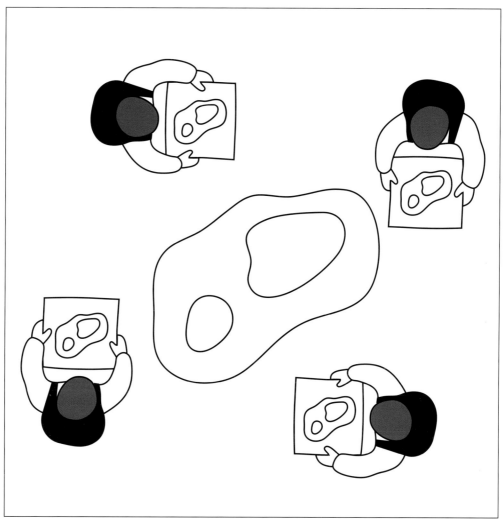

005 Setting the map by landmarks.

ignoring the "right or wrong" way up and instead keeping the map in the direction you travel, it is much easier to relate the map to the ground and identify features. On a day with good visibility this is done by identifying at least two objects and turning the map so the contours correspond. [See diagram 005.]

THE COMPASS

A professional mirror compass with luminous markings and inclinometer will give you all the compass features you need. The magnetic needle is affected by metal and electronic devices so don't hold the compass too close to any such objects when navigating or taking bearings.

FINDING NORTH True north is the direction to the North Pole from any point on the Earth. This is of little importance in navigation. Grid north is the north to

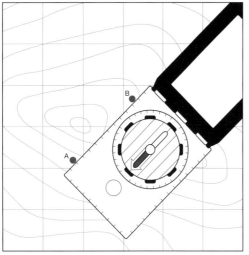

006:1 Bearings – map to compass.

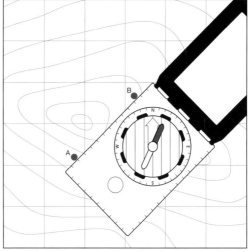

006:2 Bearings – map to compass.

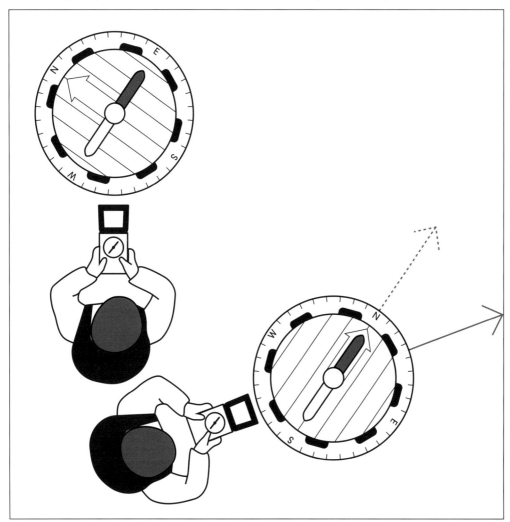

006:3 Bearings – map to compass.

which the grid line on the map points.

Magnetic north — this is the direction in which the magnetic needle of the compass points. Due to the Earth's magnetic field, the needle is pulled over to one side. Magnetic variation varies from place to place and from year to year. Information regarding magnetic variation is found in the map key.

SETTING THE MAP BY COMPASS

1. Lay an edge of the compass (with the bearing 0° on it) along a north–south grid line, make sure that the direction of travel arrow is pointing towards the north of the map (the top).
2. Set the magnetic variation on the compass housing.
3. Hold the compass firmly on the map and turn the whole package until the needle lies within the orientation arrow.

BEARINGS, MAP TO COMPASS The most common use for the compass is to take the bearing from the map, put it into the compass, and then follow the compass. When taking the bearing from the map it doesn't matter which way it is pointing.

1. Place the edge of the compass along the line joining your location, A and your destination, B. The direction of travel arrow must point in the intended direction of travel.
2. Hold the compass firmly on the map and turn the housing until the orienting lines are parallel to the north–south gridlines, with the north of the housing pointing to the north on the map.
3. Read off the bearing at the direction of travel arrow, making sure that you haven't made a 180° error. For example, if you would like to travel north–east, the bearing should be 45° and not 225°.
4. Correct the magnetic variation.
5. Hold the compass flat in front of you with the direction of travel arrow pointing straight ahead. Turn around until the red magnetic needle lies within the orientation arrow and points to the north of the housing. [See diagram 006.]

FOLLOWING A BEARING IN GOOD VISIBILITY Sight along the direction of travel arrow to find a marker directly in the line of travel. Put the compass away and go to the marker. When the marker is reached take a new bearing if necessary.

If you are good at reading the map you won't follow bearings in good visibility very often. However, every now and then it is an effective way of confirming that you are going the right way.

BEARINGS, COMPASS TO MAP There are occasions where it can be useful to take a bearing with the compass and convert it to the map. To check your position (back bearing), to identify a feature, or to take the aspect of a slope.

Checking your position Back bearing is when you take a bearing on a known feature (for example a summit) and convert it to the map. It works best when you know your approximate position, because of travelling on a linear feature such as a ridge. In such a case it is even easier to find your location by transferring the known altitude from the altimeter to the map. Back bearing is mainly used on fairly flat features where an altimeter can't really help you find your exact location.

The technique requires enough visibility for at least one object to be identified. If you have better visibility than that, there is normally no need to take a back bearing.

1. Hold the compass flat and point the direction of travel arrow towards a known feature.
2. Turn the compass housing until the orientation arrow lies under the red magnetic needle.
3. Correct the magnetic variation.
4. Place the edge of the compass on top of the known feature on the map with the orienting lines parallel to the north–south grid lines and the orientation arrow pointing to the north of the map.
5. Your position is somewhere along the edge of the compass and the extension of that line. [See diagram 007.]

Identifying a feature To identify a feature you have to know your exact location on the map. The technique is almost the same as taking a back bearing.

1. Hold the compass flat and point the direction of travel arrow towards the feature.
2. Turn the compass housing until the orientation arrow lies under the red magnetic needle.
3. Correct the magnetic variation.
4. Place the edge of the compass on top of your position on the map, with the orienting lines parallel to the north–south grid lines and the orientation arrow pointing to the north of the map.
5. The feature you are trying to identify is somewhere along the edge of the compass and the extension of that line.

Taking the aspect of a slope The direction in which a slope faces can be a useful aid if you are unsure of your exact position. Place your skis horizontally, to make it easier to find the fall line in poor visibility.

1. Point the direction of travel arrow up or down the fall line (perpendicular to your skis).
2. Turn the compass housing until the orientation arrow lies under the red magnetic needle.
3. Correct the magnetic variation.
4. Put the compass on the map and slide it in your supposed position while keeping the orientation lines parallel to the north–south grid lines and the ori-

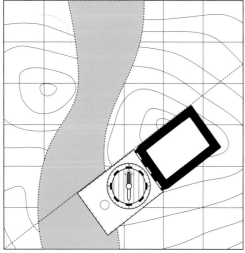

007 Back bearing.

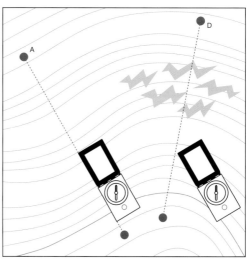

008 Aspect of the slope – line A in the example.

entation arrow pointing to the north of the map. When the edge of the compass cuts the contour lines at a right angle you have found the slope you are on.

5. With the exact altitude from your altimeter you can locate your position along the line.

This doesn't work if you're on a big uniform slope in the same aspect but it's a good technique to use when you want to stay away from danger in more varied terrain. [See diagram 008.]

THE ALTIMETER

In the mountains you are navigating both in the horizontal and the vertical plane. A compass will only help in the horizontal plane. For orientation in the vertical plane you need an altimeter. Especially when skiing, because you lose height very quickly.

Choose an altimeter, which has a measurement interval of 5 metres or less, and a chronometer function.

Since the altimeter reacts with atmospheric pressure you must reset it to the actual altitude at every known altitude (which you get from identifying your exact position on the map), otherwise it will show the wrong altitude due to changes in the atmospheric pressure. The altimeter is also affected by temperature changes, so keep it outside of your clothing when navigating in bad weather.

DEFINITE FEATURES When going up or down definite features (such as ridges, couloirs, narrow glaciers or valleys), it is easy to get a fixed position even in poor visibility. Simply transfer the altitude from the altimeter to the map. However, for this to work well, the features can't be too flat. For example, a long, flat summit plateau where 20–30 metres of vertical difference can make a big difference to the horizontal position. A GPS is a very helpful tool when navigating in such places with poor visibility.

SKIING The altimeter can be a very helpful tool for route finding while descending big mountains or glaciers, even with visibility. Study your descents carefully so you know the run by heart, take notes (mental or on a piece of paper) at what altitudes you have to do traverses. [See diagram 009.]

BAD VISIBILITY NAVIGATION

Keep the map in a plastic bag such as the Ortlieb models, and easily accessible in a pocket of your jacket. Attach the compass to your jacket using the compass lanyard so you don't lose it. Keep the compass in your pocket when you are not using it.

IF BAD WEATHER OR IF CLOUDS ARE MOVING IN FAST Be quick in taking a compass bearing on the next waypoint or fix before it disappears. A fix, or a fix-point, is a point you know the exact location of. It can be hard to find one in poor visibility.

ERRORS Be observant of the margin of error when taking bearings in the mountains. If it's snowing, cold and windy, and either your fingers are frozen stiff or you are trying to take the bearing with gloves on, it is easy to make errors when performing the following tasks:

___ When taking the bearing on the map.
___ When adding the magnetic variation.
___ When following the bearing.

As these errors could be cumulative, there is a real risk of ending up a long way from where you intended. So when taking a bearing in bad weather you need to be very thorough and keep the navigational legs (the stretches between the way-points) as short as possible (never more than 400 metres). The best way of avoiding this problem is to plan a route and prepare a route card at home, in the hut or in the tent.

PLANNING A ROUTE FOR POOR VISIBILITY When making a plan for bad weather navigation it is necessary to study the map carefully and plan the route so that it follows easily navigable terrain, and use every terrain feature that could help you. The legs should be kept short. Note your plan down on a route card.

Handrails Easily identifiable features that can be followed, such as rock walls, ridges, etc.

Attack points When going to a smaller object such as a hut, you go first to a larger feature nearby, an attack point. From this easily located feature, you keep the margin of error low by taking your bearing from a fix and keeping the last leg short.

Aiming off When going to a point on a horizontally linear feature, such as a col, take a bearing to the closest side of the ridge and follow it in, using the ridge as a handrail. This is less demanding as regards accurate navigation and avoids having to search in the wrong direction if you aren't spot-on when following the direct bearing. [See diagram 010.]

DISTANCE Estimating distance is very important when navigating without a GPS. There are two ways of finding out how far along a navigational leg you have gone.

Pacing To use pacing as a method for estimating distance, you first need to find out how many double paces you take to cover 100 metres. Mark up 100 metres with a

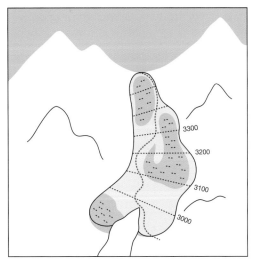

009 3300 — skier's right, 2800 — skier's left.

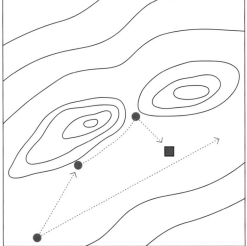

010 Instead of risking missing the hut in poor visibility, use the col as an attack point, aim off and follow the steep slope as a handrail.

climbing rope and count the number of double paces (for example, count the number of times you put your right foot down) it takes you to cover the distance when skinning. Do this on flat ground and on as steep ground as you can without having to do switchbacks, and then the angle in between the two. Put the figures in a personal pacing chart. Remember that because of the angle of the shaft it will not be the same number of paces if you change from a pair of alpine ski boots to a pair of ski touring boots.

When navigating, tick off each 100 metres as they are covered (don't calculate the total number of paces needed). Keep the legs short to minimise the risk of human error, and remember that this method does not work when doing switchbacks on steeper terrain.

Estimating time On a route card, add up the estimated time for all the legs and add extra time for pauses, etc. This gives you a time estimate for every individual leg, and an overall estimated time for the day. When moving as fast as the estimated speed, it is an efficient method for measuring distance covered. Once in the mountains you might have to adjust your speed estimate (and as a consequence the times) to reality. Never try to keep up with the time estimates; they are only there to help you make decisions.

Adjust your time estimates if you move faster or slower than expected. For example, conditions underfoot can be different to those expected.

When taking a pause, or stopping to study the map in the middle of a leg, you must stop the chronometer. Calculation of the individual legs is based on constantly moving at a certain speed.

By keeping track of the time (even in good weather) you can see whether you are way behind the overall estimated time after a few legs, and therefore whether you will be unable to complete plan A within reasonable time. If so, you can go for the back-up plan and still have a good day, instead of trying to carry on with your plan and getting into trouble, or having to turn back a couple of hours later.

A timing chart that works for most people is to estimate your walking speed and add one minute for every 10 vertical metres. You must find the formula for how fast you move on the terrain, and this can only be done through self-knowledge and evaluation of experience (you have to time yourself). On average, groups that I guide walk on skins at a speed of 3 kms/h+1 minute per 10 vertical metres.

METRES	KMS/H			
	5	4	3	2
1000	12	15	20	30
800	10	12	16	24
700	9	11	14	21
500	6	7.5	10	15
400	5	6	8	12
200	2.5	3	4	6
100	1.25	1.5	2	3

When estimating speed, you have to take into account everything that could influence it. What is the size of the group, how fit are they and how much weight is the group carrying? The altitude, and the length of the route? What are condi-

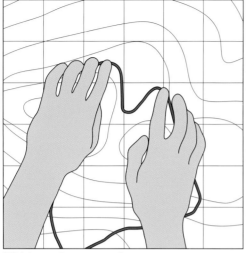
011:1 Lanyard measurement.

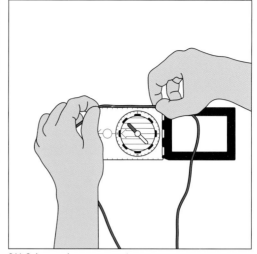
011:2 Lanyard measurement.

tions like under foot, and are you breaking trail or not? And what are the weather and wind like?

It is important to measure the distance that you will walk, not the shortest distance. Use the compass lanyard and shape it exactly to your intended route, then measure the distance on the lanyard. [See diagram 011.]

For example, if a leg is 3 cm (on a 1:25 000 map) and 60 vertical metres are gained, moving at a speed of 3 kms/h it would take you 21 minutes to complete the leg. (3 cm=750 metres, at a speed of 3 kms/h gives 15 minutes+6 minutes for the vertical=21 minutes.)

Copy the timing chart and keep the copy handy, for example on your compass, so as to minimise human error if you have to adjust your estimate when tired after a long day of navigating in bad visibility.

It is impossible to give a rule of thumb for estimating time for technical climbing or skiing, as it varies with skill and condition. You simply have to learn how fast you move from experience.

ROUTE CARD Navigating in poor visibility without a GPS often means that you can't take the shortcuts that you could with good visibility. The route card is always prepared for zero visibility. If visibility is better than expected, navigate as normal by careful map reading. If visibility becomes less good during the day you can always use the route card. Time spent preparing a route card is always time well spent if you have to navigate in poor visibility. Bear in mind that you don't have to use the route card or follow it just because you have it. Remain open-minded as always, and be prepared to re-evaluate your decisions. Be flexible and use the route card as one of the aids for navigation, not as the plan you must stick to at all times. For example:

Have an alternative plan or escape route in case the weather gets really bad or if the route takes longer than expected.

If you come across old frozen avalanche debris that is impossible to cross within a reasonable time you may have to choose another route, or completely change plans if you think that there is a risk of further avalanches.

If you run into debris from a fallen serac (scattered lumps of ice across your

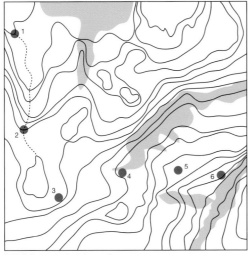

012:1 Intended route on the map.

Note.						
PLACE	ALTITUDE	+/-	BEARING	DISTANCE	SPEED	TIME
1) ROCKFACE	2400	+100	FOLLOW THE STEEP SLOPE & THEN UP THE GULLY	875m	3 KPH	27 ½ MIN
2) END OF RAVINE	2500	+20	154°	700 M	3 KPH	16 MIN
3) STEEPENING	2520	+60	71°	625 M	3 KPH	8½ MIN
4) GLACIER	2580	+70	86°	500 M	– 11 –	17 MIN
5) BOULDER	2650	+50	98°	375 M	3 KPH	10 ½
6) SECOND GLACIER	2700					1.29 H

012:2 Route card.

path) and it looks as if it will take time to cross, or the visibility doesn't allow you to see how wide the risk zone is, you will have to change your plans.

If a glacier is very open and it will take forever (and the result is going to be questionable) to ski down roped up, then perhaps the best decision is to stay in the hut and wait for better visibility. Even if that means missing your train and arriving late for work. [See diagram 012.]

THE GPS

Due to very slow speeds in mountaineering applications, only devices which combine GPS with at least a compass and barometric altimeter are a good choice. There is no question about it, if correctly used, the GPS is a fantastic tool in the mountains. Large geographical objects are not needed as waypoints (which means that you can avoid dramatic changes in terrain steepness as waypoints, and its risks regarding avalanche danger and the fall risk) and you can always get a fix-point. Most of the time the GPS will be kept in the bottom of your backpack, to be used only in poor visibility. Make sure you know how to use it before you actually need it! If you haven't used your GPS for a long time, or if you have travelled a long distance (across a continent with the GPS turned off), it can take up to 20 minutes to find its position. Make sure to check it before you go, and at the same time calibrate the compass and altimeter and make sure that you have the right map date and grid system programmed.

If you enjoy technology you can buy the maps on CD-ROM, plan your route on the computer, download the waypoints into your GPS, download pre-made routes from the web, and exchange routes with others. The latest generation of GPS units take it one step further and allow you to download topographical maps. With a small joystick, creating waypoints is quick and easy. And the risk of human error is eliminated when no coordinates are measured and programmed by hand.

To get the most out of a GPS, it is important to know its comparative strengths and weaknesses.

The benefits You can always get a fix-point — this is important when taking a bearing from the map, or when you need to notify the mountain rescue service of your exact location after an accident. On top of that, the GPS leads you directly to the waypoints (which can be imaginary points, for example on a glacier plateau) no matter what the visibility.

Things to watch The GPS might use too much battery power (especially on a multiple day tour), depending on how modern it is. Loss of battery power in cold weather is also a problem. Lithium batteries should be used, with a spare set in the backpack, as they provide full power until they suddenly die. Another aspect to take into account is that the transmission of information to the GPS device can be affected from equipment used by the US Department of Defence.

If battery power does not matter Simply program your waypoints and follow them to your goal. If precision is of importance (for example when moving between crevasses on a glacier), move between the waypoints and not along a programmed route. When choosing a route with linked waypoints, the program will make shortcuts.

If battery power does matter Only use the GPS to take fix-points when you need to back up traditional navigation, or when you need a fix to take a bearing from. In between, turn it off and keep it in your pocket. Note: If you enter the wrong coordinates in the GPS that's where you will end up. So be thorough, both when taking grid references and programming, especially if done in the mountains during bad weather.

Don't expect the GPS to take you exactly to within a metre of the waypoint. It will be close enough, but allow some distance for a safety margin if you want to stay clear of certain terrain features, such as drop-offs, etc.

You should still use the map in order to know where you are if anything should happen to the GPS.

HOW TO PRACTISE

Learning how to navigate is not difficult. But as with most skills, if you don't practise you won't be able to navigate when you need to.

COMPASS & MAP The box will allow you to practise the basics of timing, pacing and walking on a bearing.

Find a large, flat open space, and place an object (for example a backpack) on the ground. Put any bearing into the compass and walk 100 metres on that bearing, using pacing or timing. When you have completed 100 metres, turn 90° to your bearing and walk another 100 metres. Repeat this twice again, and if you have done well you will end up back at the backpack, or close to it.

Choose an easily accessible area. Take 6—10 easily identifiable waypoints on the map and make a route card. Go out and follow it precisely, both in good weather and in bad weather. You will learn a lot from analysing your actions and results.

GPS Choose an easily accessible area. Take 6—10 easily identifiable waypoints on the map and enter them in the GPS. Go out and navigate along the waypoints and get a feeling of how close you are, both when going from waypoint to waypoint and also when tying the waypoints to a route. Try this in both good weather and bad weather. After this, do the same thing but navigate traditionally, and use only the GPS as a backup or to take fix-points.

009

SKI-RELATED MOUNTAINEERING SKILLS

I have a friend who climbed a summit in the Alps a couple of years ago, in order to ski down on the other side.

He was skinning up the glacier early in the morning, and as it got steeper, he decided to put his skis on his backpack and continue on foot. As it was spring, the snow was bulletproof and he climbed a south-west face. There were good, solid steps, and the terrain wasn't too steep, so my friend carried on, his ice axe still in the backpack.

Gradually, without my friend noticing it, the terrain got steeper. So as the steps started to slope out and become even icier, he suddenly found himself in a position where falling simply wasn't an option. He was standing on slippery, sloping footsteps; wearing a pair of plastic alpine boots without Vibram soles. He couldn't reach the ice axe in his backpack, so he was forced to grab his ski poles more than half way down because it was so steep.

Then out of nowhere, a climber with crampons – and two ice axes – appeared, said hello, and climbed by, right next to my friend. Even today, I still haven't figured out why my friend didn't ask the climber for help. Instead, he just kept pushing on, and eventually made it to the summit, exhausted, and with the worst fright of his life behind him.

My friend – who is a great skier, but apparently not an experienced mountaineer, ended up taking a much bigger risk on the straight climb up to the summit, which should be easy enough, than he did skiing down the steep, exposed couloir on the other side.

If he had possessed the common mountaineering sense to put on his crampons and take out his ice axe in a safe spot before commencing the climb, he would have been safer and gone up faster.

In the mountains, always plan ahead and decide what gear or technique will help you to progress as safely as possible. Ideally, always have a selection of equipment to meet your requirements. This is not always possible, but is something that should be aimed for. Prepare yourself as much as possible before leaving home, get as much information as possible, and use the knowledge you have. If you intend climbing a steep south-facing couloir early in the morning during a spring snow cycle, you know it will be rock hard and that you need to take crampons and an ice axe. Secondly, have the right gear handy just before you need it.

On the one hand, climbing in too much snow or on dry rock with crampons is hard work and time-consuming. Perhaps it's a very short section, so the fastest way of progressing is to leave the crampons on rather than take them off and put them on again a few minutes later or vice versa. Perhaps cutting a few steps with your ice axe is faster than putting your crampons on and taking them off again. Conditions change and individual skill levels differ. Don't copy other people's solutions; make up your own mind as to what is right and acceptable for you in the prevailing conditions.

EQUIPMENT

The equipment that is carried should be useful in a variety of situations. Otherwise you will have to carry a huge backpack full of specialised gear. On the other hand, don't leave home under-equipped. The aim is for your group to be self-reliant.

TECHNIQUES

The more techniques you have at your fingertips, the more likely you are to find appropriate solutions or avoid problems before they arise. The techniques or solutions should be:
___ safe,
___ efficient and
___ require the use of minimal gear.
Bear that in mind when you are training and learning new techniques. If someone can show you a technique that lives up to these criteria and is superior to the technique you are already using, be prepared to change. Don't make techniques personal and refuse to adapt and change due to ego.

THE BASIC CLIMBING SYSTEM (PITCHING) The safest system of rope climbing is to pitch, which means that only one person climbs at a time and is protected by the rope whilst doing so. Both climbers are attached to the rope and while one is climbing, the other, who is safely attached, is managing the rope so he can arrest a fall if necessary.

Certain terms have to be known to avoid confusion:
___ To belay — To secure the person who is climbing with the rope.
___ Being "On belay" or to be belayed — Being belayed whilst climbing.
___ The belayer — The climber who belays the rope.

___ Anchor — A natural point (for example a large block) or a constructed point (for example an ice screw) on which the climber can secure himself.

___ A belay or a belay anchor — One or more anchor points tied together for greater strength.

___ To be anchored or secured — Being attached to a belay.

___ The belay — The whole system of anchor, belayer and method used to belay.

___ A pitch — The distance between two belays.

___ Runner — An article of equipment that the lead climber clips to the rope to shorten a fall.

MULTI-PITCH CLIMB Person A leads the first pitch whilst being belayed by B who is safe on the belay.

A places runners to protect the belay anchor and himself in the event of a fall.

When A runs out of rope or he finds a good place for a belay, he stops and builds a belay.

A takes in the slack rope (makes the rope tight) from B and belays him as he is climbing.

B brings the material from the belay anchor and all the runners along the way. If B should fall he would only fall the 20—30 centimetres that the rope stretches before it becomes taunt, because B is belayed from the top.

When B comes up to the belay, one of the two climbers takes over all the gear and continues onwards, to lead. [See diagram 001.]

The system remains the same whether you climb one pitch or ten pitches, whether you have been climbing for a week or ten years. The good thing about the system is that it is not difficult to learn. If you can manage the system when doing two pitches, you can manage the same system for ten pitches.

The downside of the system is that there is no learning curve as there is in skiing, where you can start skiing on blue slopes and make progress safely. The climbing system has to work right from the start! The qualities you do develop are your personal skills in handling the gear, applying the right techniques and making the right decisions. Your techniques will become faster and safer with experience, but the basic system will not change.

CLIMBING EQUIPMENT

The basics of ski mountaineering are largely to do with being well equipped and knowing when and how to use the gear.

Harness You have to ensure that the harness fits over bulky clothing, and that there are enough gear loops to carry the gear you need to have handy on the harness. A fully adjustable harness is probably the best option. It doesn't need to be well padded, because you are not likely to hang in the harness for long periods of time and you often wear a lot of clothing under the harness.

Crampons You can imagine what a broken or ill-fitting crampon can mean in an exposed place.

The crampons must not only fit well on the boot sole, but the straps and clip on system must fit your ski boot as well. As there is no standard system you simply have to take your ski boots to the shop and try different models to see what works on your boots. Just because you have a pair that works well on your summer hiking shoes doesn't mean that they are going to fit your ski boots as well.

001:1 Pitch climbing.

001:2 Pitch climbing.

001:3 Pitch climbing.

001:4 Pitch climbing.

The best all-round crampon is a general mountaineering crampon with 10–12 points; the front points should be horizontal for the best grip in hard snow and soft ice. And if you aim for steep skiing you should be able to strap them on using only one hand.

Lightweight aluminium crampons save a lot of weight and work well on hard snow but not on ice.

During wet snow conditions, the snow tends to ball up under the crampons and prevent the points from gripping properly. The best way to avoid this is by putting on specially-made anti-balling plates of plastic or silicon.

Finding crampons that work well with telemark boots can be especially difficult. Also, it is more important to use crampons on telemark boots since they bend when you kick to make steps. The crampon has to be flexible because the sole flexes continually; a rigid crampon risks being broken. Make sure that the front tip of the boot doesn't force the boot backwards in the crampon, creating a long gap between the toes and the front points. If that happens, the crampon will not be stable and the leverage will make the climbing even harder. If the front tip of the telemark boot sticks out too far it could prevent you climbing safely on the front points.

A good fit at home might change after a couple of hundred metres, so carry tools and extra straps to adjust and fix crampons, especially to start off with.

Sharpen the crampons fairly regularly. They are less effective on ice when they are blunt. Sharpening is done by hand, because heat produced by grinding tools can spoil the temper of the metal. At the same time, check the crampons for possible metal fatigue and that the strap-on-system is intact.

Climbing helmet This is not normally used as we are not on steep enough rock or ice, but you should of course wear one if you think there is the smallest risk of falling objects.

Ice axe The ice axe is a multi-tool used for everything from an aid to progressing to a snow belay.

I would recommend carrying a standard mountaineering ice axe with a straight shaft not longer than 55 cm, and a solid steel head (pick and adze). A shorter ice axe will fit inside the backpack while skiing, and you avoid the risk of the alpenstock impaling you in the neck if you fall over.

The shaft can be lightweight, as long as it's strong enough for use in a T-anchor. It should not have anything on the handle that could prevent it penetrating hard snow. Avoid a lightweight head, as this can't be used on ice. Take the wrist loop off, it only gets in the way when you are working with the tool and constantly moving it from one hand to the other.

When moving on hard snow or ice on steeper terrain it is normally more effective, and safer, to use a second ice axe. This can be a shorter technical ice axe, but make sure that it has a shaft that easily penetrates hard snow. And that it has a hammerhead instead of an adze (if you need to hammer any pitons).

Bent shafts are easier to pull out of snow, so they should be avoided as T-anchors. Always keep your ice axes sharp.

Karabiners Karabiners are used to attach all the gear in the climbing system. Because of individual design and shape they have different advantages and are used in different ways and places.

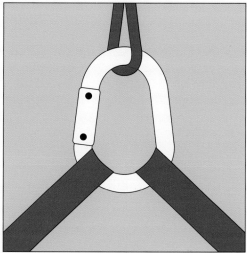

Note: A karabiner is strongest when loaded in two ways along its major axis with the gate closed.

002 Karabiner loaded in three ways.

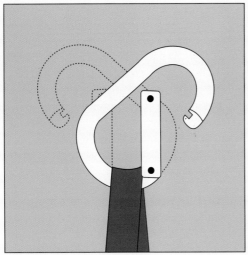

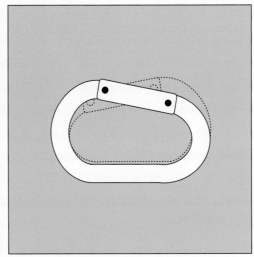

003 Two oval karabiners instead of a locking karabiner.

004 Two non-locking karabiners instead of a locking karabiner.

A karabiner is strongest when loaded in two ways along its major axis with the gate closed.

Karabiners become seriously weakened if the gates are open, if loaded over the gate or if loaded in three ways. [See diagram 002.]

The two most common types are non-locking and locking karabiners. This refers to whether the gate can be locked or not.

Non-locking karabiners have two major shapes, oval or D shape. Oval is mainly used for artificial climbing, as the lack of sharp angles makes it easier to handle when everything is under load from one's body weight. However, because of its oval shape the load is shared equally between the back bar and the less strong gate side, which makes it weaker when compared with the D shape. The D shape is stronger as it takes most of the load on the solid back. These karabiners can have either straight gates or bent gates and, together with a sling, they form a quickdraw, which is the link between the protection and the rope as you climb (a runner). The bent gate is designed to make the insertion of the rope easier and the straight gate is clipped to the equipment (ice screw, piton, etc.). Wire gates are more lightweight.

Locking karabiners Not only do these come in different shapes, they can also be self-locking or screw gate. The safe-locking system is foolproof but best avoided (accept when attaching yourself to the middle of the rope with a karabiner), because as you will see, there are certain situations in which you don't yet want the locking section to be locked.

Locking karabiners should always be used on the body for personal safety (belaying, abseiling, etc.), as there is no risk of them twisting and opening the gate. If you don't have a locking karabiner, you could use two non-locking ones.

With an oval karabiner, the gates are positioned on opposite sides. With D shaped karabiners, the gates are positioned on the same side but open in different directions. [See diagrams 003 and 004.]

Belay device The belay device should be lightweight and work for abseiling as well. It is normally used together with an HMS screw gate karabiner to avoid tangling or jamming the rope, which is possible with a smaller karabiner.

Ice screws 16–19 cm is the normal length of ice screw you should use, but you should also have at least one measuring 22 cm for making abalakovs (ice anchors for rappelling).

When carrying an ice screw on the harness while skiing, keep the protection on to avoid the teeth from shredding your clothes and to prevent injury in the case of a fall.

Snow stake This should be carried if you think there is a possibility that you may need to rappel (abseil) from a snow anchor i.e. over a bergschrund (see glacier skiing). Chop the snow stake so that it fits in your backpack, normally 55 cm in length.

Slings Two lengths should be carried. 120 (cm) slings are used for making anchors, etc.

60 (cm) slings are mainly used as extendable quickdraws, etc. Organise your slings as short as possible when they hang from the harness, to avoid getting caught somewhere or tripping over them.

THE ROPE

Ropes come in two main groups, static and dynamic. Static ropes have little elasticity and are used in situations in which you use a fixed rope and move up and down the rope a lot. Dynamic ropes are elastic in order to absorb the force of a fall, and are therefore used when climbing and in the mountains.

Rope strength The breaking strength of a climbing rope is well above any force that would be created in a fall. A single full rope has a breaking strength of about 2300 kg. A single half rope has a breaking strength of about 1500 kg.

Knots in the rope decrease its strength by between 25–45% depending on which knots are used. Running the rope over an edge also causes loss of strength. The sharper the edge, the greater the loss of strength; about 30% when over the edge of a karabiner (5 mm radius). The reason for this is that the fibres on the outer part of the curve are stretched more than those on the inside. However, for the rope to break while climbing it would have to be cut over a sharp rock edge or a razor sharp ice axe. Even stepping on the rope with crampons will not do much

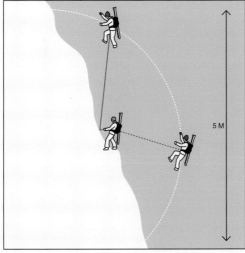

005:1 Fall factor 2.

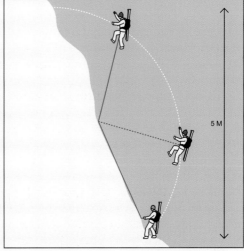

005:2 Fall factor 1.

damage, especially not on snow where the rope is pressed into the soft ground. You should examine the rope if you happen to ski over it with your edges. In these situations, a stretched rope will be more fragile than a slack.

Ropes become weaker and less dynamic when wet (less so when frozen). They also become heavier and harder to handle. Therefore, ropes used in the mountains should be dry treated.

Impact force The more dynamic the rope, the more energy it will absorb and the lower the force will be on the climber. Forces higher than 8G (8 times body weight) will cause serious injury.

The problem is that if the rope stretches a lot and arrests the fall relatively gently you will fall further and probably hurt yourself in the process.

For every fall taken the rope will stretch a little and become less dynamic. In the end, the impact forces will become too high for the rope to be used for lead climbing (the rope recovers after resting).

You must discharge the rope after a heavy fall.

Fall factors The more rope there is to absorb the fall, the less severe the force will be on the climber and on the last piece of protection (runner). The fall factor is a way of determining the hardness of a fall. The scale runs from 0—2 in climbing and the higher the number the harder the fall.

The theoretical fall factor: This assumes that there is no friction between the belayer and the last runner, allowing the entire rope to absorb the force. It is calculated by dividing the height of the fall by the length of rope available. [See diagram 005.]

$$F = \frac{\text{Height of fall}}{\text{Length of rope}}$$

The actual fall factor: Due to friction in the karabiners or against the rock, the rope can't absorb the force along the full length of rope available. This means that the impact force will be greater on the climber and the last runner than in the theoretical fall factor.

What does this mean in real life? The rope team is at its most vulnerable when one of the climbers leaves the belay and starts a new pitch. A fall before protection has been placed would mean maximum force on the system when it is the least protected. Failure of the belay anchor would, at best, only be serious. Note: To avoid this you have to place a piece of protection just after leaving the belay!

To keep the impact force low on the last runner and climber, you must reduce friction by avoiding sharp angles between runners, and allowing the rope to absorb the energy. [See diagram 006.]

Rope sizes Ropes come in two main strengths, full or half. Full (or single) ropes, roughly 9.1—11 mm thick. Half (or double) ropes, roughly 8—9 mm thick.

A single rope is used by itself, and a half rope has to be used together with another half rope (they are bought as a pair). This rule applies when climbing where forces are great in the case of a lead fall. However, if you know that you're just going to use the rope on a glacier or to abseil during a specific tour, you can carry only one piece of half rope to save weight and space. In these limited situations, forces will not be much more than body weight (unless you walk on the glacier with too much slack rope, which you shouldn't allow to happen).

The advantage with a single rope is that you can use it for everything. The disadvantages are the weight and the size (if you are not going to climb); you can only rappel half the length of the rope.

The advantages with a one-piece half rope are the weight and size. The disad-

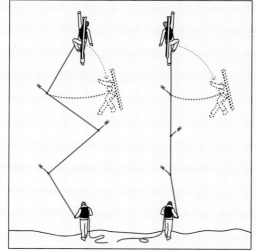

006 The actual fall factor.

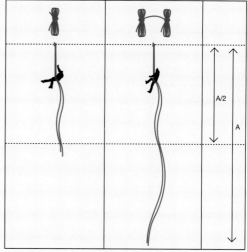

007 Rappelling on A/2 full rope, a double half rope or twin rope.

vantage is that you shouldn't use it for climbing, you can only rappel half the length of the rope.

The advantages of double half ropes are that you can avoid rope drag when climbing, and rappel the full length of the ropes. The disadvantages are the weight and size.

From a skier's point of view, you should use a single rope if you intend to climb, or use short rope technique. A one-piece half rope is good for skiing, rappelling and glacier travel while double half ropes suit long rappels.

Note: Never lead climb with a one-piece half rope. The breaking strength is not sufficient, and with thinner dimensions the risk of cutting the rope is greater.

You could however tie into both ends of a one-piece double rope and get a full strength rope to lead climb with. The disadvantage is that you will only be able to climb half the length of the actual rope length (25 metres for a 50 metre rope), but in most ski situations this is enough.

Also, you shouldn't lead climb with two full ropes. In a fall, the impact force will be too high. Use one rope when climbing, and take out the other rope when you need it for rappelling.

Rope length You can save some weight and space in your backpack by selecting the right rope length. Consider your requirements, and what you're going to do.

The advantage of a long rope is that you save a lot of time by climbing longer pitches. You can abseil longer, and if you need to rope up on a glacier you can have more people in the team. The disadvantage is that you need to carry a lot of extra rope around that you might not need (weight and space). And if you are climbing or abseiling pitches that are shorter than the capacity of the rope, you will spend a lot of time pulling rope and coiling it.

The standard length is 50 metres (164 ft), but your choice depends on planned use for that day, or general use if you only have one rope. [See diagram 007.]

Rope wear Ropes are made of nylon and therefore have a low melting point — about 250°C (Dynema and Spectra even lower). This means that sufficient heat can be created by friction to melt a rope or a sling, as one rope is pulled rapidly over another rope or sling.

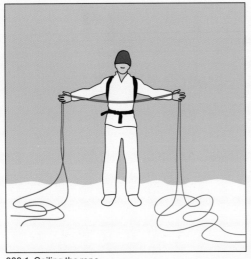

008:1 Coiling the rope.

008:2 Coiling the rope.

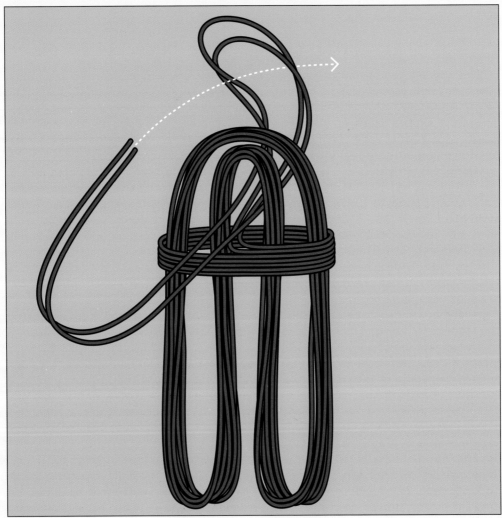

008:3 Coiling the rope.

Ultraviolet radiation damages ropes and slings, so treat all old nylon material found in the mountains (in place on belays and rappel points) with caution, and if possible avoid them. Deterioration increases with altitude, as the atmosphere blocks less ultraviolet light.

Also keep nylon equipment away from chemicals such as battery acid, for example when storing the rope in the car. Do not dry the rope in direct heat or sunlight.

Coiling the rope There are many ways of coiling rope, but I only use the one described below. It's a fast way of coiling and uncoiling rope for transportation without getting soaked by wet rope.

Lap coil: Start two arm lengths (3—4 m) from the two single ends, and drape the rope back and forth across the hand until you reach the middle of the rope.

Take the ends and whip them around the top of the rope. A bight is then pushed through the hole and the ends are pulled through the bight to secure. [See diagram 008.]

When uncoiling, do the same thing but backwards. Don't try to throw the rope on the ground and pull the ends in. Even though this seems faster you always end up with a big, time consuming mess.

KNOTS

Here are the knots you need to know for ski-mountaineering. Each knot has certain advantages, making it the best choice, or only choice, in certain situations.

Overhand knot This is used to tie a stop knot to secure the rope end when rappelling or after another knot has been tied. [See knot 1.]

Overhand knot, joining ropes of equal dimension for rappelling When tying two ropes together for rappelling, leave at least a 50 cm long tail, and tighten the knot carefully by pulling the four ends one by one. The advantage of the overhand knot is that when retrieving the rope after rappelling, the knot rolls outward away from the rock and the flat side reduces the chance of the knot jamming on the way down. The disadvantage is that the overhand knot should only be used on ropes of equal dimension. [See knot 2.]

Overhand loop This is used to make a loop to clip into on the middle of the rope. The advantages are that the knot is small and quick to make, and that it doesn't use much rope. The disadvantage is that it is difficult to untie after it has been loaded. [See knot 3.]

Overhand slip-knot This is used to prevent slings being lifted off rock spikes when used as protection, and to tie off partially driven pitons or ice screws. [See knot 4.]

Figure of eight This is used to tie into the harness, and to tie around an object for a fixed rope. The advantage is that it is foolproof. The disadvantage is that it is harder to untie after it has been loaded, compared with a bowline. [See knot 5.]

Figure of eight loop This is used to make a loop to clip into on the middle of the rope. The advantage is that it is easy to untie after it has been loaded. The disadvantage is that it is a big knot that uses a lot of rope. [See knot 6.]

Bowline This is used to tie into the harness, or to tie around an object for a fixed rope. The advantage is that it is easy to untie after it has been loaded. The disadvantage is that it is easy to get wrong. [See knot 7.]

Double bowline This is used to tie-in the middle person(s) of a rope team. The advantages are that it is safer than attaching the middle person to the rope with a

Knot 1 Overhand knot.

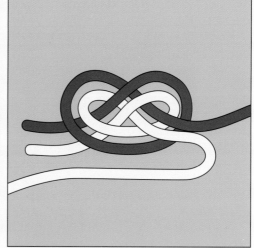

Knot 2:1 Overhand knot.

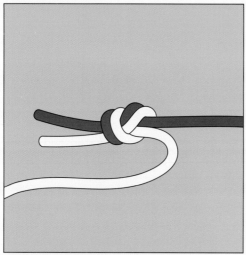

Knot 2:2 Overhand knot.

Knot 3 Overhand loop.

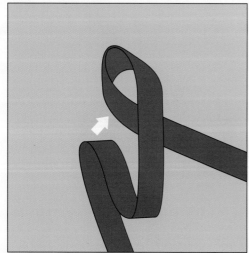

Knot 4:1 Overhand slip-knot.

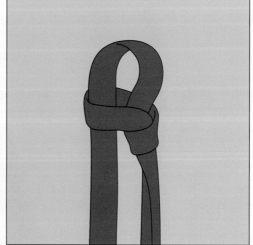

Knot 4:2 Overhand slip-knot.

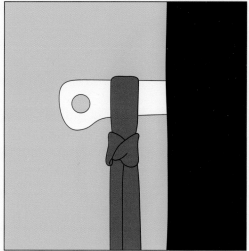

Knot 4:3 Overhand slip-knot.

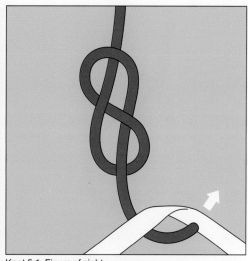

Knot 5:1 Figure of eight.

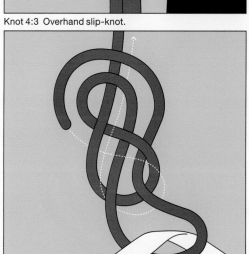

Knot 5:2 Figure of eight.

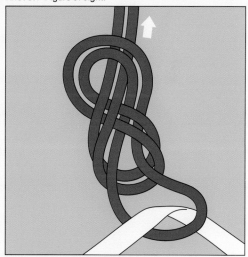

Knot 5:3 Figure of eight.

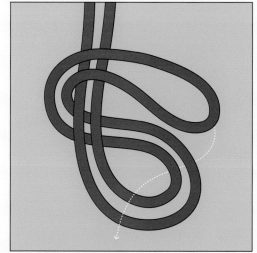

Knot 6:1 Figure of eight loop.

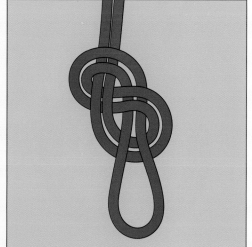

Knot 6:2 Figure of eight loop.

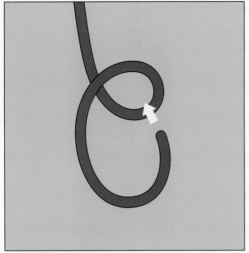

Knot 7:1 Bowline.

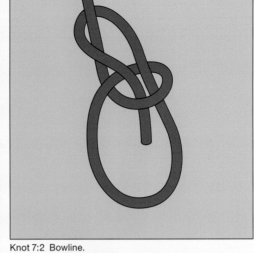

Knot 7:2 Bowline.

Knot 7:3 Bowline.

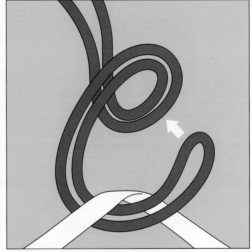

Knot 8:1 Double bowline.

Knot 8:2 Double bowline.

Knot 9 Double fisherman's knot.

karabiner, and easy to untie after it has been loaded. The disadvantage is that it takes a bit longer to tie compared with an overhand loop. [See knot 8.]

Double fisherman's knot This is used for joining ropes. The tails sticking out should be 1 cm x the rope's diameter in mm.

The advantages are that it is possible to join ropes of different diameters, and it is good for fixed knots, e.g. prusik cords, etc. The disadvantage is that it is very hard to untie after it has been loaded. [See knot 9.]

Tape knot This is used for joining tapes. The tails sticking out should be five times the width of the tape.

The advantage is that this is the most suitable knot for joining tapes. The disadvantage is that it comes untied easily and must be tightened with bodyweight. Should not be used on Dynema/Spectra tape. [See knot 10.]

Clove hitch This is used to tie into belay and around objects. It needs to be tightened before use. The advantages are that it is easy to adjust when in place, and easy to untie after it has been loaded. The disadvantages are that it's not very strong, and works best on soft and flexible ropes. [See knot 11.]

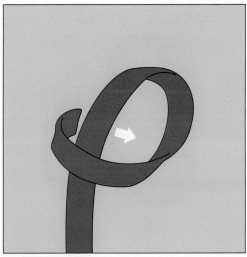

Knot 10:1 Tape knot.

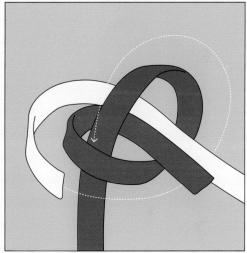

Knot 10:2 Tape knot.

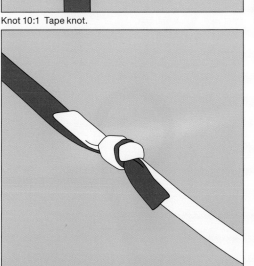

Knot 10:3 Tape knot.

Note: Tape knot is used for joining tapes. The tails sticking out should be five times the width of the tape.

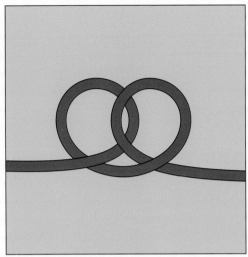

Knot 11:1 Clove hitch.

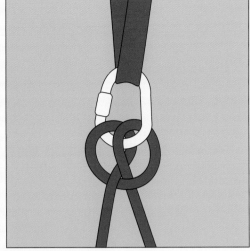

Knot 11:2 Clove hitch.

Knot 12:1 Alpine butterfly.

Knot 12:2 Alpine butterfly.

Knot 12:3 Alpine butterfly.

Knot 13:1 Italian hitch.

Knot 13:2 Italian hitch.

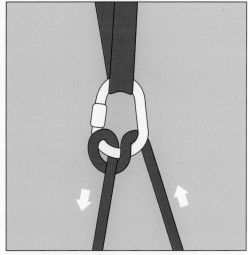

Knot 13:3 Italian hitch.

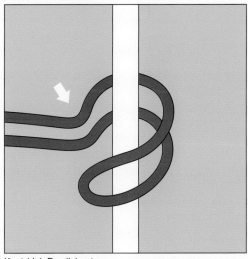

Knot 14:1 Prusik knot.

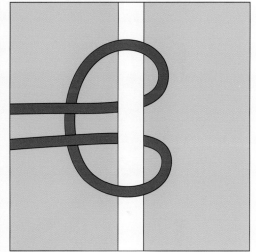

Knot 14:2 Prusik knot.

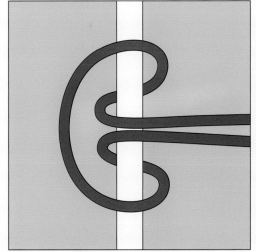

Knot 14:3 Prusik knot.

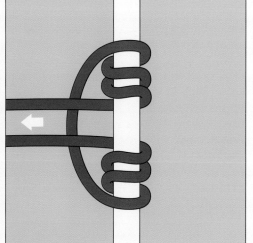

Knot 14:4 Prusik knot.

Knot 15 French prusik.

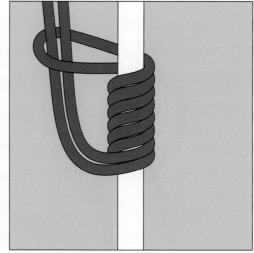

Knot 16:1 Klemheist.

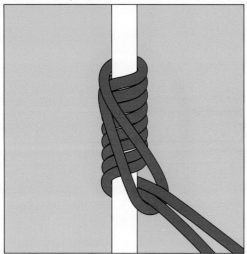

Knot 16:2 Klemheist.

Note: The prusik loop must be of a smaller dimension to grip the rope. The newer the rope and/or prusik loop, the less grip there will be. Rub the prusik loop against a rock to roughen it. Add another loop if it isn't gripping. On icy ropes you may have to use mechanical ascenders to be effective.

Alpine butterfly This is used as a stop-knot on the middle of the rope between two skiers who have roped up on a glacier. The advantage is that it doesn't have a flat side, so creates a lot of friction when it's digging into the snow. The disadvantage is that it uses a lot of rope. [See knot 12.]

Italian hitch This is used to belay a lead climber, or to lower someone. The advantage is that you don't need a belay device. The disadvantage is that it can twist the rope badly. [See knot 13.]

Prusik knots In certain situations (for example, climbing the rope or hoisting someone) you need a short cord of a smaller dimension than the rope you are using. By winding the thinner prusik loops around the thicker climbing rope with different sliding friction knots, the prusik will grip the climbing rope when loaded.

The prusik loop consists of a cord 6–7 mm thick and 135 cm long, tied together with a double fisherman's knot. You should carry three loops to be able to deal with every scenario.

Note: The prusik loop must be of a smaller dimension to grip the rope. The newer the rope and/or prusik loop, the less grip there will be. Rub the prusik loop against a rock to roughen it. Add another loop if it isn't gripping. On icy ropes you may have to use mechanical ascenders to be effective.

Prusik knots are used on wet and icy ropes. The advantage is that they grip very well. The disadvantage is that they don't slide very well. [See knot 14.]

French prusik: This is used almost every time a prusik knot is required. The advantage is that it can be untied under load. The disadvantage is that it can become undone by itself when under load if you don't fully understand how it works. [See knot 15.]

Klemheist Is used to make prusik knots with slings or tape. [See knot 16.]

PROGRESSING WITH SKIS ON THE BACKPACK

General rules of snow stability and group discipline don't change when you put your skis on the backpack. Generally speaking, don't climb next to each other in large numbers, even if there are good steps. You don't know if the group who made the steps were keeping distance and whether your group is now putting more load on the snow cover than they did.

There are various ways of attaching the skis to the backpack. Just make sure that they're stable and not in the way. Attaching them to the backpack and unattaching them should also be easy and quick, even with gloves on. If you need to put them on the backpack for down climbing, and you need to down climb facing away from the slope, make sure they are attached high enough not to get stuck in the snow.

FRESH SNOW Climbing or walking on foot in fresh snow can be very difficult, even impossible if there's a lot of snow. Conditions are safer and easier if you ski during the days immediately after a snowfall, allowing the snow to transform.

On less steep terrain, progression will be much easier on skis with skins (see ski touring). When you feel the terrain is too steep to continue on skis, create a platform (by compressing the snow with your skis) so you can put the skis on the backpack comfortably.

Crampons are best avoided. They are more often a hindrance in soft snow. The exception is if you suspect the snow will turn hard in a place where you can't put the crampons on safely, or if you suspect that the snow overlays ice or rock. Then you need to put them on beforehand. Make sure you keep the crampons clear of snow clumps building up. In bad conditions you will need to knock the clumps off with your poles or ice axe after each step.

If you expect any of the above conditions, and therefore put on crampons, take out your ice axe as well, or at least keep it within easy reach under the shoulder strap of your backpack. [See diagram 009.]

The normal scenario would be to go without crampons, holding the poles for balance (keeping an upright position over your feet). You need to hold the poles lower down the steeper it is. If the snow gets harder you can turn the poles upside down and push them into the snow for safety.

Face the snow and kick forward; not too high. Make a tamping motion or two (or as many as you have to in very soft snow) to create a solid step that will support your body weight.

009:1 When in doubt, keep the ice axe handy under your shoulder strap.

009:2

009:3

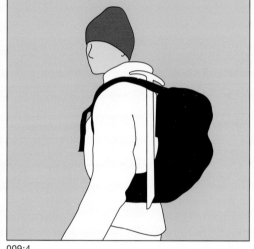

009:4

Transfer your weight onto the step carefully, without breaking the step. If it is fragile, spread your body weight by leaning forward slightly and putting some weight on your knee and hands (holding the poles mid-way). Then start again with the other foot, kicking a new step.

Progress in such conditions needs patience and endurance. There are many different types of snow, so adapt to the snow and try to balance. The aim is to progress as efficiently as possible without wasting all your energy. As always in the mountains, try to move at a steady pace.

<u>HARD SNOW</u> **Crampons & ice axe** The right time to use crampons is when you only succeed in making a footstep a few centimetres deep with several hard kicks in the snow. Or when more time and energy are expended in kicking steps over longer sections than putting the crampons on.

Walking on flat ground is pretty straightforward, just remember to walk with your feet a bit further apart than usual, to avoid the front point getting caught

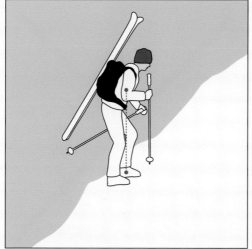

010:1 Balance over the feet.

010:2 Balance over the feet.

010:3 Incorrect position on the inner edges.

010:4 Correct "flat foot" position.

in your ski pants and causing you to trip over. On hard snow your body weight is sufficient to drive the points of the crampons into the ground. On ice you have to use more effort. Skiers tend to want to edge the crampons as they do with the skis, but this will cause the crampons to lose grip. Instead you have to strive to keep the crampons flat on the ground so that all the points grip.

When the terrain becomes sloping you need to flex your knee a bit to keep the foot flat and all the crampon points on the ground. This movement doesn't come naturally, so a bit of practise is needed to make it second nature. [See diagram 010:4.]

This is very difficult to do with a stiff ski boot (keeping the top buckles loose makes it easier). When it becomes unstable, switch over and climb on the front points. Lower your heel to prevent your calf aching, and let the second pair of points on the crampons grip the snow as well. [See diagram 011.]

The aim is to establish rhythm between your feet and the ice axe and to keep your balance all the time. The ice axe should always be held in the upper hand so

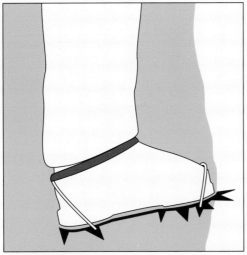

011:1 Correct stance.

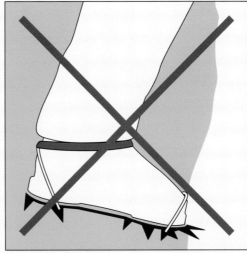

011:2 Incorrect stance.

012:1 Progressing on snow.

012:2 Self-belay.

013 Anchoring the shaft.

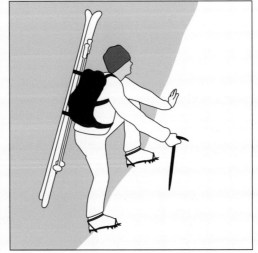

014 Dagger technique.

you can shove it down into the snow as a self-belay and catch a slip before it turns into a fall. I hold the axe in a self-arrest position with the pick pointing back, to be able to self-arrest quickly if the self-belay fails. Other people claim that the correct method is to have the pick pointing forward to minimise the chance of injury in a slip, and give a more comfortable grip. [See diagram 012:1.]

The rhythm is simple; ice axe, first step (cross your legs), second step.

You only have to shove the ice axe shaft into the snow as deep as you think it needs to be to hold for a self-belay in the event of a slip. Then move the ice axe when your body is in the most balanced position.

Don't be lazy in hard snow, shove the ice axe down if exposed and you want to have a real chance of preventing a fall — and change ice axe techniques if you have to.

When it gets steeper and you're facing the slope, you must anchor the shaft to the surface more perpendicularly. Hold the ice axe in your stronger hand. [See diagram 013.]

If the snow is hard when it gets steeper you can use the dagger technique. This can be used with one or two ice axes. Either place your hand on the head of the axe and drive the pick into the snow at waist height. [See diagram 014.]

Or with your hands on the shaft, just under the head, drive the pick into the snow in front of you. This style is a bit more strenuous but it feels more secure on steeper ground.

On most steep sections, use two axes for speed and safety. The icier or harder the conditions are, the more likely you are to use two tools. However, you can come across short, steep sections when you only have one ice axe.

1. Hold the bottom of the shaft of the ice axe, and with a full swing plant the ice axe as high above your head as you can reach. Make sure you get a good placement that you can trust (your life will depend on it).
2. Put your other hand on the axe head, and move up until your shoulder is level with the axe.
3. When your feet are well placed a bit wider apart and you're in balance, put your weak hand flat on the snow, or if possible dig your fingers into the snow and create a handhold. Then move the ice axe and replace it higher up. This way you secure yourself while moving your feet, and you move the ice axe while still balanced. [See diagram 015.]

Using two axes is pretty straightforward Place the first axe. Step up (the higher you step up the harder it will be to lock off with the lower axe, but the faster you will climb). Place the second axe as high as possible. Step up. Move the first axe and replace it as high as possible. If it is less steep, use the high or low dagger position for both tools. [See diagram 016.]

To remove an ice axe, just reverse the motion you used when you placed the axe, by rocking the axe back and forth on the same plane as the pick. Not sideways as you then risk breaking the pick. [See diagram 017.]

Cutting steps Sometimes it is faster to cut a few steps for a short section than have the whole group put on crampons and take them off again. It takes some practise to master this without using brute force all the time. Let the swing do the job.

The steps should be cut when you're standing securely on two steps, with good balance. The steps should slant inwards, not too spaced out, and should be big enough for everyone's feet. The group should be able to move safely and efficiently.

If the snow is very hard, use your feet (kicking) to perfect the step when you're standing on it. Everyone in the group has to make sure that they don't damage

015:1 Steep section with one ice axe.

015:2 Steep section with one ice axe.

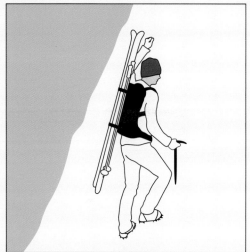

015:3 Steep section with one ice axe.

016 Dagger position.

the steps, making it harder and less safe for the person following them.

Diagonal ascent (when it's not too steep) Use your pick and make three blows from above and three blows from the side. If you need to, remove the snow in between with the adze. [See diagram 018.]

To make it safe and easy to change direction, you have to create a good platform. Use your pick and give seven blows from above in the shape of a half moon, then another five blows from the side forming a horizontal line below. If you need to, remove the snow in between with the adze. [See diagram 019.]

Straight up Five blows from above with the pick, and with the adze remove the snow in between. Don't start too high up. [See diagram 020.]

Straight down (facing outward) Two blows forming a V, then with the adze remove the snow in between. Make sure you dig your toe in, and do not destroy the step when you move on to the next one. If you roll your foot you make the step slant outwards which then renders it unsafe for anyone coming after you. [See diagram 021.]

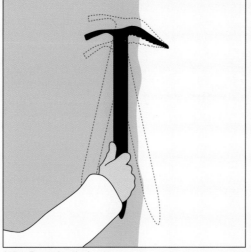

017:1 Removing the ice axe.

017:2 Removing the ice axe.

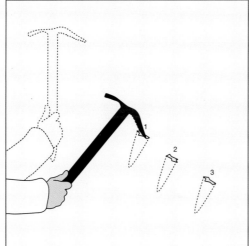

018:1 Cutting steps.

018:2 Cutting steps.

On ice You will probably use crampons on ice but sometimes it's good to cut steps on ice. This makes it easier to get all the crampon points into the ice when using stiff ski boots.

You'll get the perfect arm/axe length by gripping the shaft in the right place. And by swinging the axe in an arc, the adze will clear away some ice effortlessly as a part of the swing. This also works when cutting diagonal steps in hard snow. If you get the wrong angle or length, the adze will just cut too steeply and stick. [See diagram 022.]

<u>**SELF-ARREST**</u> Practise self-arrest on a slope which has a safe run out. Practise with a backpack and without a backpack (the most likely scenario is with a backpack, possibly even with skis on the backpack).

The most important thing to learn and understand is the limit of the self-arrest. If you gain speed on hard snow or ice on steeper terrain it's unlikely that you will stop yourself from sliding. Knowing this will force you to make sure that the slide doesn't happen in the first place, e.g. by making sure that the ice axe(s) is/are well planted, by staying in balance on the crampons or by roping up.

Stopping a slide (without crampons or ice axe) This is the most likely scenario if you start sliding after a fall in which both skis have released.

First, try to get in a position where your feet are down hill and facing the snow, then push yourself up on your hands and feet. If you push your hands up too fast, your feet will get caught in the snow and you will make a back flip. Try to be calm and measured. If you still have a pole, use it as an ice axe to stop the slide.

Sliding on your back. [See diagram 023.]

Sliding head–first. [See diagram 024.]

Stopping a slide with skis still on If you still have your skis on, try to get them downhill and use the skis (ski edges) to stop the slide.

Stopping a slide with crampons & ice axe Bend your legs and keep the crampons away from the snow (it's easy to break your ankle if the front points get snagged).

The basic breaking position.

Head–first. [See diagram 025.]

On your back. [See diagram 026.]

On your back, head–first. [See diagram 027.]

When wearing a backpack, try to roll over on your stomach and then perform the self–arrest from that position.

Note: Always practise without crampons and harness to avoid hurting yourself. Take care with the ice axe! When wearing a backpack, make sure you don't have sharp objects in the backpack that can cause injury. Make sure that the slope has a safe run out.

ROPING UP

Most of the time you will probably climb unroped to reach the descents but whenever you feel exposed and insecure, rope up.

BELAYING If a fall is stopped statically — that is with no rope moving through the belay device — all the force will be put on the rope system (rope, climber, runners and belay anchor). It is much better to allow some rope to slip through the belay device (which the belay plate and the Italian hitch do naturally), and convert some of the energy of the fall into friction. This is the main reason why we don't use any pinching belay devices in mountaineering when we place our own protection (Grigri is the most well–known). However, if there's not enough friction the fall will be too long with the risk of injury from hitting something.

There are two main ways of belaying. In the event of a fall, the force transmitted onto the belay anchor will vary depending on which method you're using. They all have advantages and disadvantages.

Direct belay The force of a fall is taken directly on the anchor, which should be a solid belay anchor used for belaying the second climber. Here, forces are low (body weight).

In its simplest form the anchor could be running the rope behind a spike, flake or pinnacle and holding the fall by the friction created between the rope and the rock. It could also be using an Italian hitch or a guide plate directly in the belay anchor.

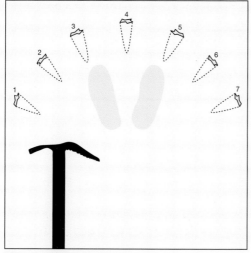

019:1 Cutting a platform.

019:2 Cutting a platform.

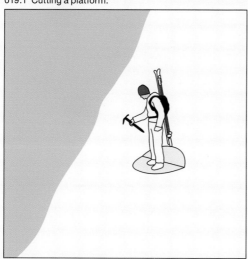

019:3 Cutting a platform.

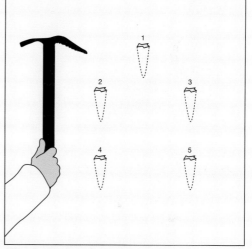

020:1 Cutting steps for climbing straight up.

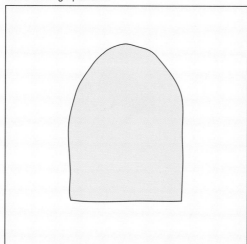

020:2 Cutting steps for climbing straight up.

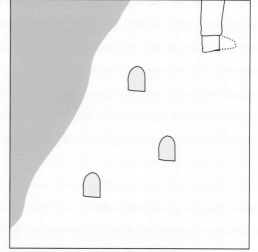

020:3 Cutting steps for climbing straight up.

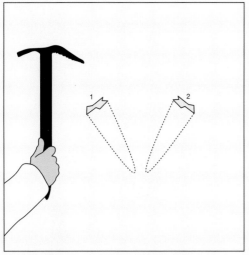

021:1 Cutting steps for climbing straight down.

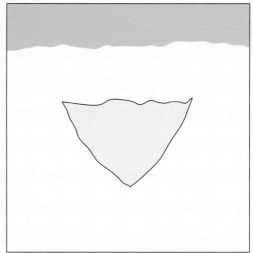

021:2 Cutting steps for climbing straight down.

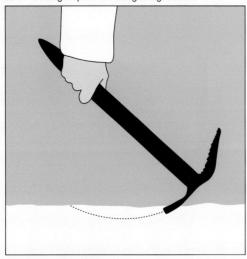

022 Steep cutting swing.

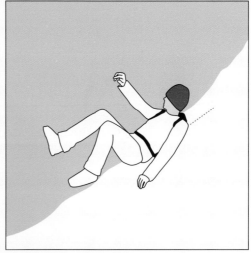

023:1 Self-arrest without ice axe.

023:2 Self-arrest without ice axe.

023:3 Self-arrest without ice axe.

024:1 Self-arrest without ice axe.

024:2 Self-arrest without ice axe.

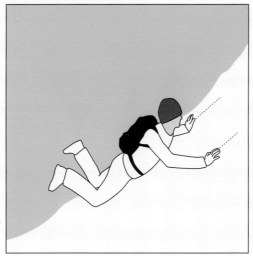

024:3 Self-arrest without ice axe.

024:4 Self-arrest without ice axe.

Advantage: Speed (in its simplest form), comfort (if someone is hanging a lot on the rope, you don't have to take the weight in you harness). Disadvantage: Should only be done on rock or ice, as the belay anchor is not allowed to fail! [See diagram 028.]

Indirect belay This is mainly used on hanging belays when the belayer is hanging in the belay anchor and belaying the second climber from the harness. Any downward force will go straight onto the anchor. The advantage is that directional pulls that were not anticipated when constructing the anchor could be absorbed by the belayer, but the anchor still has to be bombproof. [See diagram 029.] However, if you for some reason don't trust the anchor 100% (not uncommon for belays in winter snow) you must absorb most of the fall energy with your body to protect the anchor. This often involves good foot placement and sometimes sitting down to use the terrain in an optimal way.

   Note: This is a must when you don't trust the anchor 100% and it's impossible to construct something better. If you have to you have to!

025:1 Self-arrest with an ice axe.

025:2 Self-arrest with an ice axe.

025:3 Self-arrest with an ice axe.

025:4 Self-arrest with an ice axe.

025:5 Self-arrest with an ice axe.

025:6 Self-arrest with an ice axe.

027:1 Self-arrest with an ice axe.

027:2 Self-arrest with an ice axe.

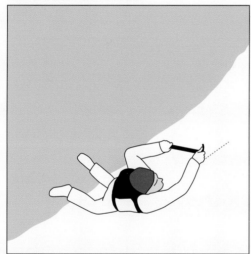

027:3 Self-arrest with an ice axe.

027:4 Self-arrest with an ice axe.

If it is impossible to get a reasonably strong anchor, the most common solution would be to continue on running belay. The second climber undoes the belay and both climbers climb simultaneously with the rope taught until the lead climber finds a place where he can build a belay. If necessary (if the climbing is difficult) the lead climber's backpack with skis should be left hanging from some piece of protection. When the second climber reaches the backpack he can attach it to the other end of the rope lowered by the lead climber from the belay anchor. You have to improvise. Again, certain terms have to be known in order to avoid confusion:

__ Live rope: The rope that runs between the belayer and climber (whether a leader or a second).

__ Dead rope: After it's been passed through the belay system (except for when you belay a lead climber; then it is a live rope).

__ Feeling hand: The hand that is on the live rope.

__ Braking hand: The hand on the dead rope (locking off).

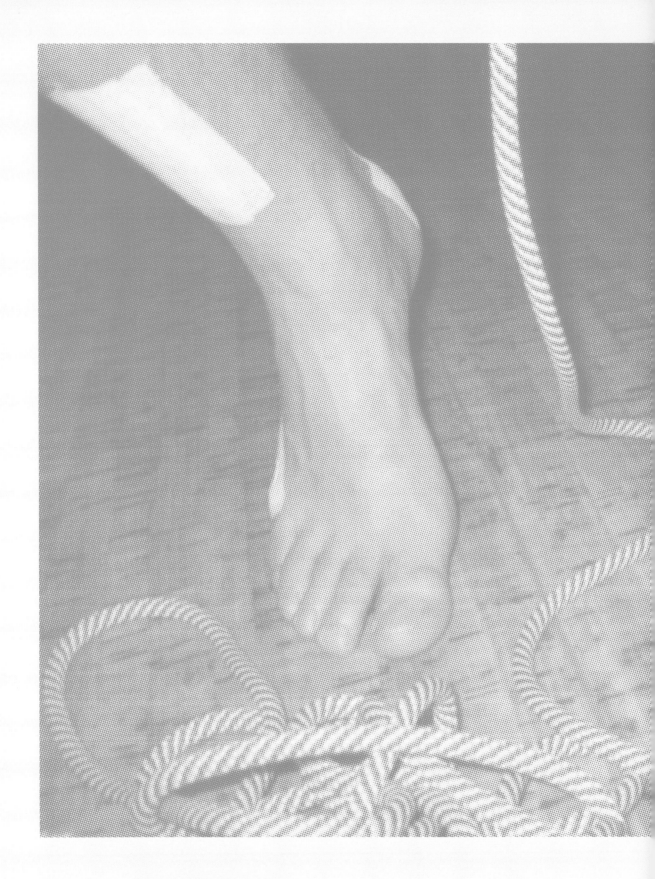

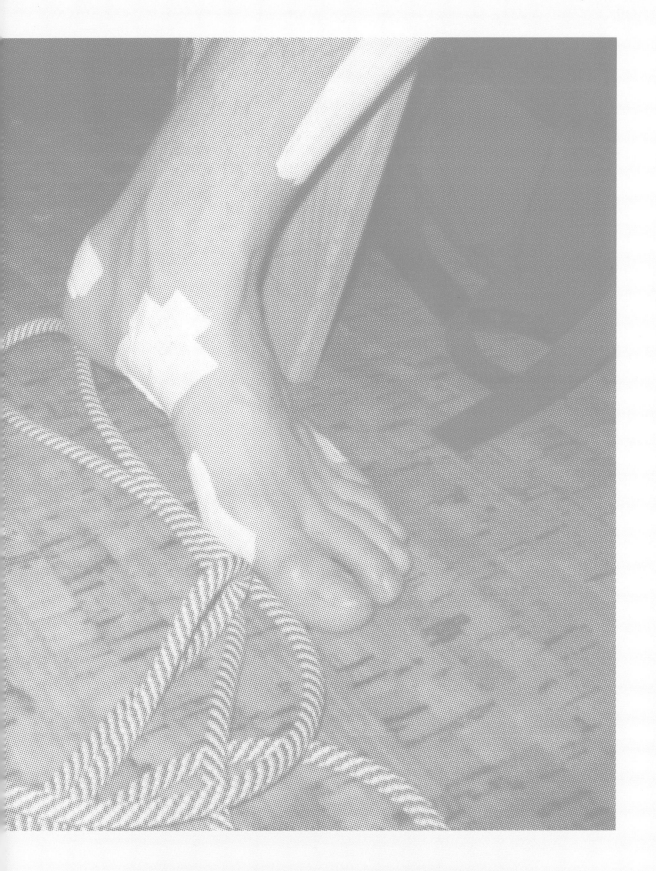

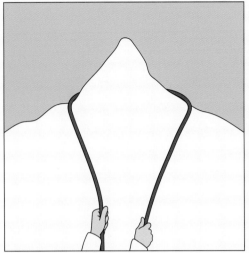

028 Direct belay over a spike.

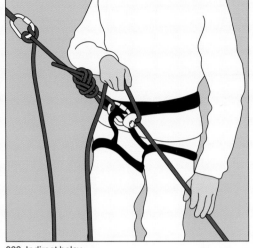

029 Indirect belay.

Belaying a lead climber Don't belay too far away from the slope, because if the lead climber falls you can be slammed into the wall and lose your grip on the live rope. [See diagram 030.]

The belayer must be attached to an anchor that can take an upward pull if he weighs less than the lead climber. [See diagram 031.]

To pay out, the feeling hand pulls the rope through the device/hitch, while the break hand holds the dead rope parallel to the live rope (for easy running). The brake hand should always be prepared to brake and must therefore always stay on the dead rope.

Slide your hands into position to start a new cycle.

Belay plates: Using a belay plate is the standard method of belaying a lead climber. It is also used for rappelling. [See diagram 032.]

Italian hitch: This is an essential technique to know if you drop your belay plate. If you are using double rope and clipping them separately, you must use one karabiner for each knot and separate the two with a third karabiner to give the knots some room to turn.

Belaying the second climber with an indirect belay To take in rope, simply pull the live rope towards the device/hitch, and at the same time pull the rope through with the brake hand. Cross over the feeling hand and hold on to the dead rope. With the dead rope guarded by the feeling hand you can replace your brake hand.

Then replace the feeling hand on the live rope and the cycle starts over again.

<u>BELAY PLATES OR ITALIAN HITCH</u>   **Belaying the second climber with a direct belay** A guide plate or magic plate is a self-locking device that can only be used for belaying the second climber. It is always placed in the master point of the belay anchor, which means it is a direct belay. The live rope goes on top of the dead rope and locks it off while loaded.

Simply feed the live rope towards the plate and pull the dead rope away with the other hand.

The advantage of a self-locking device is that you don't have to pay attention the whole time. So if someone is moving slowly you have time, for example, to eat and drink whilst belaying. If needed, it can be quickly turned into a hoist. The

030:1 Belaying unattached and too far away.

030:2 Belaying unattached and too far away.

031:1 Attached to belay.

031:2 Attached to belay.

disadvantage is that this is not straightforward if for any reason you want to lower the second climber. [See diagram 033.]

Italian hitch as a direct belay: The HMS karabiner is placed in the master point of the belay anchor. The advantage is that it is not self-locking, which makes lowering someone easy. The disadvantage is that the rope can twist, as you have to hold on to the rope the whole time.

Note: If a belay has to be redirected, it should be to the master point as it creates a pulley at the redirected point, which means that the load at this point is multiplied. [See diagram 034.]

PITCHING When pitch climbing, you need clear, concise communication between climbers that won't be misunderstood. This is important both for safety and speed.

Basic climbing calls:

__ The lead climber has attached himself to the new anchor and calls: "Safe".

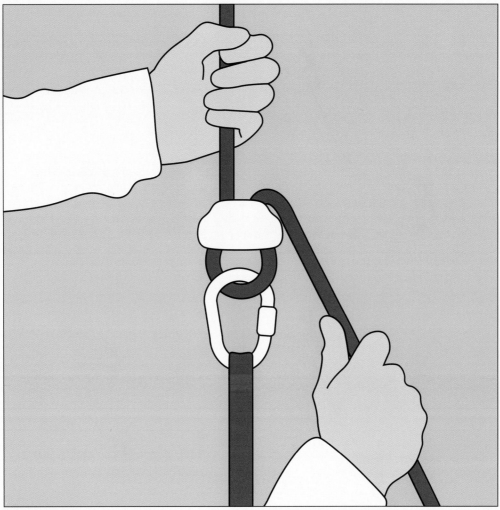

032 Belay plates.

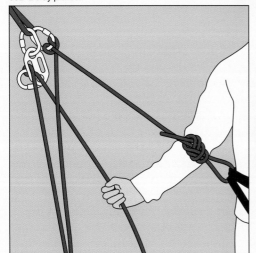

033 Direct belay of a second climber with a guide's plate.

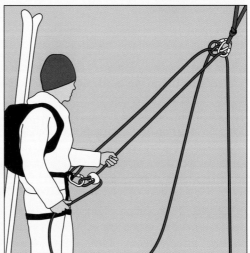

034 Belaying a second climber by redirecting through the anchor.

___ The second climber removes the rope from the belay device and replies: "Rope free" or "Okay".

___ The lead climber pulls in the rope as quickly as possible until it's stretched to the second climber. The second climber confirms with: "That's me".

___ The lead climber puts him on belay and calls: "You're on belay".

___ The second climber dismantles the belay, and before starting to climb calls: "Climbing".

___ The leader can simply confirm with: "Okay".

Additional climbing calls are: "Slack"; the rope is too tight, more rope is required, "Take in"; the rope is not tight enough.

Hearing one another can sometimes be difficult during a long pitch, when you're out of sight and the wind is taking every word. In such conditions it is often faster to plan pitches and build belays so you stay in sight of one another. Decide on a system, so the second climber knows when he is on belay. One effective way is to start belaying before the rope is stretched to the second climber, so the leader is taking in the last metres of slack through the belay device and the second climber knows that as soon as the rope is stretched he is being belayed. This method requires visibility. Don't assume that the rope is taught for the second climber just because you pull in the rope hard from the top; it could be stuck halfway down.

When you decide to start pitching, you begin by building a belay. This is the basis of all safe climbing. You have to be able to choose the right place for the belay, find and place the anchor points, tie onto them and choose the correct method to belay the rope.

Whenever you decide to stop and build a belay anchor, make sure you do it properly. No matter what!

ANCHORS There are two main types of anchor, single and multiple. Your choice depends on what is available. Your priorities are in this order: First safety – to withstand any potential load it may be subjected to – and then speed – quick to set up and dismantle and requiring a minimum of equipment.

As speed is safety, it is actually wrong to place and tie three anchors together to a complicated belay system (overkill) if pulling the rope behind a spike will provide equal safety (tying onto the anchor using either slings or the rope). Personally, I prefer slings but you need to know both methods so you can improvise and adapt.

Slings With slings it's straightforward to escape the system if you need to perform a companion rescue. It's easy to switch over if you would like to lead more than one pitch in a row.

The disadvantage is that you need a lot of slings if you don't place your anchor points close enough. Sometimes it's impossible to place them close enough.

Rope The advantage is that it's already there. It works even if the points are spread out. The disadvantage is that it could be very complicated to escape; you have to lead every second pitch to be effective.

Single anchor & body belay Consists of one point and is always chosen for speed. Either it's full strength and therefore you don't need more than one point e.g. a spike. [See diagram 035.]

Or the terrain is easy, so you anticipate stopping a slip rather than a fall, e.g. holding only body weight for a short while and not the full force of a lead fall. [See diagram 036.] The live rope has to go in under the arm.

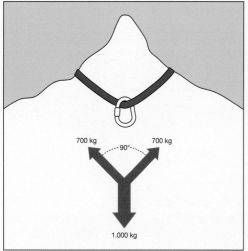

035:1 Single anchor.

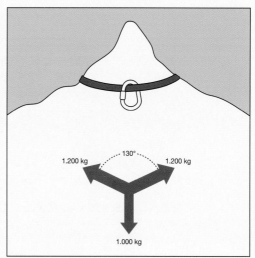

035:2 Incorrect single anchor.

036 Body belay using terrain features.

Note: When progress is too slow due to overprotecting the lead, you have probably chosen the wrong route for your skill level and will probably not even have fun doing it. This means that you're taking a bigger risk and getting less fun out of it! What's the point? Challenge yourself but don't be stupid.

Multiple anchors No matter if it is ice screws, pitons, nuts or bolts — the method of tying the anchors together stays the same. The standard belay consists of two anchors that are:

__ Bombproof — the anchors are not allowed to fail.

__ Equalised — the force put on the belay should be equally distributed over the anchors.

__ Independent — tight sling/rope to both points. If one of the anchors fails, there shouldn't be a shock load onto the other one.

At least one of the anchors should be attached with a locking karabiner. Make sure the gate can't be opened. Place the gate facing away from the snow/ice/rock.

The angle should be kept small to distribute the load equally on both anchor points. [See diagram 037.]

The different ways to tie the anchors together with slings (one 120 cm sling should be enough) are equalised sling, equalised sling with clove hitches, and self-equalising sling.

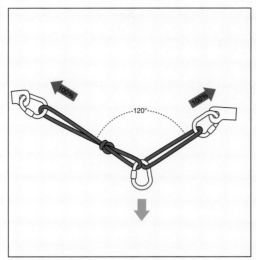

037:1 Distribution of the load on anchor points.

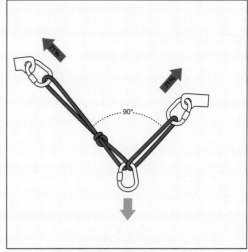

037:2 Distribution of the load on anchor points.

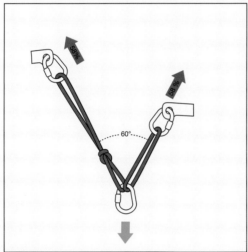

037:3 Distribution of the load on anchor points.

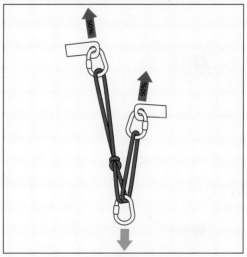

037:4 Distribution of the load on anchor points.

038 Equalised sling.

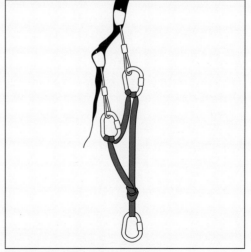

039 Equalised sling with clove hitches.

Equalised sling: Use an overhand or figure of eight loop, depending on how much sling you have. The advantage is that it's fast. The disadvantage is that the anchors need to be close; you should have at least one locking karabiner in the anchors. [See diagram 038.]

Equalised sling with clove hitches: There has to be slack in the "dead sling" between the two anchors; otherwise the load won't be equally distributed. The advantages are that the anchors can be further apart, and that it's possible to use it without locking karabiners. The disadvantage is that if you don't use a locking karabiner in the anchors, you have to be extra careful that the gates can't be opened and weaken the strength of the belay. [See diagram 039.]

Self-equalising sling: This is used when each anchor is of equal strength or weakness (where equalising is of great importance to create a stronger point), and the direction of the force is difficult to anticipate or might vary.

The advantages are that it's fast, has no knots, and is self-equalising (it doesn't matter if the direction of the load is different from what was anticipated). The disadvantage is that it doesn't live up to the third criterion; if one anchor fails the shock load will be greater on the other anchor! Normally used on bolted anchors. One should have locking karabiners in the anchors. [See diagram 040.]

A knot can be added to reduce the impact force should one of the anchors fail. [See diagram 041.]

Tying together more than two points Start with equalising two points, then equalise the new master point with the third point to create the real master point. [See diagram 042.]

Protecting the anchor for upward pull When the weight difference between climbers is great and the belays are not multi-directional e.g. stoppers and friends, just add the protection and clip it to the anchor in the easiest way with a quickdraw.

If you have problems with knots freezing up, put a clove hitch in a locking karabiner and use it as a master point. [See diagram 043.]

BELAY PLACEMENT A belay should of course always be built in places where you can build a strong belay, and should be placed:
___ In safe places protected from rock or ice fall.
___ In places where a good belay anchor can be built quickly.
___ In places where you can stand comfortably (ledges) protected from the wind.
___ In places that allow you to communicate easily.
If the terrain doesn't vary (snow or ice flank), then climb as far as the rope allows you before building the belay anchor.

Belay organisation Your aim is to move as quickly as possible, and you save a lot of time by having a well-organised rope. When you build the belay, have a plan ready for where you want to stand, how to tie on, etc. Taking a few extra seconds in planning and efficient rope handling will save you minutes of problem-solving later on.

Figure out where the rope should go, re-stack once, do it quickly, and make it clean. If you are on a ledge, just stack the rope in a pile on the ground, efficiently and quickly. If you are on a hanging belay or a ridge where the rope could get stuck if it hangs down, drape the rope back and forth across your attachment to the belay anchor. Make the coils shorter as you go.

Note: Don't use any short-cut solutions. It's usually best to take time to solve the problem, or do things properly in the first place, rather than hoping that it

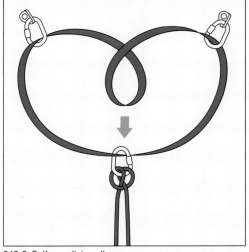

040:2 Self-equalising sling.

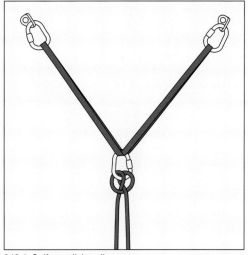

040:1 Self-equalising sling.

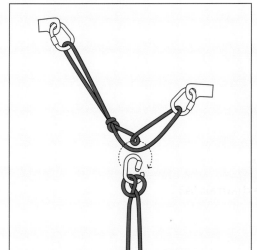

041:1 Self-equalising sling with an added knot.

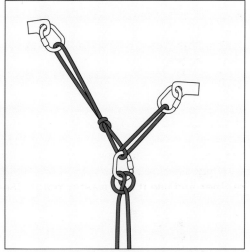

041:2 Self-equalising sling with an added knot.

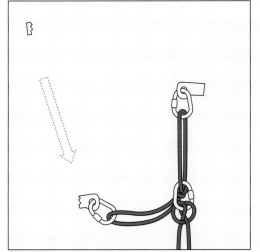

041:3 Self-equalising sling with an added knot.

Note: Self–equalising sling. This is used when each anchor is of equal strength or weakness (where equalising is of great importance to create a stronger point), and the direction of the force is difficult to anticipate or might vary.

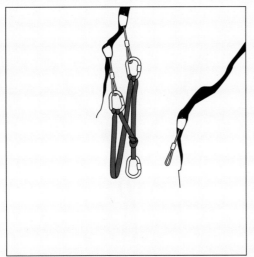

042:1 Tying together more than two points.

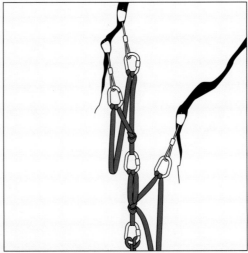

042:2 Tying together more than two points.

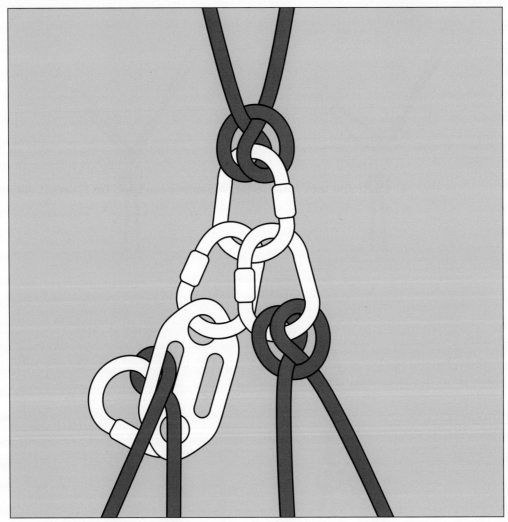

043 Locking karabiner as a master point.

will work out. The classic example is pulling the rope from the bottom of the stack instead of taking the extra seconds to re-stack it — you'll have to spend minutes untangling the rope.

Do not run the dead rope around the live rope or under it. This just creates a time consuming mess by adding friction to the system or twisting and jamming the rope.

PROTECTION STRATEGIES & PLACING RUNNERS Runners are placed along the way as the lead climber is progressing. Placing and taking out protection is time-consuming for the rope team, which again forces you to consider safety in speed.

However there are certain rules:
___ Use protection that is simple, quick and easy to remove.
___ Place protection soon after leaving the anchor, to protect from a factor 2 fall.
___ If possible, use bigger, stronger pieces of protection at the beginning of the pitch, where potential impact force is high.
___ Place protection to protect you from long falls, from falling onto ledges, etc., and below difficult sections or moves where a fall is more likely to happen. Remember to protect the rope from sharp edges and rock falls.
___ Place protection to protect the second climber on traverses. Place a protection after the hard moves as well, otherwise the second climber will have to remove the protection before doing the hard moves and therefore risks long pendulum falls.
___ Reduce rope drag with long slings. This also reduces the impact force if you fall.
Some materials are stronger than others. To get a strong anchor, you should protect yourself on rock, ice or snow. However, material quality may vary in any given place, so you have to assess which material is the strongest.

If you don't trust the slings, pitons or bolts that are already in place — what does the general condition look like and what has it been used for? Does it show signs of damage, rust or corrosion?

Clipping into protection The link between the rope and the protection (the quick-draw) should be long enough, or be extended to allow the rope to move with a minimum of friction and to prevent the rope from lifting out the protection. [See diagram 044.]

Use 60 cm slings as quickdraws. They are easy and quick to extend, and they can be placed as protection over spikes and be used in many other situations. [See diagram 045.]

Protection that could fail or be lifted out by the movement of the rope are friends and stoppers. If there is a risk of the rope manipulating your protection and weakening it, you must extend the runner. Even if at first sight this looks like you're going to get a longer fall, it might be the opposite.

Clip the rope correctly into the karabiner to reduce the risk of the rope un-clipping itself. The gate should face away from the intended climbing direction. [See diagrams 046 and 047.]

Place karabiners so the gates can't be opened or the karabiners break over an edge. [See diagrams 048 and 049.]

Note: When progress is too slow due to overprotecting the lead, you have probably chosen the wrong route for your skill level and will probably not even have fun doing it. This means that you're taking a bigger risk and getting less fun out of it! What's the point? Challenge yourself but don't be stupid.

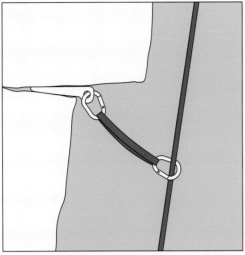

044:1 Preventing rope drag.

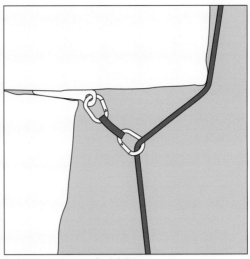

044:2 Incorrect use of quickdraw.

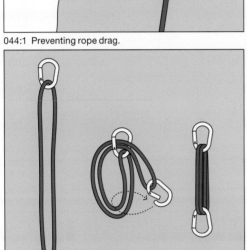

045:1 60 cm sling as quickdraw.

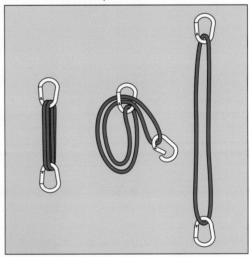

045:2 60 cm sling as quickdraw.

046:1 The gate facing the correct way.

046:2 The gate facing the correct way.

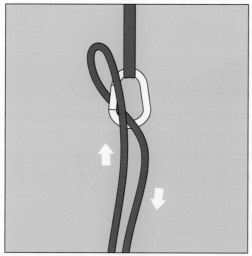

047:1 The gate facing the wrong way.

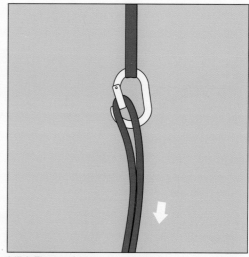

047:2 The gate facing the wrong way.

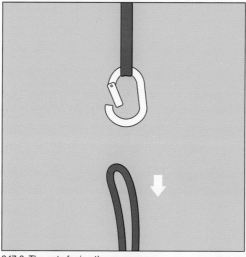

047:3 The gate facing the wrong way.

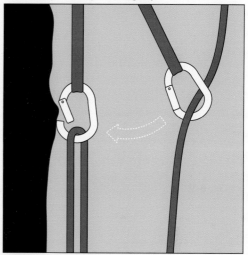

048:1 The gate facing the wrong way.

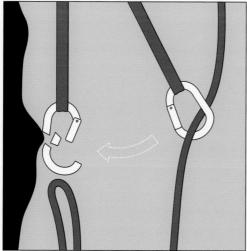

048:2 Incorrect length of the sling.

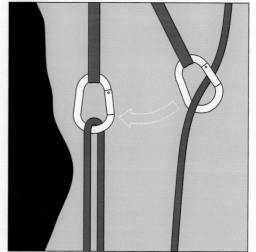

048:3 Correct length of the sling.

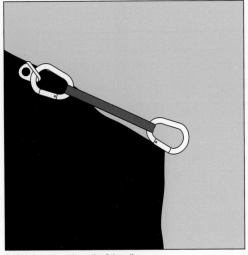

049:1 Incorrect length of the sling.

049:2 Correct length of the sling.

PROGRESSING IN MIXED TERRAIN

You are most likely to climb snow or ice to reach skiable terrain. Perhaps you will encounter some "easier" rock sections, turning it to mixed terrain. Don't be fooled by the word easy; in ski boots and crampons and with skis on your back, even easy rock passages covered in snow can demand the full range of skills and protection to allow safe progression.

<u>ON SNOW</u> It's not the depth of the snow anchor that gives it strength, but the quality of the snow. If you reach a layer of depth hoar (sugar snow) when you bury the anchor, you must place the anchor in a more settled, stronger layer, higher up in the snow pack.

T-anchor This could be made either with the ice axe or the skis, depending on purpose and snow quality. The ice axe alternative is mainly used for belays when pitching snow. Chop out a platform on the belay so you can stand comfortably. [See diagram 050.]

H-anchor Turning the ice axe T-anchor into an H-anchor with skis makes it much stronger. It could be used to make a belay stronger, but it is used mainly for crevasse rescue. [See diagram 051.]

Turning the ski T-anchor into an H-anchor with the help of the poles makes it much stronger. Mainly used for crevasse rescue in soft snow. [See diagram 052.]

Single ski belay Could be used as a fast belay at the top (when you don't have to put the skis back on the backpack), or to lower someone. [See diagrams 053 and 054.]

<u>BODY BELAYS</u> Many body belays involve sitting down, which won't work with the skis on the backpack. However it's good to know at least one method for use in loose snow conditions on fairly easy terrain; just remember to take your backpack off before sitting down. [See diagram 055.]

Standing body belay Fast on easier terrain and in hard snow conditions. [See diagram 056.]

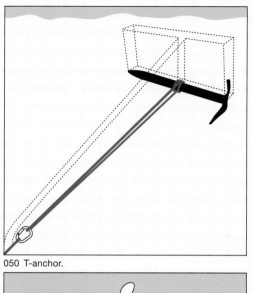

050 T-anchor.

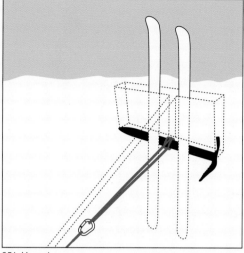

051 H-anchor.

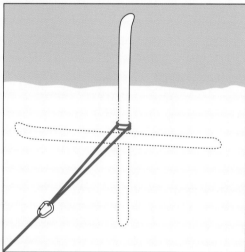

052 Ski anchor.

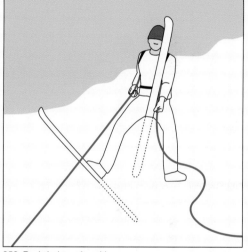

053 Body belay using skis.

Runners are not normally used in this type of snow climbing. Place in rock or ice if you have to. If possible climb on snow and belay on rock, or secondly on ice.

If very steep, hard summer snow is climbed in late spring and early summer and snow stakes can be used as protection/anchors. Use the ice axe to drive the snow stake into the snow. Count the number of times you have to hammer it to drive it in all the way. 20 times means solid, 10 times limited, and if less than that, make a T–anchor. [See diagram 057.]

<u>ON ICE</u> Protection and belays are both made with ice screws. The ice screws should be carried in a special karabiner or rack in the harness.

Using the adze, clear away the top layer of ice (until you reach firm, solid ice), and place the ice screw at chest height where you are stronger and can use your body weight to put pressure on the ice screw. Chop a platform out on the belay so you can stand comfortably.

054 Quick body belay.

Note: Many body belays involve sitting down, which won't work with the skis on the backpack. However it's good to know at least one method for use in loose snow conditions on fairly easy terrain.

055:1 Sitting body belay.

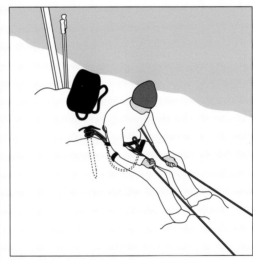

055:2 Sitting body belay.

056 Standing body belay on the ice axe.

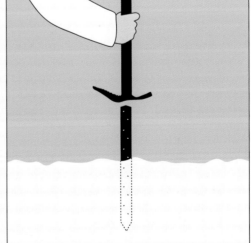

057 Placing a snowstake.

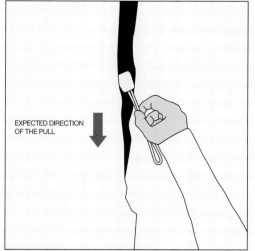

058:1 Placing a stopper.

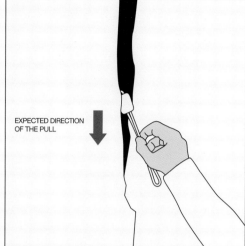

058:2 Placing a stopper.

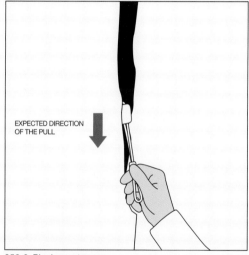

058:3 Placing a stopper.

Note: If a crack is iced–up you will have to place a piton, and if not, you will probably use a stopper or a friend.

<u>ON ROCK</u> If rock is snow covered, climb with crampons and with the ice axe within reach (to aid progression and for clearing away snow and ice to place protection).

Rock protection The two main methods of protecting yourself on rock (or building belays) are to place slings over spikes and to put protection in cracks. If a crack is iced–up you will have to place a piton, and if not, you will probably use a stopper or a friend. It is most important that the protection can hold a fall in the expected direction of the pull.

Placing a stopper:

1. Find a place where the crack is wide but getting narrower. If it's a vertical crack, place the stopper from the top and down; if horizontal from the side. [See diagram 058.]
2. Try to get as much metal as possible in contact with the rock (by testing different sizes and sides of the stoppers). [See diagram 59.]
3. Choose the largest size that will fit the crack and make sure it can take some outward pull as well.

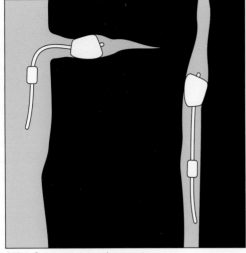

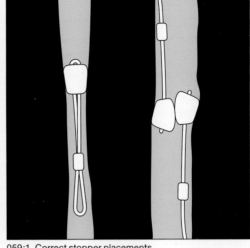

059:1 Correct stopper placements.　　　059:1 Correct stopper placements.

Always try to get the best available placement in the circumstances. If you are not happy with that and you don't feel that it is reliable then you just have to find a good placement as soon as you can.

To remove it, just move it in the opposite direction from which it was placed (it's normally obvious). If it's stuck, use the spike on your ice axe to tap it or lift it out.

Note: This is not to be used when there is any ice in a close to parallel crack.

Camming devices & friends These should be placed with the stem in the expected pull direction, in perfectly parallel cracks. All the cams work against the rock and should be in a symmetrical position on both sides of the stem. They are the strongest of the mid-range of the expansion spectrum. [See diagram 060.]

Note: Camming devices and friends should not be used when ice is present in the crack.

Place them in a solid crack, as they create a lot of expanding force when loaded, and therefore risk exploding flakes and moving blocks.

Over-camming (placing a friend that is too big for the crack) can result in it being impossible to remove the friend, while under-camming (placing a friend that is too small for the crack) is unsafe.

If you use a quickdraw that is too short (to clip the rope), the ensuing rope movement tends to make the friend walk deeper into the crack, ending up in a position where it can't hold a fall or is impossible to remove.

Placing them in non-parallel cracks — if a crack is flared (the opening is wider) the placement could be as good as useless. In an expanding crack (wider on the inside) — the friend will open up completely and be useless if it starts walking.

Pitons As with stoppers, the bigger the gear, the stronger it is. Knifeblades are not supposed to be used as runners but if nothing else works you have no choice. However, they work well for body weight (belaying the second climber and rappel anchor).

To place (drive) pitons you will need to use the hammerhead on your second ice axe. If you didn't plan to place any pitons but you have to, or you have to hammer pitons that are already in place (for example before rappelling) and you don't have the second ice axe, then hit the piton with the top of your normal ice axe.

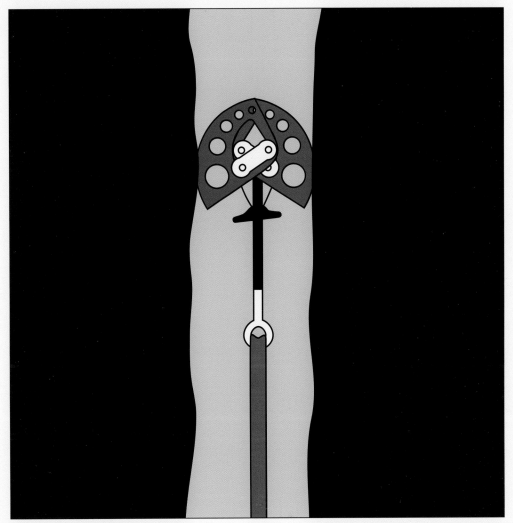

060 Correct friend placement.

Look locally for places wider than the crack. By choosing the right size piton, you should be able to place the piton a half to two-thirds in by hand. Clear away ice if you have to.

Horizontal cracks are better than vertical cracks, because rotation is reduced. Ideally, the eye should be pointing downwards when placed in a horizontal crack. Place knifeblades in vertical cracks with the eye uppermost so any load will twist the blade more firmly into the crack. [See diagram 061.]

Placing angles: Keep the three points of the V in contact with the rock.

Hammer the rest of the piton in place. A sound piton rings with a higher pitched "ping" with each strike. When driven, tap it on the side along the crack to test for rotation. If it moves, replace it with a bigger size. [See diagram 062.]

Don't hit when the eye is in contact with the rock.

When a piton can't be driven in all the way — if you have to use the placement, stop hammering to avoid loosening it. Use a sling to tie off the piton as close to the rock as possible with an overhand slip-knot. [See diagram 063.]

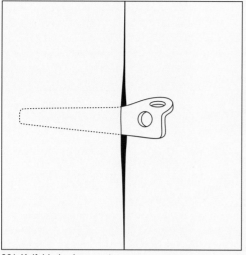

061 Knifeblade placement.

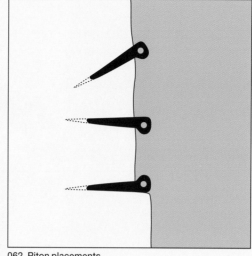

062 Piton placements.

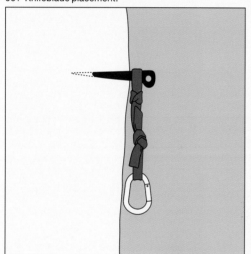

063 Tied-off piton.

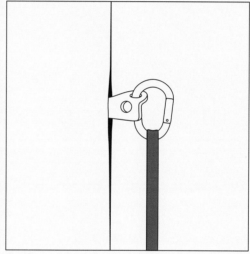

064 Correct way to clip a piton.

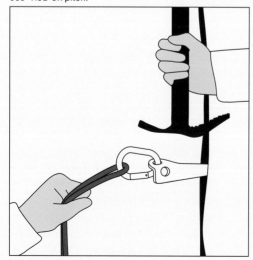

065 Removing piton.

Note: When clipping a karabiner to the piton, you have to take care not to place the karabiner in such a way that it could break under load. Clip it from the inside and out. [See diagram 070:2.]

When clipping a karabiner to the piton, you have to take care not to place the karabiner in such a way that it could break under load. Clip it from the inside and out. [See diagram 070:2.]

When removing pitons, clip a quickdraw to the piton and hold onto it with one hand, then clip it to yourself or the rope. Pound the pin back and forth along the axis of the crack, as far as it will go in each direction. Once it's loose enough to be moved sideways easily, you can try to pull the quickdraw. Always leave fixed pitons in place on the way, unless they are dangerous to use. [See diagram 065.]

CLIMBING: THREE IN THE TEAM While a climbing rope team most often consists of two people, a group of skiers consists of three to four people more often than not. If you are four people, simply form two rope teams. But if you are three or five people, there have to be three people in one rope team.

Use one rope in order to save weight if you don't have to make any long rappels.

If you have to make a long rappel you will use one rope and have another rope in the backpack, unless you are two rope teams. Then you can rappel the full rope length by rappelling together and using both teams' ropes.

If using one rope you will have to know how to tie-in to the middle of the rope.

To avoid bulky knots, use either a fisherman's knot or a bowline. The loop should be secured with a locking karabiner.

The most common use (for speed) is an overhand loop and attach with a safelock karabiner. An overhand knot should be placed to allow movement for the middle climber. [See diagram 066.]

The distance between the second climber and third climber should be "as short as possible but as long as necessary" — most often two to three metres, (so the third climber isn't too close to the second climber's crampons in the event of a fall).

MOVING TOGETHER

Pitching is safe but time consuming. Climbing unroped is fast but doesn't allow for any mistakes. In between the two, you have the possibility of moving together with either a running belay or short roping.

Short roping is a technique for situations where one or both of the team members are very experienced and skilled and therefore is used mainly by mountain guides. Even though it might look easy, it's the rope technique that is the hardest to master because there are so many variables to take into account. That is why mountain guides spend years perfecting this technique before they become certified.

In the winter, the main situation use for short roping is in situations where one skier/climber is much more experienced/stronger than the other (e.g. mountain guide and clients). So this is not very likely to happen with a recreational skier. Just be aware that roping up is not enough! In itself, the rope does not provide safety. To make the system safe and effective, the leader has to be very creative and must work actively. A slip must be stopped before it turns into a fall. If used in the wrong way, it means that if one person falls, everyone falls.

Shortening the rope This is an effective way of transporting the rope over easy sections. You don't have to untie, coil the rope, put it in the backpack, and have to stop a few minutes later when you need to rope again, take it out of the backpack, uncoil the rope and tie-in again.

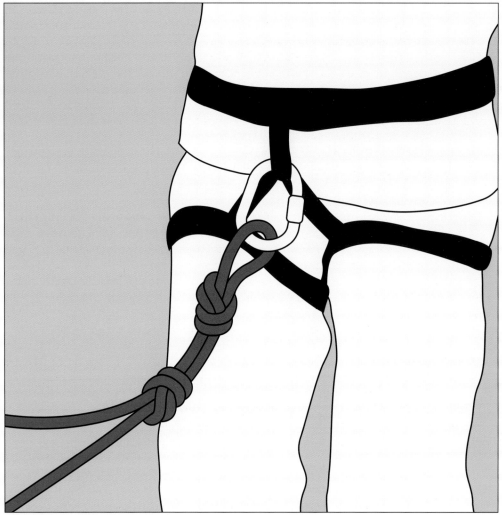

066 Attaching a climber to the middle of the rope using a safe-lock karabiner.

On the other hand, simply walking with 50 metres of rope between each person is not safe or practical, and in a lot of cases it is not even possible. The most efficient solution is to shorten the rope, which is done by taking coils.

Taking coils This is the method used when you constantly change the distance between the climbers. For example; going from pitch climbing with 50 metres rope out to running belay with 15 metres rope out, to a snow ridge using approximately only 8 metres of the rope.

If you are just transporting the rope over easy terrain, both climbers can take coils. If you are climbing with running belay, the lead climber should take all the coils. You never know when you need to change the distance or technique.

To allow movement, a single rope, not longer than 50 metres, should be used.

The rope should be pulled through the harness loop to get a low tie-in point (which makes it easier to take a fall or hold someone directly with the harness). Wear the backpack while taking the coils (it will also prevent the coils from sliding off your shoulder). [See diagram 067.]

If you have tied-off the coils incorrectly, they will strangle you when loaded. Make a test simply by pulling the live rope and make sure that no coils become tight.

Leaving the prepared rope in the backpack This technique is useful when you are expecting to use the same length and you want to avoid getting too warm when wearing all the coils. You are still able to extend the rope without having to take the backpack off, and to make the rope shorter simply take coils.

Don't use this method in situations where you risk a leader fall, as you're attached to the rope with a karabiner. Attach yourself to the rope with a safe-lock karabiner in harness loop and an overhand loop. [See diagram 068.]

In most cases it's faster to move the rope and the team together like this. But if you only have an easy pitch in the middle of technical terrain, it may be faster to run up one at a time and take in the rope from the top in the easiest possible way by using your hands.

The simple rule for rope length is 'as short as possible – as long as is needed.'

SHORT ROPING ON SNOW RIDGES

SHORT ROPING ON SNOW RIDGES This is a situation in which you add safety to progress easily without reducing speed too much. The idea is that if one person slips and the other team member is unable to stop it before it turns into a fall he would have to jump onto the opposite side of the ridge.

The rope length between the first and second person should normally be between 8–15 metres, and the leader takes coils by hand so the team can move together very closely to one another (maximum 2 metres apart) to avoid pendulum falls.

Hold the ice axe in your upper hand (if possible), and keep the coils locked off in the other hand. [See diagram 069.]

The rope should be kept tight to the second person at all times. Your arm should be slightly bent and there should still be slack in the rope when you stretch your arm. When used correctly, your bent arm functions as suspension and gives the leader enough time to get into a position with a low balancing point, preventing the slip turning into a fall. From the feel of the rope you should always know what is going on in the rope team behind you. It doesn't take much to pull the leader off balance if the force from a slip of the second climber is transferred into a straight arm or directly into the leader's harness. [See diagrams 070 and 071.]

When progressing, move together on different sides of the ridge where possible. The rope length should be 8–10 metres. [See diagram 072.]

Move behind each other on the ridge if this is not possible. The biggest problems with this are the cornices. Remember that they always break much further in than you would expect.

If there are well-formed cornices, you have to traverse a bit lower down on the opposite side to keep well away from them.

Rope length should be a bit longer (10–15 metres) to give you enough time to run the few steps up hill and jump to the other side if someone in the team should start sliding. [See diagram 073.]

The biggest problem with jumping to the other side of the ridge is communication. If it's so steep that one of you is hanging more or less freely in the rope, counterbalanced by the other person, you can't just climb up. The options could be anything from climbing the rope simultaneously to fixing the rope at a belay (for upward pull) and climbing up the rope to establish communication and find a solution. You will have to improvise, but do realise that it could be very time consuming, so take your time and avoid ending up in this situation in the first place.

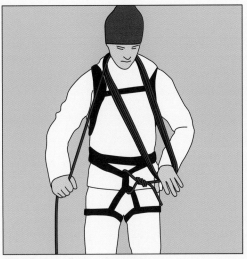

067:1 Taking coils.

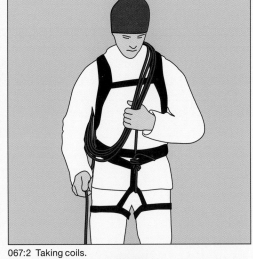

067:2 Taking coils.

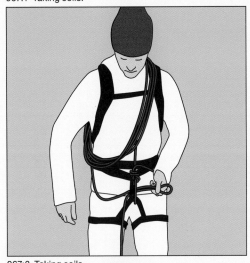

067:3 Taking coils.

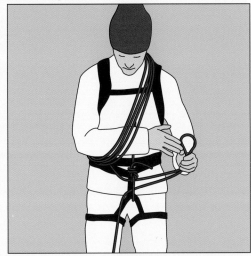

067:4 Taking coils.

067:5 Taking coils.

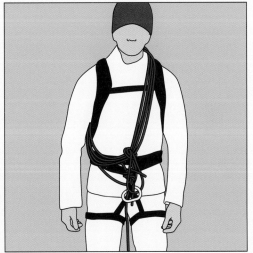

067:6 Taking coils.

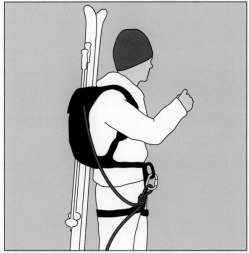

068 Shortening the rope without coils.

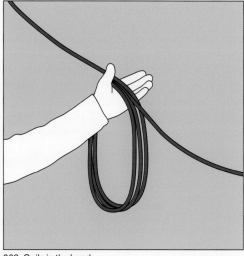

069 Coils in the hand.

070 Moving together.

071 Moving together on a snow flank.

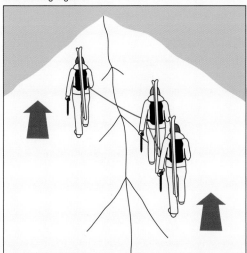

072 Moving together on a snow ridge.

Note: The rope should be kept tight to the second person at all times. Your arm should be slightly bent and there should still be slack in the rope when you stretch your arm. When used correctly, your bent arm functions as suspension and gives the leader enough time to get into a position with a low balancing point, preventing the slip turning into a fall.

RUNNING BELAY Climbing with a running belay allows you to move together with a good safety margin. You both simply climb at the same time, at the same speed and the rope stretched at all times. The lead climber places protection, and there should be protection on the rope at all times — natural (the rope behind spikes and flakes) or gear. When the leader starts to run out of gear he has to stop at a good place so that he can get the gear from the second climber.

Safety depends on:
__ Applying the technique in the right terrain — That is terrain where the team moves comfortably with little risk of a fall.
__ Protection — There must be a certain amount of protection on the rope at all times. The protection must be placed to hold a fall from either end of the rope.
__ Stretched rope – This means that the climbers have to adapt to the slowest climber's speed to keep the rope stretched at all times.

Rock On rock you should have roughly 15 metres of rope between the climbers and there should be two runners (could be natural) on the rope at all times. [See diagram 074.]

073 Moving together on a snow ridge.

074 Running belay on rock.

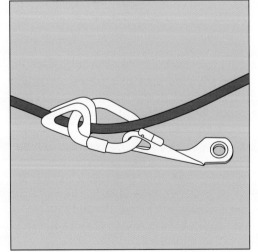

075 Running belay on ice.

Note: Climbing with a running belay allows you to move together with a good safety margin. You both simply climb at the same time, at the same speed and the rope stretched at all times. The lead climber places protection, and there should be protection on the rope at all times.

Ice When one climber is stronger than the other he could climb a full pitch from the belay. When he is out of rope he places an ice screw with a TIBLOC (a mechanical rope ascender that allows the rope to be moved in one direction but blocks the other). The rope has to run inside the locking karabiner (allowed to move up but blocked from going in the other direction).

Apart from everything mentioned before, safety depends on the use of a short locking karabiner. If the second climber falls, the karabiner will move from following the rope upwards to being pulled into a downward position before it can arrest the fall. If this distance is too far (karabiner too big or the use of a sling), there's a large risk that the force will pull the leader off the ice and the team's safety is then reliant on one ice screw. [See diagram 075.]

Clear away enough snow in front of the ice screw and behind it to allow the rope to run without becoming jammed. With a 50 metre rope, three ice screws and two TIBLOCS, you can climb 150 metres before having to stop to build a belay. Adapt to the terrain and choose a technique that enables you to progress as fast as possible while still maintaining safety. [See diagram 076.]

RAPPELLING

<u>CORD AND TAPE</u> Cord of 6—8 mm diameter, or tape, should be carried together with a knife for building rappelling anchors. Apart from nylon, there are other materials like Kevlar and Spectra which are lightweight and extremely strong (5.5 mm is enough). But due to their low melting point (lower than nylon), care should be taken when they could become shock loaded. You must pull the knots tight with your full body weight, otherwise there is a risk that the cord will burn off from the friction created when the knot is tightened by the shock load. Even if these materials are excellent for rappelling anchors, they are still expensive, and normal nylon cord that you buy by the metre is fine as you normally don't rappel that much anyway. If you use Kevlar and Spectra you must use a triple fisherman's knot.

Tubular tape is still lightweight and a bit stronger than dynamic cord.

If found in place, treat it with more respect than an old rope, as the large surface area and thin volume makes it more susceptible to damage from sunlight and friction. If you run out of cord/tape and slings to make rappel anchors, you have to start cutting bits off the end of the rope.

<u>RAPPEL ANCHORS</u> If there's no rappel anchor in place you'll have to build one. Get a sound anchor at any price; the anchor must be 100% bombproof! Building your own anchor means leaving gear behind. It is part of the game and you try, of course, to make the anchors as cheap as possible (choosing stoppers instead of friends, etc.) but your life is worth more. Don't be cheap! As long as the rappel is part of the plan there shouldn't be any problems, as you'll bring the gear needed for the anchors.

On rock You need to carry rock protection and cord/tape. To build a single anchor, a spike, flake or block, simply tie a sling around the object and pull the rope through. Make sure that the sling is not too tight.

To build a multiple anchor, tie the points together with the cord or tape (without using karabiners).

On ice You need to carry a 22 cm ice screw, a hook and cord/tape. To build an an-

076 Framework for rope technique.

chor, build two abalakovs and tie them together. Roughly 4 metres of cord is needed for one anchor. [See diagram 077.]

On snow You need to carry a snow stake and cord/tape. A plank will work instead of the snow stake. To build an anchor, make a T-anchor. The most likely use for it is to get over a bergschrund (see Glacier skiing).

ECONOMY ANCHORS The problems arise when you have to start rappelling and need to save gear in order to build enough rappel anchors to reach the ground.

Note: This is an emergency approach that you should use only if you need all the gear to reach the ground!

Above the economy rappel anchor you place a bombproof piece of protection or construct a solid anchor as a back up. Pull the rope through the economy anchor as usual.

Attach a sling from the back up to the rope. There should be enough slack in the sling from the back up to allow all the weight to be on the rappel anchor, but not enough to create a big shock load if the rappel anchor should fail.

The heaviest persons rappel first, with all the gear being protected by the back up. The idea is that if it holds for the heaviest person then it should hold for the lightest person, who takes away the back up before rappelling to leave as

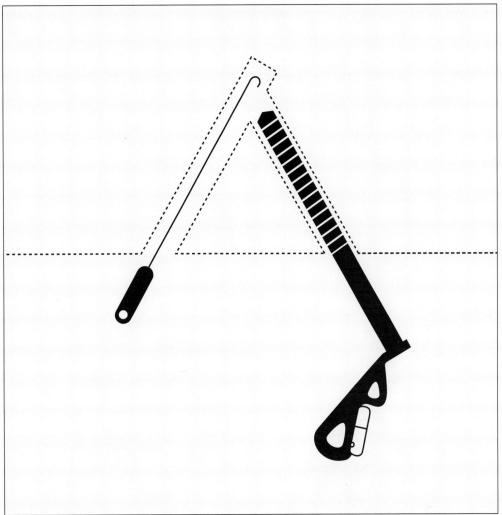

077:1 Building an Abalakov.

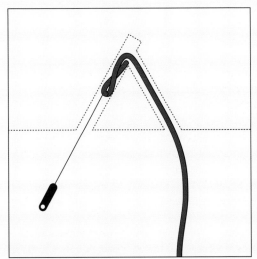

077:2 Building an Abalakov.

077:3 Building an Abalakov.

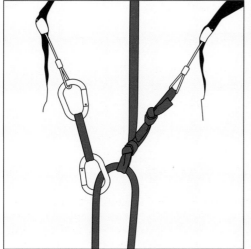

078 Rappel anchor with back up.

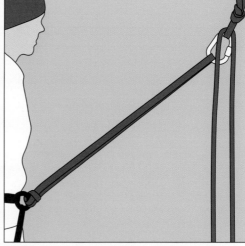

079 Attached to the rappel anchor using a cow's tail.

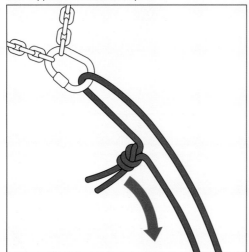

080 The knot on the correct side of the anchor.

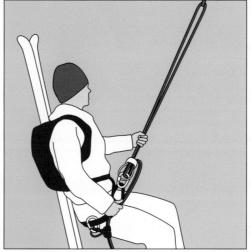

081 Rappelling.

little gear as possible behind. [See diagram 078.]

On rock Use hardwear for one of the points in a multiple anchor. For the other point(s) simply tie knots on the cord/tape that you wedge into a crack like a stopper. Use the ice axe to get the knot in a good position.

On ice Make a single abalakov and you could get away with using only one metre of cord/tape. Note: Try to build the anchor as high as possible in relation to the take-off point, and if possible where you can stand comfortably.

Attach yourself to the anchor with a cow's tail. [See diagram 079.]

If you are using double ropes, feed one rope end through from the top and join the ropes together (see overhand and double fisherman's knot) on the under side of the anchor, to reduce friction against the rock when you pull down the rope. [See diagram 080.]

If you are using a single rope, just pull the rope through until you reach the middle of the rope. If you don't know whether you will reach the ground or another ledge, tie an overhand knot on each rope 50 cm away from the ends.

Feed out the rope from the anchor, still holding the ends (or attach the ends to the harness with a karabiner).

When the whole rope is hanging down, make a small ball with the rope ends (to get some weight) and throw the ends down.

Connect yourself to the rope with your device — the same rule applies as when belaying, namely the brake hand must never leave the rope. To back it up (in case of a rock fall, etc.) attach a French prusik to the rope and place it in the leg loop on the same side as your brake hand.

Keep your feet flat on the rock and slightly apart (for balance) as you rappel down. Be careful not to knock down any rocks or ice, and check the position of the rope above your head to make sure that it doesn't get stuck in a crack, etc. [See diagram 081.]

If you don't reach the ground in one rappel, stop where it looks easy to build a new anchor. Then attach yourself to the new anchor with the cow's tail and undo yourself from the rope. Try to pull down the rope. If it works, the last climber can attach himself to the rope and rappel. If it doesn't work, the last climber has to adjust the anchor to reduce friction.

When everyone is down at the new anchor and attached with cow tails, pull down the rope and repeat until the ground is reached. [See diagram 082.]

If there is steep snow where you reach the ground, create a good ledge for putting on the skis while still being secured by the rope — either by kicking or using a shovel.

PULLING DOWN & RETRIEVING THE ROPES The last person to rappel down makes sure that there are no loose rocks on the ledge that could be pulled down by the rope, and that the rope will not get stuck in a crack when being pulled down.

Be careful when pulling down the rope; it's easy to pull down loose rocks at the same time (wear helmets if doing a multiple rappel on rock).

If you have different dimensions on the ropes when rappelling on rock, prepare the rappel so you pull in the thinner rope, as thicker ropes tend to get stuck less when they fall. Make sure that the ropes are not twisted. [See diagram 083.]

Move out from the slope, if possible, to get a less sharp angle at the anchor (less friction) if you can't pull the rope down and try to pull from that position. If that still doesn't work you will have to climb up the rope (on both ends!) back up to the anchor and find a solution. [See diagram 084.]

You can also use mechanical ascending devices.

If you've pulled one rope end half way up before it got stuck, move out from the slope, if possible, to get a less sharp angle at the anchor (less friction) and try to pull from that position.

If that doesn't work, put your prusiks on the rope and try to pull the rope down using your body weight.

If that doesn't work, and there's not enough rope to lead-climb back up with the end that you've already pulled down, you must cut the rope and continue to rappel with what's left. You can't climb up on the single rope as it could come loose at any time.

IMPROVISED RAPPELLING DEVICE If you lose your rappelling device you can build one with karabiners. [See diagram 085.]

If possible, avoid rappelling with an Italian hitch as the twist in the rope makes it more likely to get stuck when you pull the rope down.

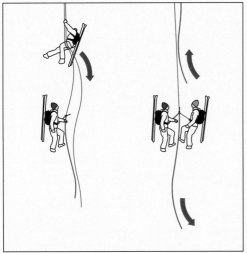

082:1 Multiple rappel sequence.

082:2 Multiple rappel sequence.

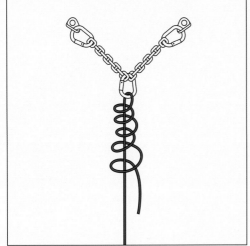

083 Separate the rope ends before pulling down the rope.

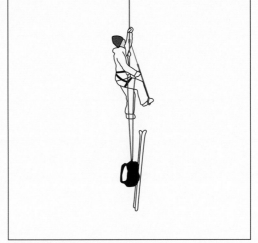

084 Prusik climbing up the rope.

Tactics & problem-solving How to avoid building rappel anchors on snow if you have, for example, a short but steep, exposed snow slope down to a rock anchor, from which you're going to rappel down to a skiable couloir:

___ Skier A makes a single ski belay while skier B puts skis and poles on the backpack.

___ Skier B down climbs while being belayed by skier A.

If it's exposed, skier B has to place runners (rock or ice) on the rope to protect skier A when it's his turn to down climb. At least one runner should be placed next to the anchor to avoid a factor 2 fall. If it isn't possible to place runners (only snow), rappelling from a snow anchor at the top is the safest option.

___ Skier B builds a rock anchor and belays skier A while he's down climbing (and removes the eventual runners). No gear is left behind.

___ When both are at the anchor, rappel as usual.

085 Improvised rappelling device using karabiners.

COMPANION RESCUE FOR SKI RELATED MOUNTAINEERING SITUATIONS

Companion rescue is quite a big topic, and with a bit of imagination one can easily come up with nightmare scenarios. However, it is generally easier to companion rescue in ski mountaineering than in climbing and general mountaineering. This is because we are not very often on terrain where an injured person is free-hanging with his full body weight on the rope, with no possibility of lowering him down to lower, angled ground.

If possible always rappel down together. Lower the injured person down and rappel after him. Remember to lower just half the rope length if you need to rappel after. Otherwise rappel the full rope length and down climb after.

If time is an issue, and you can reach easier, angled terrain by rappelling or

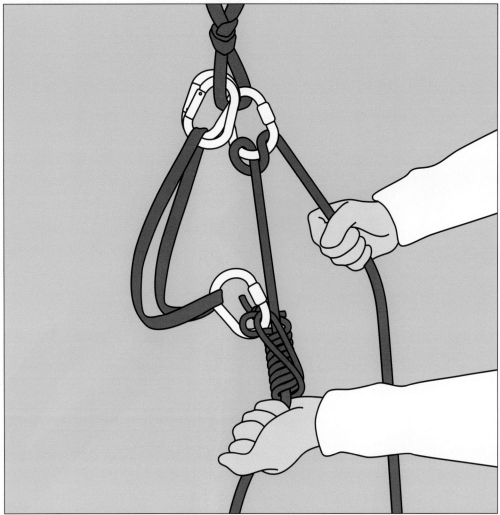

086:1 Lower past a knot.

lowering on two or more simple ropes tied together, you do that and leave the ropes behind. Then you would need to know how to lower past a knot and how to rappel past a knot.

LOWER PAST A KNOT
1. Lower with an Italian hitch. Use a French prusik in a 60 cm sling as an auto block.
2. When you reach the knot, let the auto block take the weight. Make a backup a metre back on the rope. An overhand knot on the bight is attached to the central loop with a karabiner.
3. Move the Italian hitch to the rope on the other side of the knot and tie it off.
4. Pull on the auto block and let the rope slide through until the weight is transferred to the tied-off Italian hitch.

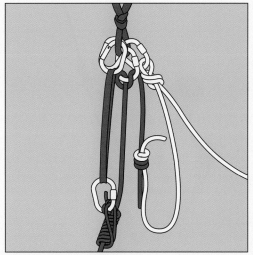
086:2 Lower past a knot.

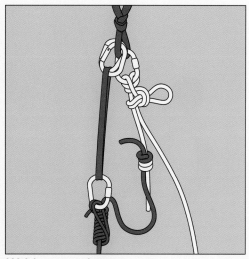
086:3 Lower past a knot.

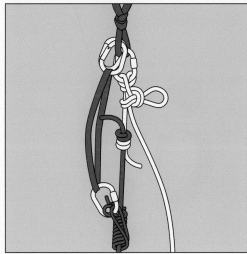
086:4 Lower past a knot.

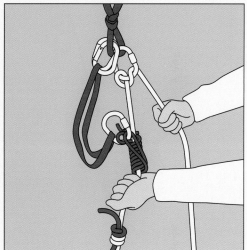
086:5 Lower past a knot.

5. Remove the prusik and replace it as a new auto block above the knot. Remove the backup, untie the Italian hitch and continue lowering. [See diagram 086.]

RAPPELLING PAST A KNOT
1. Place another French prusik above the rappelling device.
2. Make an overhand knot on the bight, one and a half metres below the knot, and attach it as a backup to the work loop of your harness, using a screw gate karabiner.
3. Remove the rappelling device, and replace it below the knot. Add a French prusik to the leg loop. Pull in the upper auto block and transfer your weight over to the rappelling device, which is being locked off by the auto block on the leg loop.
4. Remove the backup and continue rappelling. [See diagram 087.]

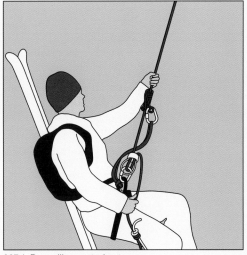

087:1 Rappelling past a knot.

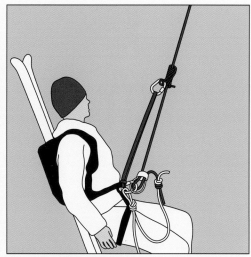

087:2 Rappelling past a knot.

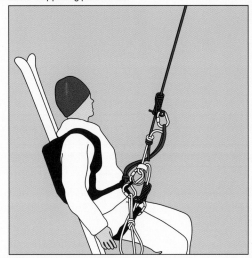

087:3 Rappelling past a knot.

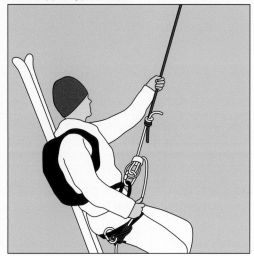

087:4 Rappelling past a knot.

ADJUSTING TO THE TERRAIN

In popular areas you can find guidebooks that will give you all the information you need. Aim low when you come to a new area or if you are using a new guidebook. Get a feeling of how accurate the book is as regards grades, times, what gear to bring and general information.

Make sure that the guidebook is not too old. Conditions change. What used to be an easy glacier to climb could now be a smooth rock slab and impossible to climb. If guidebooks are unavailable you will have to observe, using binoculars and talking to locals.

When you arrive in a place you haven't visited before, ask yourself a couple of questions before filling you backpack: Where are we? What are we going to do? What are the conditions like? Who's coming?

After answering these questions, you can decide what to take. Standard equipment consists of ice axe and crampons. Optional equipment consists of a second ice axe, helmet, harness, rope(s), gear for building anchors (both belay and rappel).

For protection on snow: A snow stake for rappelling.

For protection on ice: Two quickdraws (60 cm slings), two ice screws for possible shorter ice sections, three or four ice screws if the ice/snow slope is not too steep but could involve several pitches and sections on ice, five or six ice screws if the ice/snow is steeper and involves several pitches and sections on ice.

For protection on rock: Four quickdraws (60 cm slings), four stoppers (size 3, 5, 7 and 9), two friends, a few pitons. This is a full rack for normal use with skis on the back. If the rock section is short, strip the rack, starting with the friends and saving the pitons.

010

GLACIER SKIING

A tape recorder. And a set of fondue forks.

Those were the essential tools in my backpack the first time I did the Haute Route.

When I came up to Mont-Fort for the very first time, and squinted east towards the Matterhorn, I immediately felt drawn to the breathtaking landscape of rock, snow and ice. A friend had told me about the Haute Route and, fascinated as I was by the glaciers, I decided to traverse the mountains over to Zermatt as soon as possible. There was just one problem. My friends and I were skiers and rock climbers, not mountaineers. However, we solved that minor problem efficiently by ignoring it.

In the middle of February we took off, with huge backpacks and skinny telemark skis. It was early in the season, so we had to break trail and navigate the whole way. It was a good experience, not necessarily in the sense that I enjoyed every minute of it, but rather in the sense that I learned a lot. For starters, we didn't have a clue as to how to perform a crevasse rescue. So we put fresh tracks on those huge glaciers at random, with the rope between us stretched like a guitar string, all the while praying to God that no one would fall into a crevasse. We shouted things like "No problem" and "Let's improvise" to each other. I knew how to prusik-climb a rope, but I had no idea what it meant to arrest a fall. Consequently I hoped that it would be me down in the hole and not the opposite.

The days were long and tough, and we were forced to make decisions we weren't at all used to making. But eating that cheese fondue at the end of the day, with the sun setting and the Doors playing through the half-broken speakers, made it all worthwhile. And when we finally made it to Zermatt, we felt like heroes coming out of a war zone.

Every time I do the Haute Route nowadays, I cannot help laughing when I pass certain places and the memories come back. The serious part of me always ends up wishing that I had some source of useful mountaineering information back then. My energy and love for the mountains were endless, but the constant trial and error did not always make the progression fast or even very enjoyable.

Nevertheless – if I had a book like this back then, I would still wish that I had read between the lines. A set of fondue forks in one's backpack may not be lightweight, but it's life quality. It was right, back then and it's right today.

The major concern when it comes to glacier skiing is of course the crevasses. As long as the crevasses are open they are easily avoided, but during the winter most of them are hidden under the snow. Therefore, detecting them is hard or impossible. A lot of people think that mountain guides know where all the crevasses are located, and that's how they choose the routes up and down the glaciers. The answer is no, they don't know. Only through understanding how glaciers work will you know where crevasses are likely to form. And only by choosing the right timing (when the glaciers have filled up and snow bridges are stable) and the right technique (rope up or not) will you be able to ski and travel as safely as possible on the glaciers.

GLACIERS

A glacier will begin to form when the excess snow left from the previous winter forms a permanent snowfield. If this cycle is repeated over a period of time, the snow at the bottom will eventually turn into ice from the pressure of the weight of snow above.

Some 20–30 metres down in a glacier, the pressure of the weight of ice above transforms it into a dense, plastic-like material that is soft enough to flow slowly downhill with the force of gravity. The plastic-like ice will follow the terrain features, while the top 20–30 metres of the ice (that is still brittle and hard due to less pressure) will break up and form crevasses, bergschrunds, ice falls and seracs. The colder it is and the closer to the poles you are, the deeper the crevasses. The steeper the slope, the faster the glacier moves, creating acceleration and compression zones. [See diagram 001.]

Ice falls and seracs (ice towers) will form whenever the glacier flows over a pronounced steepening or over a cliff. These are very unstable, and pose a great danger to skiers. You should avoid moving below them at all times, as there is no way of knowing when they will collapse and fall. If for some reason you choose to expose yourself, keep exposure time to an absolute minimum. It may be an acceptable risk to spend five minutes skiing through a risk zone, but unacceptable to walk uphill exposing yourself for an hour. [See diagram 002.]

The majority of glaciers in the world move 1 metre or less per day, but the fastest, such as those found in Greenland and Antarctica, can move as much as up to 20 metres per day. It is therefore wise to observe the activity before moving into new areas.

ROUTE CHOICE

On a complex glacier, all your ski mountaineering skills are put to the test. When making a route choice you have to consider all the dangers, such as crevasses, falling seracs, avalanche danger, etc. Your understanding of where the crevasses are likely to form together with local knowledge, guidebooks and maps will help you with your choice of route. On the map you can identify all the terrain features that favour the formation of crevasses and other dangers, so study it carefully! But remember to check how old the map is. Glaciers (especially in the Alps) can change a lot from one year to another.

When crossing the glacier and bergschrund early in the morning, a good halogen head torch will make route finding easier and faster.

Crevasses are formed by the flow of the glacier, and consequently are not permanent features. Some will open and others will close, but the areas where they are likely to form will remain the same because the terrain features that cause them are permanent.

Bergschrund The bergschrund forms at the head of the glacier where the ice is thick enough to form plastic flow, and starts to tear itself away from its upper edge of brittle ice. Crossing it, both on the way up and the way down, can be either straightforward or very difficult. When going up you have to look for a place to cross where it is not too wide or where there is a snow bridge. When coming from above on steeper terrain, it can be difficult to see where the best place to cross is located. If possible, make sure you have that information beforehand. For example, by studying your descent route from another place. If the bergschrund is very open, falling is not an option when skiing above. In the majority of cases a bergschrund is crossed fairly easily by skiing or with a small, controlled jump. If for any reason you decide that it is not safe to jump across, you must be prepared to make a rappel anchor on either rock, ice or snow, as it may not be possible to choose where it is best to rappel.

Convex slopes Crevasses form when the glacier flows over convex slopes and forces the brittle ice to crack up.

Glacier bends Crevasses form where a glacier makes a turn, more so on the outside edge but also on the inside edge where the flow is obstructed.

Rognons or nunataks Crevasses develop around rock formations that protrude through the ice and obstruct the glacial flow. Wind channels, often tens of metres wide, normally form around nunataks. These are never covered by a snow bridge but are difficult to see nevertheless, especially in poor visibility and if you are skiing too fast.

Glaciers changing in width Crevasses are also likely to form where two glaciers meet or where the distance between valley walls either becomes narrower or expands. Take extra care where it expands, as crevasses tend to form along the direction of travel. [See diagram 003.]

Other hazards to consider Falling seracs — avoid exposing yourself under potentially dangerous seracs.

Getting off the glacier could be problematic late in the season, due to snow melting and leaving nothing other than an ice dome or a smooth slab to cross on. Either time it so you ski it when there is snow cover or rappel off.

White-out — Route finding can be difficult enough on a glacier, without the added difficulty of not being able to see crevasses until you are almost standing on top of them, or weaving in and out of the dead ends between the crevasses. It is wise to avoid the most crevassed glaciers if you do not have up-to-date GPS waypoints through the labyrinth. By that I mean that someone walked or skied the route and took waypoints the week before! Conditions can change fast on a glacier due both to the movement of the glacier and the snow accumulation/ melting. It is not enough to take the waypoints from the map as this won't tell you where all the crevasses are.

Avalanche danger and terrain-traps — In general the same rules apply. But because there is no heat from below, and therefore less temperature gradient within the snow pack, avalanches are less likely to occur on glaciers. However, avalanches are often triggered at the mountainsides, continuing out onto the glaciers.

Moulins or glacier wells — These are found on the flat sections lower down.

They look like round depressions, and are normally too small for a skier to fall into. But keep your eyes open as they are normally very deep.

EQUIPMENT

This is a basic glacier skiing kit. If you have to rappel or climb you will have to add equipment. Always consider your requirements according to route choice, conditions and experience. With ski touring bindings and a pair of skins you will have the extra option of being able to walk back uphill when it comes to solving problems. As always when skiing, everyone in the group must carry basic personal equipment (transceiver, shovel and probe).

PERSONAL EQUIPMENT

Ice axe and crampons You are on a glacier and could have use for them, for example for crevasse rescue.

Harness Everyone in the group should always wear a harness when skiing on a glacier, so as to be prepared if anyone should fall into a crevasse. Put a locking karabiner in the harness and leave it unlocked, making it easier if needed to clip in the rope when a loop is being lowered down.

Rappelling gear Rappel device and prusik slings. For rappelling and crevasse rescue.

Ice screw An ice screw and a 120 cm sling neatly hanging in the harness from a locking karabiner. One brand makes an ice screw with a turning "head" that will allow you to have the cow tail connected to the screw while placing it. It is a fast option, and therefore good for safety.

In addition to the basic group equipment you need a rope and gear for crevasse rescue and an abalakov kit.

GROUP EQUIPMENT

Rope A half rope is enough provided it is only used for roping up on the glacier, or rescue or rappelling (but of course you can use a single rope, it will just be heavier). Depending on how many you are in the group, the rope should be 30—50 metres long. If that is not enough, carry two ropes instead of a longer rope.

Slings A 120 cm sling and two 60 cm slings. Together with the 120 cm sling that you already have in your harness, this is sufficient for building an anchor and have slings to climb the rope if needed.

Ice screw Together with the ice screw on your harness, this makes two ice screws for building an anchor.

Karabiners Four or five (mainly locking) karabiners in addition to the two you are already carrying.

Rope ascenders Two lightweight rope ascenders, for example TIBLOC or Ropemans.

Traxion and block A Mini traxion and a block to minimise friction in the hoist system.

001 Glacier with crevasses.

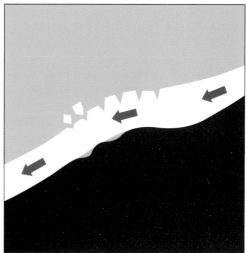

002 Ice falls and seracs.

003 Crevasses formed along the glacier.

Note: Crevasses are also likely to form where two glaciers meet or where the distance between valley walls either becomes narrower or expands. Take extra care where it expands, as crevasses tend to form along the direction of travel.

TACTICS

Skiing roped up is not skiing. It is a way of transporting yourself safely across a glacier when the conditions are bad. There are no secret tricks to make it pleasant and fun. That's why you choose to ski the glaciers when they are in good enough condition to allow you to ski at least mainly unroped. However with a bit of experience, roping up for a shorter, problematic section won't be time consuming.

Conditions are good when snow bridges are formed by cornices. Cornices can either grow from both sides (and meet in the middle to form snow bridges). Or if one wind direction dominates, the snow bridges will form from one side and the cornice will grow across to the other side.

It takes a few cycles of snow, wind, melt and freeze for them to form and become stable. So you have to be careful in early winter.

In the spring when the days are warm you have to find out whether the snow freezes during the night and that you are off the glacier before the snow bridges become too weak. Eventually, many of them will collapse during late spring or early summer.

Bear in mind that certain winters will be better than others. Don't assume you can ski the same lines every winter.

PREPARATIONS What do you hang from your harness? It is not necessary to ski around looking like a Christmas tree as long as you are skiing unroped. It is uncomfortable, and you risk injuring yourself if you take a fall and land on the equipment. It is also very dangerous to have long slings hanging from the harness (when walking in exposed places), as there is a risk of hooking a leg and tripping over.

As long as you might need to stop and take out the rope from the backpack, for example for a crevasse rescue, you might as well leave all the gear that you will only use together with the rope in the backpack with it. That will most often leave you with nothing more than a locking karabiner prepared in the front of the harness and another locking karabiner with an ice screw and a 120 cm sling hanging from one of the gear loops. That is enough gear to solve the most likely problem, falling into a crevasse and landing on a second snow bridge a bit further down. Then you can secure yourself from falling further down simply by placing the ice screw and attaching yourself to it with a cow's tail from your harness. You still have a free locking karabiner to clip into the rope that your friends will lower down.

Where within the group do you place the group equipment, and is it sufficient with only one crevasse rescue kit in the group? The last person in the group should carry the rope and the crevasse rescue kit, because he is less likely to fall into a crevasse, at least as long as he is skiing in the tracks left by those in front of him.

What happens if the person with the rope and the crevasse rescue kit falls into a crevasse? The easiest way is to avoid the problem. Both the person at the front of the group and the person at the back can carry a rope and a crevasse rescue kit. However this is rarely done on small, straightforward glaciers.

If the person carrying the rope and rescue gear falls into a crevasse, you are out of luck and there is not much you can do. If he is not injured he can try to aid climb out of the crevasse using two ice screws.

Note: Here is an emergency procedure that should be avoided if you can get help! You are committing yourself to one ice screw without any back up!

1. Place a sling in the first ice screw and step in it to reach higher up. Make sure that you are attached to the ice screw with a cow's tail from your harness.
2. Place the second ice screw higher up and attach yourself to it with another cow's tail. Hang in the ice screw to transfer your weight to the second ice screw.
3. Remove the first ice screw and place the sling in the second ice screw so you can step up high and start all over again.

The real problem starts if there is a lot of snow on top of the ice. Again it comes down to improvising. Maybe everyone else in the group can tie the slings from their harnesses together and lower a karabiner down so that the person in the crevasse can attach the rope thus allowing them to pull it up and continue with a standard crevasse rescue.

SKIING Keep your eyes open. Don't just look down the fall line. Scan the whole terrain regularly to detect any crevasses open 30 metres out to the side, that could continue in under your intended ski line. Don't ski too fast. Give yourself enough time to react when you detect something suspicious. (I've even seen people skiing into crevasses that were completely open and clearly visible. There are better-suited terrain and situations on which to blast down a mountain, than those you encounter when finding your way down a glacier). If you crash and both skis release, stay where you are and someone in the group will have to hand you your skis.

When stopping to regroup, have at least two ski lengths between each person. This is to avoid the possibility of everyone in the group standing on the same snow bridge. You should also avoid stopping on the prolongation of a snow bridge or a crevasse. All snow bridges should be passed perpendicularly. If you are uncertain about the stability of the snow bridges you must rope up.

ROPING UP Never walk on a snow covered glacier on foot without being roped up! That is the basic rule. When you are on skis it's a different situation, because your weight is spread over a larger area. This means keeping your skis on if you stop for a picnic, or if you have to go to the toilet. If you need to put the skins on, take one ski at a time, always keeping at least one ski underfoot.

When walking on foot, you have no idea where all the crevasses are so don't gamble. This is mainly a common situation for snowboarders when passing flat sections. But it could also happen when you would like to climb somewhat steeper sections, with your skis on your backpack.

When you are laying the first track skinning uphill there is no good argument for not being roped up. Walking in an old track is not a guarantee either. (I've heard of people suddenly falling in, even when in the tenth group to pass that day.) You have to consider what the greatest risk is. If the glacier is not too complex, has a lot of tracks and is in very good condition, maybe it's more important to be able to move fast and avoid time-related problems later in the day. It can be especially time consuming for an inexperienced group doing a lot of switchbacks while being roped up. You rarely rope on small, straightforward glaciers but when in doubt it is better to be safe than sorry.

In bad visibility; if you can't see where you're going you have to rope up.

In bad conditions; when the glacier is very open and/or when you don't trust the snow bridges.

HOW TO ROPE UP Rope up in exactly the same way as when you short rope. Excess rope needed for a possible crevasse rescue situation is best either kept in your backpack, or take coils. You can leave a somewhat longer distance between the first and second skiers. They should also be the best skiers. The most experienced skier skis in front so he can navigate and find a good route. [See diagram 004.] Note: The distance between group members is determined by the width of the crevasses.

When moving roped up:
__ The rope should be kept taught at all time. This means that the rope between the individuals in the group should just be touching the ground. If you have slack in the system it will be more difficult to arrest a fall, and there will be a greater risk of the person falling into the crevasse being injured.

Note: The distance between group members is determined by the width of the crevasses.

004 Distances on the rope.

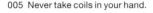

005 Never take coils in your hand.

006 Alpine butterflies.

__ Keep the ice axe handy under the shoulder strap of your backpack so you can get into a self-arrest position quickly and shove the skis down in the snow. This is generally not a problem if the snow is soft, because there is a great deal of friction on the rope when it cuts into the snow bridge.

__ Never take coils in your hand if you get slack in the rope whilst moving on a snow covered glacier. If someone should fall in, you risk losing your hand when the rope becomes taught. Instead, stop and wait until the rope comes taught as the person in front of you moves away. [See diagram 005.]

Skiing roped up most often means snow ploughing. As skiing roped up can be very difficult for inexperienced skiers, when in bad visibility (never bad conditions) you could rope up the two best skiers and let everyone else in the group follow exactly in their tracks. If there are only two persons on the rope, the distance between them has to be 20—30 metres, and two alpine butterflies could be tied on the rope two metres and four metres behind the first skier. This is to add friction if the first skier should fall into a crevasse. The alpine butterfly is used because it does not have a flat side and therefore creates a lot of friction. If the second skier should fall in, the first skier should have no difficulty in arresting his fall, since he will be downhill. If you are on flat ground, add two knots on the rope in front of the second skier as well. [See diagram 006.]

CREVASSE RESCUE

A crevasse rescue in winter could be very different to a crevasse rescue in summer. The amount of light, dry snow makes building solid anchors more complicated, and creates much more friction in the hoist systems because the rope cuts into the snow. In the winter there is a greater need for special equipment to reduce the friction, compared to the summer. Of course, it can be done only using prusik slings and karabiners, but the time that takes if there is a lot of snow (friction in the hoist system) and you are hoisting alone, is simply not acceptable. However you should know how to do it without the special equipment. Make sure you avoid dropping your skis into the crevasse, as it could be a long way back to civilisation. There are two possible scenarios when it comes to crevasse rescue. Either someone falls in whilst roped up, or not roped up. The easiest scenario is if you are roped up. If hanging in the rope in the crevasse it is of course always possible to prusik climb up the rope. Simply attach the skis to the backpack and climb up the rope.

ROPED UP If the rope has been kept taught you rarely actually fall into the crevasse. You are more likely to get stuck at backpack depth after your legs have gone through, or you fall up to your armpits and stop with your arms held sideways above the snow. Then it is most likely to be a matter of pulling the person out of the hole by walking backwards (he helps by crawling). If the person falls in completely you have to start hoisting.

A skier hanging in his harness is subject to major risks, such as hypothermia, lack of oxygen and blood supply.

Hypothermia: The temperature in the crevasse is much lower than on the surface. Compounding the problem, hypothermia is accelerated by the shock of an accident.

Hanging inactive from a harness can entail serious physiological problems. If the victim is unconscious, it's an emergency.

Basic 3:1 hoist or Z pulley: Works well when two or more persons are hoisting. If you practise a lot, it will also work when you're alone. But that can be time consuming because of friction.

1. The person closest behind the victim has to build an anchor while the rest of the rope team are keeping the rope taught, preventing the victim from falling further into the crevasse.
2. Make an anchor with ice screws or an H-anchor using the ice axe and the skis, or the skis and the poles.
3. Place a French prusik on the live rope and clip it to the anchor with a locking karabiner. Make sure that the live rope is inside the karabiner. Slide the prusik as far away as possible until the sling in the anchor becomes taught. Dig a hole under the prusik (to make sure that it will grab the rope) and slowly crawl away from the anchor so as to carefully transfer the weight to the anchor, all the while making sure that the prusik grips (if not, add a lap).
4. Clip yourself to the live rope with a cow's tail for your personal safety, and

007:1 Crevasse rescue.

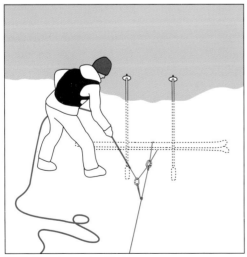

007:2 H-anchor made with skis .

Note: Don't forget the option of calling for help or waiting for help.

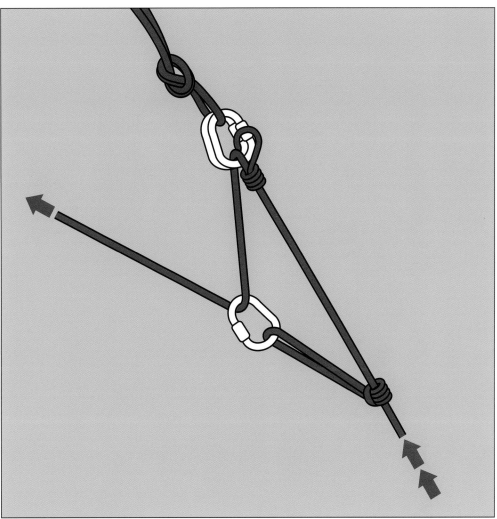

007:3 Basic 3:1 hoist or Z pulley.

walk out to the edge to establish contact. If needed untie. Your safety comes now from the cow's tail. Attach yourself to a prusik on the live rope when working on the edge, to prevent yourself from falling on top of the victim if the cornice should break.

5. Shove your backpack in under the live rope. This is most easily done by sitting down and pushing the backpack forward, using your legs. Clip the waist belt around the rope to make sure that you don't lose the backpack in the crevasse.

6. Very carefully dig or kick away the cornice (in small chunks so you don't kill the victim).

7. When you have created a passage wide enough for the victim to get through place another prusik on the live rope prepared for pull in the opposite direction and clip the slack rope (that comes out from the anchor) to the prusik.

8. Start hoisting and check where the victim is regularly so you don't squash him under the cornice. It might be impossible to hear someone scream. And

007:4 Backpack used to avoid the rope cutting into the snow.

whenever you need to you let the prusik at the anchor take the weight and slide the second prusik down the rope before you start pulling again. [See diagram 007.]

If you realise after point 5 that the victim is injured and needs immediate medical care.

1. Create a back up by making an overhand loop on the slack rope and clipping it to the anchor.
2. Everyone in the rope team attaches himself/herself to the live rope (using a cow's tail) and untie.
3. Rappel down on the slack rope and do whatever is necessary.
4. Prusik climb up the rope and continue as before with point 6.

As mentioned before, this can be very time consuming due to the friction. In the faster and more modern version you swap the prusik for a Mini traxion and TI-BLOC. Note: Don't use the TIBLOC as an auto-block, as it can release if it touches the ground. The advantage of using mechanical devices is that they work on wet, slightly frozen ropes and friction is reduced. The disadvantage is that the system is not easily reversed.

1. The person closest behind the victim has to build an anchor while the rest of the rope team are keeping the rope taught, preventing the victim falling further into the crevasse.
2. Make an anchor with ice screws or an H-anchor using the ice axe and the skis, or the skis and the poles.
3. Place the Mini traxion on the live rope and clip it to the anchor with a locking karabiner. Make sure that the device is correctly placed and that the live rope is locked. Slide the Mini traxion as far away as possible until the sling in the anchor becomes tight.
4. Clip yourself to the live rope with a cow's tail for your personal safety and walk out to the edge to establish contact. If necessary untie. Your safety now depends on the cow's tail. Attach yourself to a prusik on the live rope when working on the edge, to avoid falling on top of the victim should the cornice break.
5. Shove your backpack in under the live rope. This is most easily done by sitting down and pushing the backpack forward with your legs. Clip the waist belt around the rope to make sure you don't lose the backpack in the crevasse.
6. Very carefully dig or kick away the cornice (in small chunks so you don't kill the victim).
7. When you have created a passage wide enough for the victim to get through, place a TIBLOC and a pulley on the rope prepared for pulling in the opposite direction, and clip the slack rope (that comes out from the anchor) to the pulley.
8. Start hoisting and check regularly where the victim is so you don't squash him under the cornice. It could be impossible to hear someone scream. And whenever you need to, let the Mini traxion take the weight and slide the TIBLOC down the rope before you start pulling again. [See diagram 008.]

If a person in the middle of the team falls in, it would normally be the person downhill making the anchor and hoist while the person uphill holds the weight. If conditions are unfavourable downhill (crevasse, etc.) the person uphill will have to make the anchor.

ASSISTED HOIST If you have two ropes in the group but have only used one to tie-in, you can improvise if the live rope gets jammed. But if you don't have an extra rope you could use the assisted hoist. This can be used when the rope has cut in a long way into the cornice, or if you are only two in the rope and have tied an alpine butterfly on the rope, which also creates a lot of friction when hoisting.

The victim has to be conscious and unharmed. A maximum of a third of the rope can be used between the anchor and the victim. These criteria must be fulfilled, otherwise you have to proceed with a standard 3:1 hoist.

1. Create a back up by making an overhand loop on the slack rope and clipping it to the anchor.
2. If there are more people in the rope team, they should attach themselves to the live rope (using a cow's tail) and untie.
3. Clip yourself to the live rope with a cow's tail for your personal safety and walk out to the edge two metres from where the live rope is.
4. Kick away the cornice (now you can be less careful, as you are not directly above the victim). Establish contact.
5. Adjust your tie-in point so the rope to the anchor is taught while standing on the edge (don't forget the stretch in the rope).

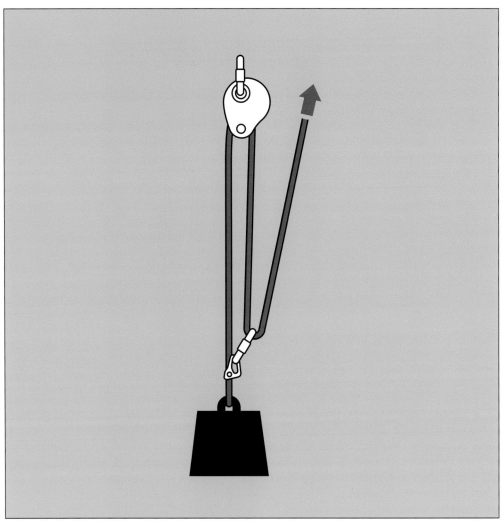

008:1 3:1 hoist or Z pulley using a Mini traxion and a TIBLOC.

008:2 Backpack used to avoid rope cutting into the snow.

Note: Don't use the TIBLOC as an auto-block, as it can release if it touches the ground. The advantage of using mechanical devices is that they work on wet, slightly frozen ropes and friction is reduced. The disadvantage is that the system is not easily reversed.

009:1 Assisted hoist.

009:2 Mini traxion being lowered.

010 Crevasse rescue of unroped skier.

011 Practising crevasse rescue with a back up rope.

6. Lower the Mini traxion with the slack rope that goes from your harness. The victim should attach it to the work loop in his harness so that the device locks while hanging from it but slides when you are pulling in the other end. Make sure the rope is not twisted.

7. The victim is pulling in the rope coming from your harness and you're pulling in the rope coming from his. (If you have adjusted your tie-in point too loosely you will be pulled over the edge at this point, due to rope stretch when the victim hangs from your harness. He should actually be hanging from the anchor, and the force should only be redirected through your harness). Hoist until the victim is up. [See diagram 009.]

UNROPED If someone falls in you have to clip that person to the rope as quickly as possible, because he might be standing on a fragile snow bridge that could collapse any second.

If the person is conscious

1. Have two persons sit down and shove the tails of the skis down in the snow to anchor them. The person farthest away from the crevasse holds on to the rope with a body belay and the person in front of him simply holds on to the rope with his hands.
2. Make an overhand loop on the other end of the rope and lower it down to the victim, who clips the rope to his harness.
3. The persons who are sitting down pull the rope taught and attach it to their harnesses with a clove hitch, making sure that the rope is taught between them. [See diagram 010.]

Now that you have secured the victim from falling further down, you can build an anchor and proceed exactly as you would if you were roped up from the beginning.

If the person is unconscious

1. Build an anchor.
2. Attach the rope to the anchor and rappel down on a single rope.
3. Tie-in the victim and prusik climb up the rope.
4. Pull the rope taught.

Now that you have secured the victim from falling further down; proceed exactly as you would if you were roped up from the beginning. Note: Don't forget the option of calling for help or waiting for help.

HOW TO PRACTISE

Practise on the stairs, on a balcony, etc., with a heavy backpack so you know what to do when you are up on the glacier. Find a crevasse that is open, if possible not too deep, and it is good if you can walk out from it. The area around it should have no crevasses, so you can move freely around when practising. Before sending a person down you should make sure that there are no cornices on the sides that could collapse on to "the victim". The first time you do this you could practise with a heavy backpack instead of a person. If you are uncertain, hire a mountain guide to do the exercise with you.

Rope up three or four persons, and have one extra person along to take care of the safety aspect during the exercise. Check that coils are correctly tied off. Build a back up anchor that is only there for the exercise, and let the victim tie-in to the back up rope that is attached to the anchor with an Italian hitch. The group should ski towards the crevasse, and when the victim falls in they must arrest the fall. Keep some slack in the back up rope so that the group takes the full force and weight of the victim.

When the group has stopped the fall, the safety person can tie off the Italian hitch with just a bit of slack in the rope to the victim. This way he can now move freely and make sure that everything is fine as well as staying in contact with the victim.

Now proceed according to the steps given under 3:1 hoist. If any one rappells down simulating an exercise with an unconscious victim, the person should be attached to a back up rope. If you are practising assisted hoist, there should be a back up on the person on the edge as well. Remember to pull the back up rope tight (to avoid shock load should anything fail) as the victim is being hoisted.

011

STEEP SKIING

At 9 p.m., my client for the following day called and told me he couldn't ski because he had twisted his knee. I half felt sorry for him, but I started making plans. A day off was just the thing I'd been waiting for.

For years I had been looking at this run from all possible angles, but always when the conditions had not been right, and for some reason or other I had not managed to ski it. Of course, what makes this line so attractive is its size – 2135 vertical metres in the fall line – and its beauty. Of equal importance is the fact that due to its characteristics, good skiing conditions on it are very rare. In this case, good conditions mean a good snow base and a big dump on top of it, followed by roughly a week of stable weather, windless and cold, to let the snow settle and make the run sufficiently safe

It is one thing to have snow all the way down to the valley on this run. To have both snow and a stable snow pack, is another. The aspect faces south-west, turning south south-east towards the end. Together with the big vertical drop, and the end at low altitude – 1087 metres above sea level – the timing is made extremely complicated.

I had been monitoring terrain conditions and Internet weather forecasts for about a week, so I knew that the conditions were perfect. But I also knew that in another two days it would be too late. So I had resigned myself to the fact that once again I would miss out on the run. Then came the call.

After a morning climb up over the East Ridge to the summit of Bec des Rosses, the tips of my skis were finally pointing down the steep top couloir. The snow was hard but smooth and the edges of our skis were gripping beautifully. It is not quite as steep after the couloir, and the snow was fantastic. We stayed in the sections facing as far west as possible, because there the snow was light, cold and boot deep. Once we ceased having to concentrate on the tricky, steep top section, everyone was laughing the whole way. Eventually we were forced over to the south-eastern facing slopes, but there we encountered perfect spring snow. In fact, we didn't have any route-finding problems all morning, because we had studied the run from different angles for so long.

We also knew that the following day the run would be impossible, as up top where we had enjoyed perfect powder, there would be breakable crust, or down low there would be frozen ice chunks (or dangerous conditions if it didn't freeze overnight). That fact, combined with our anticipation for this run, made the sun-drenched lunch in Verbier that ended our day seem truly perfect.

What one perceives as steep is, of course, dependent on personal ski ability and experience. Perception of steepness also varies with conditions (a steep slope that feels mellow in soft snow conditions can feel very exposed in hard conditions) but in this chapter it means slopes from approximately 40°, to a bit less than 50°, as opposed to extreme skiing on slopes of around 50° and above.

EQUIPMENT

Most equipment required, and its use, has been covered in previous chapters. When deciding what to put in the backpack, gather information and anticipate conditions and difficulties. There are a few extra points worth mentioning.

Skis & poles Wide skis without too much waist are best. The advantage of such skis is that they will still float in bad snow, so you avoid falling over. Also, they prevent you being thrown off balance when your ski boot touches the slope in hard snow conditions. When skiing on steep, exposed runs you should choose shorter skis (170–180 cm for tall people). These are lighter and more manoeuvrable. Some extreme skiers tune the edges of their skis to 87° underfoot, from 10 cm in front of the binding to 10 cm behind it. It is important to be aware of the fact that it takes a lot of practise to be able to ski with such a ski without catching an edge. The poles should be thin enough to be held in one hand while holding an ice axe in the other hand. The pole handle should be slim so you can turn the pole upside down and shove it into the snow, using it as an ice axe.

Bindings Bindings should be set high of course (losing a ski in this terrain is not an option) but should never be cranked to the maximum! If the spring can't flex the risk of the bindings releasing from impact or shock is increased.

When choosing bindings there are two ways to go. Choose either a lightweight ski touring binding such as the Diamir Freeride, or a sturdy alpine binding with a pair of alpine trekkers for the approach.

Boots Ski touring boots are best avoided on very steep, exposed slopes as they lack precision and are too soft to help you regain your balance if you make a mistake, especially if you have too much back weight. Alpine ski boots with vibram soles are ideal in those situations. However, some alpine boots with vibram soles do not fit into an alpine ski binding, so remember to check.

Crampons Lightweight are best avoided, as they do not work on ice. They should have an easy clip-on system that you can handle with only one hand.

HOW TO PRACTISE

The techniques for skiing steep terrain must be practised in advance.

THE TURN Stay focused and be prepared for the unexpected. Always try to link your turns together to help you stay in balance. You also have the option to side slip at the end of each turn, for speed control. Try to develop a rhythm to your turns. Make sure to turn short and control your speed completely after each turn. [See diagram 001.]

1. Put your weight on the downhill ski, turn your upper body slightly outwards, and face downhill. With a little controlled speed, plant the pole to the side below the binding, more downhill than a normal pole plant. Look at the snow

"The turn" 4 steps.

001:1

001:2

001:3

001:4

and try to anticipate what the turn will be like; breakable, soft or hard.

2. Transfer your weight onto the uphill ski and start the turn by pushing away (extending) your uphill leg. At the same time, your shoulders and torso should be facing downhill. Push your downhill pole and hand forward and in front of you (the folding pole plant) to avoid coming out of the turn too fast and being thrown off balance onto the tails of the skis.

3. Try to jump around as little as possible (the closer to the ground you are the more control you will have). If possible, keep your skis on the snow through-out the whole turn. Continue pushing your downhill pole and hand in front of you throughout the whole turn.

4. Keep your speed down and stay in control by allowing the turn to finish at 90° to the fall line (you should be able to stop straight away after coming out of the turn). Stay cantered over the downhill ski, and if the skis unexpectedly get stuck in the snow, you must be prepared to go for the next turn immedi-

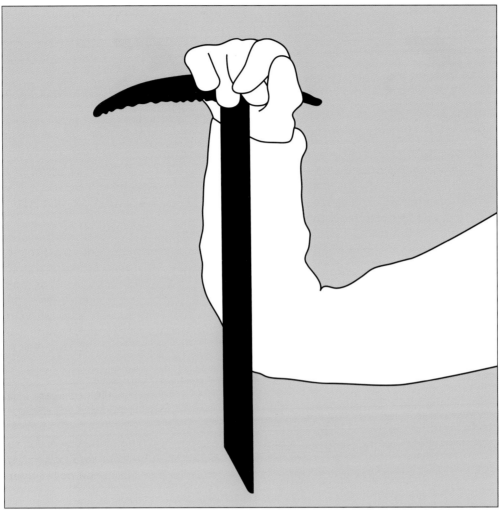

002:1 With this grip you can choose to use either the pick or the shaft. This means that the axe will not slide out of your hand as it could if you fall while only holding on to the shaft.

002:2 See 002:1.

Note: Make sure you allow the snow conditions to decide when a steep slope is okay to ski, so you don't go just because you are ready and want to proceed.

ately to avoid cart wheeling down the slope. When your upper body position is as in step 1, you are ready to start the next turn.

Ski small steep runs with a safe run out (no rocks, trees or crevasses at the bottom of the run). By choosing runs close to the lifts you can do laps in different conditions.

Practise skiing, side-slipping and side-stepping with the poles in one hand and the ice axe in the other hand. [See diagram 002.]

Find a slope that is 10 metres high and 50° steep and practise taking off the skis and putting on the crampons with one hand while holding on to an ice axe with the other hand.

When you feel confident, start skiing on more exposed runs. But progress slowly and choose runs where you feel at ease, or feel excited, rather than scared. Safety depends on staying on your feet and on your skis. If you are scared you will stiffen up and will be more likely to fall.

APPROACH When an object has been chosen, timing is essential. Not only for the snow conditions, but also for your own physical condition and, most important of all, your mental condition. But make sure you allow the snow conditions to decide when a steep slope is okay to ski, so you don't go just because you are ready and want to proceed. Wait for the right day when you are prepared and the snow is soft. Bear in mind that in a continental snow pack, most high altitude steep runs come into condition at the end of the season (April–June for the northern hemisphere).

If you have not climbed your line before descending, make sure that you have a good idea where you are going, as route finding can be hard when coming from above, especially if the run is convex. Study the line from a distance, from pictures, in guidebooks, on the map and memorise your route.

If a more serious run has been chosen, climb it before skiing down in order to get to know the run and the conditions. You should then be able to avoid being thrown off balance due to unexpected snow conditions or thin snow cover over rock or ice.

003 If it is exposed you can turn the uphill pole upside down and shove it in to the snow as an ice axe. In this way, you are anchored while working.

If the slough is building up behind you, you must continue descending diagonally in the same direction, either left or right (in this case skier's left).

If possible, stay on the spines.

004:1 When in doubt, keep the ice axe handy under your shoulder strap.

004:2

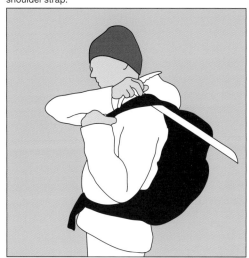

004:3

004:4

ENTERING Steep terrain is all about control; make sure you are in control when you enter the run. If you attack too hard you risk a nasty surprise and losing control.

If there is an old frozen side-slipping track that is more narrow than your skis, making it impossible to side-slip without the tips or the tails of your skis getting caught, try to loosen the snow by moving the skis back and forth. If this does not work, the solution could be to hold your pole upside down and, by using the weight of the handle, swing the pole and knock the sides off, making the track wide enough for your skis. [See diagram 003.] Through practise, a line can be found directly through the narrows to a wider section below to dissipate speed. Steep skiing is often not about each turn, but rather the flow of linked turns through changing degrees of steepness, snow quality, and slope weaknesses. The ability to forecast those changes and to use them to advantage is what makes one skier smoother than another. For example a short narrow section can be straight-shot or the "puddle" of soft snow, part way up the side of the couloir, can be used to slow down and give time to set-up for the next section.

DESCENDING Take it easy; keep your speed down, stay focused and in control. Only jump over obstacles that are in your way when you know that you can stick the landing. If you are not sure whether you can, you must find another solution; down climbing or rappelling.

If you are uncertain whether the conditions could be hard pack or not, keep the ice axe handy under the shoulder strap of your backpack and the crampons easily accessible from your pack. [See diagram 004.] If the conditions make a short section much worse than you expected, your climbing gear (axe, crampons, rope, etc.) can offer you other options than skiing down.

Slough management Skiing steep runs in cold snow conditions often means having to think about how to manage the slough, and the steeper the run the faster the slough moves. One method is to traverse back and forth a few times at the top of the run to let it slough out before you start descending.

012

SKI TOURING

Two officials of some kind had followed our descent with binoculars. They now claimed that we had skied through the newly planted forest. We hadn't but we knew that any attempt to convince these mysterious men of our innocence would result in the same old, by now quite annoying, answers.

Consequently, by the time the police arrived, we were quite frustrated by these unreasonable officials. We were also extremely stressed out, as we knew that the fine for skiing in the newly planted forest was 15000 Austrian schillings – and a suspended ski pass for the rest of the season.

As the police car arrived, we just saw a huge white grin through the windscreen. We shot each other a glance, with sinking hearts. We might as well pack our bags and go home; that grin looked just like Stone Face.

In those days, the police in St Anton used to chase every ski bum and make life hard for them in general. The fine for basically any "crime" was 100 schillings. It could be any little thing. If no reason existed, they would invent one. In fact, people never left home without having an extra 100 schillings in their back pocket, because if you weren't able to pay the fine in cash, you had to spend the night at the police station. And I never heard of anyone who managed to talk his or her way out of a 100 schillings fine. Especially not when Officer Stone Face was involved.

Officer Stone Face was known to hate ski bums more than all the other policemen put together. And of course it was Stone Face who was driving up to the officials and us. We would have to try and plead our case to the toughest police officer in all of St Anton.

Having identified ourselves, we were told by Stone Face to get our passports and come down to the police station in two hours. But then he changed that to one hour, with an even wider grin. Which left us no time to shower and meant us having to take a taxi to get there in time. He knew that, of course.

When we got to the police station – after 59 minutes – the officers there were very polite. And Stone Face was nowhere to be seen. To us this meant that one of the guys in our group had called his boss, who owned just about half the town, and he had promised to talk to the police before we got there.

The desk sergeant told us that we had committed a serious crime, and that he would have to fine us accordingly: 500 schillings. We could not believe our ears. 500 schillings! And we got to keep our ski passes. That night, we had a big coming-back-from-the-dead-party to celebrate. (And to think, I did not even have to use my emergency 100 schillings.) At the time, my first ever ski touring drama seemed quite dramatic and scary. But as long as you don't have to experience anything worse than that, you should be extremely grateful. And to top it off, six months after the incident I received an official document from the Austrian government. They informed me that I had the right to an attorney if I wanted to appeal against the fine.

I didn't exercise that right.

Ski touring is the culmination of all the techniques, starting before you even leave home with a weather forecast check and taking into consideration avalanche hazards and general conditions.

Where are we going to find the best snow? Is that run I've been looking at for so long in good condition? Are we going to pass the south-facing slope too late in the day? Is that steep slope still going to be bullet proof when we need to descend, or will it have time to warm up? Has that couloir slid due to the heat, leaving us with nothing but refrozen chunks that are impossible to ski?

Have a look at maps and guidebooks. Make a time estimate. Once your plans have been made, pack the gear you will need. Basic safety equipment should always be in your backpack; items such as shovel, probe, first aid kit, navigation kit, means of communication, etc.

EQUIPMENT

Most of the equipment has been covered in the previous chapters, but there are still a few things worth mentioning.

Ski touring boots Depending on your goal, a ski touring boot is more comfortable to walk and climb in, but less stable when skiing. In general, the more lightweight the boot, the worse it skis.

Lightweight skis & bindings These are fantastic for going uphill and traversing areas, such as the "haute-route" in the Alps, and they ski well enough to get down most things. However, if the skiing is demanding and/or the skiing is your way of having fun, rather than a means of transportation, take your normal skis.

Skins & knives When skinning on hard packed snow you will need knives (crampons for skis).

Sleeping bag This is not normally needed if staying in a guarded hut, but always check to be sure. There are two options.

A down bag has the smallest pack size and gives the greatest warmth to weight ratio, as long as it is dry. Once moist, it doesn't warm at all (the air between the feathers provides the insulation). A down bag works best in really cold conditions, with little moisture in the air.

A bag filled with synthetic fibre for insulation is not as compact or warm compared to its weight, but it will keep you warm in a moist environment.

Spare clothes You must bring extra clothes to keep dry and warm in when not moving. This is always a compromise. You can't carry all the gear it would be nice to have, but you still need to stay warm. The bare minimum, even if staying in a hut, should be:

A pair of thin gloves to use when skinning. It does not matter if they become wet from transpiration since you have your dry ski gloves to keep you warm.

An extra pair of thermals and socks to put on when stopping for the night. You will stay warmer if you are dry next to the skin.

A puffball or extra fleece to keep the upper body warm. Staying warm when you are drained of energy could be difficult.

Head torch This should be carried for working, and for finding your way in the dark, even if it is just to find your way to the toilet during the night.

Stove A stove that runs on white gas is very efficient for melting snow. A stove that runs on butane cartridges is very convenient, but doesn't perform as well in cold temperatures. Whichever type of stove you choose, experiment with it in a place where results don't have serious consequences. Make sure you can handle the stove and that it is reliable in very cold temperatures. Record boiling times and fuel consumption so you know how much fuel to bring. In cold temperatures, there is a risk of O-rings and rubber ball-seals freezing and not sealing the fuel properly, so bring spare parts for replacement if possible.

Repair kit Consider whether you need to make additions to the basic repair kit.

SKINNING

A well-set track is a work of art that reduces steepness to comfortable levels, without compromising elevation gain. It moves the group through the terrain with a minimum of effort and maximum speed. It flows through the terrain, gaining elevation through contouring, avoiding sudden changes in direction and technique. It also avoids areas where options are limited and choices are forced upon the group rather than chosen freely. This is not always possible, but is something to strive for.

Strive to ensure that everyone in the group has a steady heartbeat. This is achieved by having a well-set track, a steady pace, and rhythm. Be efficient and avoid unnecessary stops. Try to take breaks when you do have to stop and change techniques, for example when stopping to take skins off or to put on crampons. Otherwise, have a stop of about five minutes every hour, to drink and build up energy. [See diagrams 001, 002 and 003.]

CHANGING DIRECTION When skinning uphill, you have two major ways of changing direction (although there are intermediate variations). The easiest way is to simply change direction when walking, by making a turn whilst keeping the skis on the ground the whole time. This only works on fairly low-angled terrain. As soon as the terrain becomes too steep, you have to use the kick turn to change direction. [See diagram 004.]

If the terrain is very steep, or if hard packed snow makes it impossible to do the kick turn, you can try this method. [See diagram 005.]

If you have to use this technique the whole way up a slope, you will probably go faster and more safely by putting the skis on the backpack and kicking steps straight up. (That is if the snow is not soft; in that case progression on foot will be too slow and too much hard work.)

USING THE KNIVES On hard packed snow put on the knives, but if the terrain is steep it may be more efficient to put the skis on the backpack and walk straight up. Use an ice axe so you can self-arrest in the case of a slide.

CARETAKING Make sure you take good care of your skins, so that they function throughout the day.

In cold conditions (colder than –10°C) When you are in the mountains in cold conditions, knee deep snow, and the only way out is a couple of hours skinning you realise just how important your skins are. The last thing you want is for the skins to behave like dry toilet paper, literally impossible to stick to the skis. The best way to prevent this from happening is to keep the skins warm by storing them under your jacket and mid-layer whenever they are not glued under your skis (e.g. when you are skiing). Then they will most likely stick to your skis the

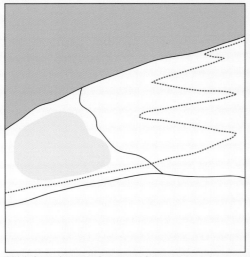

001:1 A poorly set track on a moraine crest.

001:2 A well-set track on a moraine crest.

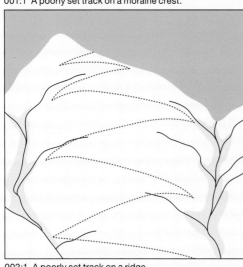

002:1 A poorly set track on a ridge.

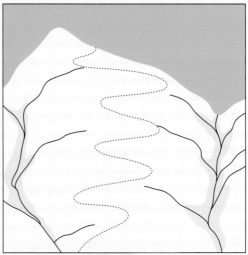

002:2 A well-set track on a ridge.

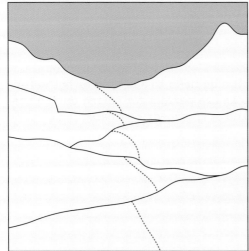

003:1 A poorly set track in benched terrain.

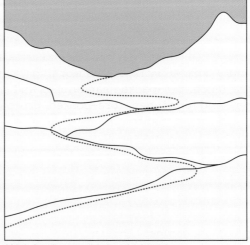

003:1 A well-set track in benched terrain.

next time you need to use them. To be on the safe side, a pair of spare skins can be carried in the group together with extra straps and a can of glue designed for this purpose.

In warm conditions When it's thawing in the sun but freezing in the shade and you have to go between the two, the skins are going to get soaked from the wet snow. Once you enter the shade, the cold, dry snow will stick under the skis and build up. This results in very heavy skis that are impossible to slide on, making it very hard work to get anywhere at all. Sometimes this is not even caused by shade. The different angles at which the sun hits the ground are enough to create these conditions. The best way to prevent the problem is to wax the skins before you go out, and make sure that they do not get wet, or at least, less wet.

OVERNIGHT

When working out time estimations, you will realise that a lot of runs simply won't be possible to finish in a day, even if they are fairly close to a ski resort and lifts. Your only option is to spend the night in the mountains and start early the next morning, or next night (you may have to leave between 02.00—06.00). Consider your departure carefully. If you start unnecessarily early you may waste energy, not using time efficiently, as most things are more time-consuming when it's dark. It may be wiser to sleep an extra hour and thus be more efficient once you get going, spending only one hour in the dark. However, you must start early enough to have a good safety margin.

Prepare all your gear and if possible pack the backpack in the evening when it is still light, so as to be more efficient in the morning when it is easy to lose time. Just wake up, get dressed, have breakfast, and go.

Whatever your objective, you have to decide where to spend the night. The choice of accommodation is the deciding factor in choosing which gear to carry.

Hydration As a result of skinning uphill with a heavy backpack, you will become dehydrated and need to drink a lot to re-hydrate. As you cannot carry the amount of water you need, you must start melting snow as soon as possible. Drink a lot of water, and after a while you can supplement for recovery. Continue to drink until your urine is straw-coloured and copious. Melt enough water to have some ready for breakfast and for the next day as well.

Food Try to have food that is as simple to cook as possible, so as to save fuel for melting snow.

For breakfast; prepare breakfast bags at home containing cereals, dried fruit and powdered milk. In the morning you will only need to add cold or hot water. For lunch; pre-packed sandwiches and snacks are perfect for eating during the day. And for dinner — pre-cooked, pre-packed or freeze-dried meals.

Only take food that you really like, so you actually eat it. Add hot instant drinks to every meal, especially in the morning, as they make it easier to get going.

<u>MOUNTAIN HUTS</u> Staying in a mountain hut makes life in the mountains so much easier. You will travel faster and lighter when you are not carrying a tent and all the extra gear that goes with it, and you will definitely enjoy the skiing more with a lighter pack. Another major bonus with a hut is that it is possible to dry boots and clothes. Even better if it is a hut with a guardian, as in the Alps, where you won't even need to carry food (for dinner and breakfast) or a sleeping bag.

The Kick Turn.

004:1 Place your skis across the fall line.

004:2 Put your weight on your downhill ski and change the direction of your uphill ski.

004:3 Transfer your weight to your uphill ski and place your uphill ski pole as far away as possible.

004:4 Keep your balance by using your poles, lift up your downhill ski, bend your knee and rotate your heel towards the ground to ensure that the ski tip doesn't get stuck during the kick turn. Flick the ski with your heel and, in one sweeping motion, place the ski parallel to the other one.

Mountain huts have their own tradition of use everywhere in the world. Find out what the local customs are and adapt to them. Do you need to book in advance or pick up a key somewhere in the valley? Are there any cooking facilities, and do you need to carry a sleeping bag?

However, there are a couple of universal rules. Always do your best to make everyone in the hut feel welcome and comfortable. Do not disturb people who are sleeping, as they may have to get up in the middle of the night and therefore need every minute of sleep. When you leave, take your rubbish back to the valley for proper disposal. And don't forget to pay for the accommodation; the money is needed for maintenance, otherwise the huts won't be there in the future.

004:5 The turn is complete.

Note: In hard snow conditions you will probably go faster and more safely by putting the skis on the backpack and kicking steps straight up.

SNOW & WINTER CAMPING Setting up tents will be faster and easier, but in cold conditions a good snow shelter will be sturdier and warmer (because of snow insulation).

TENTS Use a quality, lightweight four-season tent that is self-supporting and sturdy enough to withstand high winds and snow. It should have a vestibule for storage and cooking.

During a storm, drifting snow will build up on the tent and there will be a risk of the tent poles breaking. In extreme cases, the people inside may even suffocate. To keep the tent clear of snow, you will need to shake the tent walls and shovel out regularly.

Select a spot that is as flat as possible and is protected from hazards such as crevasses, avalanches and falling seracs. Note recent wind patterns and try to find a place that is protected from the wind. If staying several nights, take care not to choose an accumulation zone (if a storm should come in).

Compact an area large enough for the tent and for movement around it. Flatten the tent area thoroughly to get rid of uncomfortable lumps. Build snow walls around the tent (if the site is expected to be exposed to wind), facing the expected wind direction. The snow walls can be 1–2 metres high and should be located 5–10 metres from the tent. If you position the walls too close to the tent there is a risk of drifting snow building up behind them due to turbulence, and burying the tent. [See diagram 006.]

Skis, poles and ice axes make solid anchors, but of course you cannot use them when they are holding down the tent. If you are leaving the tent at the same spot for several days you could either take tent stakes designed for snow or fill nylon stuff sacks with snow and bury them.

Cooking In bad weather, and with the possibility of remaining in your sleeping bag, you will often cook in the vestibule.

Place the stove on a metal shovel blade. It becomes a stable platform that won't melt. Keep the fuel insulated from the snow so that the stove can work more efficiently. Light the stove near the tent opening so it can be tossed out if there

Alternative Switch.

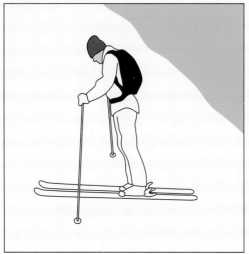

005:1 Place your skis across the fall line.

005:2 Keep your balance using the poles. Move your uphill ski backwards, behind and then below your downhill ski. Place it in the opposite direction.

005:3 Keep your balance using the poles. Move the downhill ski backwards.

005:4 Place the ski parallel to the other ski.

is a leak. Ensure that there is plenty of ventilation to avoid carbon monoxide poisoning.

Sleeping Ground insulation: Good insulation under your sleeping bag is essential for a good, warm night's sleep. A thin pad of closed-cell foam in combination with a thin, small Therm-a-Rest will give you both insulation and comfort.

Warmth: In the evening, when melting water for the next day, put the tightly sealed water bottles with hot water in next to the sleeping bag. If they are too hot you can wrap them in some clothing. They will keep you warmer, dry your clothes and prevent the water freezing during the night. Put on dry socks and thermals.

. Drying gear: When going to bed, put socks, thermals and liners in the sleeping bag. But if possible, not at the bottom of the sleeping bag, as the extremities probably won't produce enough heat to dry them.

005:5 The turn is complete.

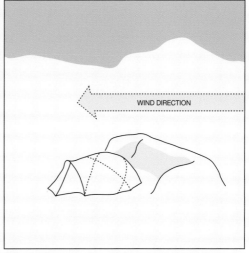

006 A winter camp. Snow walls and tent opening facing away from the wind.

Pee bottle: Have a wide-mouthed, one-litre bottle with a tight seal to prevent your bladder from ruining your night's sleep. Men simply pee in the bottle while remaining in the sleeping bag, seal it to avoid spilling when taking it out of the sleeping bag, and pour it out outside the tent while still in the sleeping bag. You hardly have to wake up. Women need to carry an adapter and to kneel while peeing, but that is still better than getting dressed and having to go outside.

SNOW CAVES & EMERGENCY SHELTERS Remaining several nights at the same place, when conditions are too extreme for a tent (because of wind and/or very low temperatures), or in an emergency, is a situation in which it makes sense to build a snow shelter. Try to keep clothes dry while working. Limit yourself to a moderate work pace to avoid excessive sweating. Put a Gore-Tex bivy sack over your sleeping bag to keep it dry.

Select a spot with enough snow (if in doubt, probe to make sure), and protected from hazards such as crevasses, avalanches and falling seracs. Likely locations are found in streambeds, under cornices and other places where snow has accumulated. Possible changes in the weather and snow build-up must be taken into account. If snow accumulates, it increases the risk of avalanches, burial and suffocation. [See diagram 007.]

Steeper slopes are easier to dig into as gravity takes care of snow removal. If possible, locate the door high up on the slope to make snow removal easier. Otherwise, you may have to remove the same snow two or three times.

Moving the snow in blocks is faster than moving powder snow or small chunks. Also, you will be more efficient if you have enough room to manoeuvre in whenever possible.

Snow cave The most efficient snow cave to dig is a cave with two (or more) doors, as several people can dig at the same time. Mark two (shoulder-width) doors in the snow, 1.5 metres apart. Dig 1 metre in before joining the two tunnels, and make sure that you leave the central pillar intact. Enlarge the hole to the desired size. The floor-wall intersection should be a smooth right angle for making best use of the space. Round off the wall–ceiling to create a half–sphere. Block up the larger of the two doorways with blocks from outside or debris. [See diagram 008.]

   Note: When digging a snow cave, make sure you have enough ventilation at all times (lack of oxygen can go unnoticed). This is not easy during a storm or in strong wind, as large ventilation holes and even the main door can get covered in snow in no time. If the entrance gets snowed in, the snow can be dug out and stored in the hole.

Emergency snow shelter An emergency snow shelter must be quick and easy to build, because of the circumstances. Dig a shoulder–width circular tunnel, 1 metre into a steep bank. Cut a bench to sit on and space for head and shoulders. Once inside and protected from the elements, you can enlarge the space. If the snow doesn't let you cut blocks for the door, use skis or a backpack. [See diagram 009.]

   Note: Make sure there is sufficient ventilation. If possible, take off wet boots, socks and clothes and put on dry ones, to conserve body heat. Put on all the warm

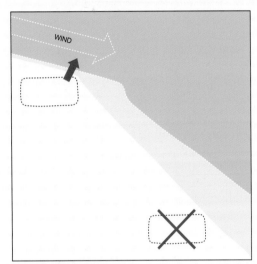

007 Placement of snow cave.

Note: When digging a snow cave, make sure you have enough ventilation at all times (lack of oxygen can go unnoticed). This is not easy during a storm or in strong wind, as large ventilation holes and even the main door can get covered in snow in no time. If the entrance gets snowed in, the snow can be dug out and stored in the hole.

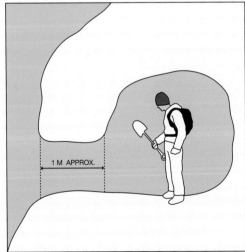

008:1 A two-door hole seen from the side.

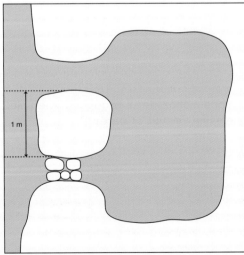

008:2 A two-door hole seen from above.

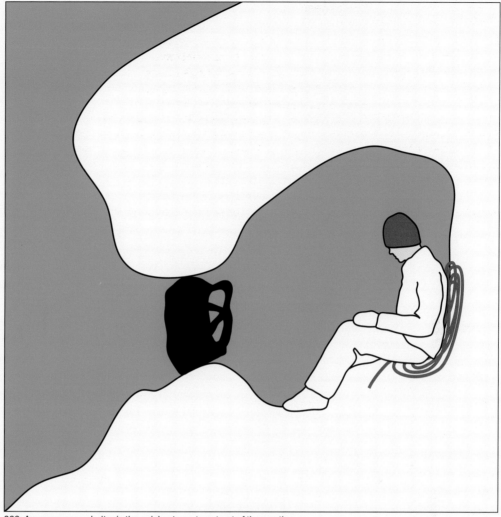

009 An emergency shelter is the quickest way to get out of the weather.

clothing you have or need, especially a hat. Loosen things such as belts that can impede circulation. Insulate yourself from the snow by sitting on ropes and backpacks, etc., and huddle together for warmth as much as possible.

Carbon monoxide (CO) poisoning Carbon monoxide is a gas that builds up during incomplete combustion, irrespective of type of burner used. Double the amount of carbon monoxide is produced when melting snow on a burner, than when heating the same amount of water.

In the open air, where carbon monoxide can disperse, there is no danger. However, in enclosed areas, for example, small tents and snow bivouacs, carbon monoxide is dangerous. Carbon monoxide gas remains close to the floor at first, but after a while it fills the whole bivouac.

Oxygen is absorbed from your lungs into your blood by attaching itself to the red blood cells, and carbon monoxide prevents this. The body reacts quickly and tries to compensate for the lack of oxygen in the blood with an increased heart rate. In serious cases of carbon monoxide poisoning, lack of oxygen can lead to unconsciousness or death.

Symptoms: Rapid pulse, weakness, cold sweats, headache.

Treatment: For mild carbon monoxide poisoning — rest and fresh air. It is important not to exert yourself (skiing) while symptoms remain. More serious cases of carbon monoxide poisoning require hospital treatment.

Carbon dioxide (CO2) poisoning Carbon monoxide (CO) must not be confused with carbon dioxide (CO2). Carbon dioxide is created during all combustion and is also present in air a person exhales. A high concentration of carbon dioxide can build up in a confined space that has poor or non-existent ventilation, for example a cramped emergency bivouac containing many people.

You may also be affected by carbon dioxide poisoning if you have to stay in a snow bivouac for many days due to bad weather. A build up of ice on the inner walls of the bivouac prevents oxygen from the snow entering the chamber. If this happens, scrape away the ice and make sure that the ventilation shafts are working.

Rapid breathing is a symptom of carbon dioxide poisoning. The treatment is fresh air.

CHOOSING A ROUTE

For popular areas, you can find guidebooks that will give you most of the information you need. Aim low when you come to a new area or when you use a new guidebook. Get a feeling of how accurate the book is as regards grades, times, what gear to bring and general information.

Make sure the guidebook is not too old. Conditions change. A glacier that used to be easy to climb could now be a smooth rock slab, and impossible to climb.

If guidebooks are unavailable, you will have to gain information with binoculars and by talking to people.

RATINGS Guide books in different areas use different systems for rating tours and/or descents, but the system used in the Alps is the most common and most developed. It is divided into two parts.

Overall difficulty The UIAA (Union Internationale des Associations d'Alpinisme) rating system for alpine climbing is used to rate overall difficulty, commitment level and to some extent technical difficulty. It includes the following: Length of itinerary (including approach and ascent), length of technical descent, exposure (consequences of a fall), objective dangers, altitude and remoteness.

GRADE	FRENCH	ENGLISH
F	Facile	Easy
PD	Peu Difficile	A little Difficult
AD	Assez Difficile	A little more Difficult
D	Difficile	Difficult
TD	Tres Difficile	Very Difficult
ED	Extremement Difficile	Extremely Difficult
EX or ABO	Exceptionellement Difficile	Exceptionally Difficult

Pluses and minuses represent the upper and lower end of each grade.

Technical difficulty The technical difficulty of the actual descent with skis or snowboard is divided into seven grades.

S1 An easy run.

S2 Slopes up to 25°.

S3 Large slopes up to 35°.

S4 Slopes up to 45°, if they are not too exposed, or less steep if there are narrow passages.

S5 Slopes between 45°–50°, the steeper a slope is (with this grade) the less exposed it will be, and vice versa.

S6 50° if it is very exposed, if not it could be steeper than 55°.

S7 Slopes with passages steeper than 60° or jumps over obstacles in very steep terrain.

So a route could, for example, have the grade D–, S5. Just remember that the difficulty will always vary with the snow conditions, so just because you skied an S5 graded slope in soft snow it doesn't necessarily mean that you will enjoy skiing (or even should ski) the same grade in other snow conditions.

ABOUT THE AUTHOR

Name Jimmy Odén.
Born 1971.
Nationality Swedish.
Lives in Verbier, Switzerland, since 1993.
Occupation UIAGM mountain guide, Bureau des guides — Verbier.
Membership Swedish Mountain Guide Association (serves on the training committee) and Swiss Mountain Guide Association.
Other Has been skiing full-time for 15 years in the Alps, Scandinavia, Greenland and elsewhere. www.freeskiing.nu

In the writing of this book, I have been given invaluable help from the following group of experts, authorities in their respective fields and generally accomplished professionals.

THE REFERENCE GROUP

Manuel Genswein — World-leading expert when it comes to companion avalanche rescue. www.genswein.com

Pierre Rizzardo — UIAGM guide. Member of the French Mountain Guide Association. President of Bureau des Guides — La Grave. Member of the training committee for the Swedish Mountain Guide Association. www.guidelagrave.com

Per Ås — Swedish and French UIAGM mountain guide who lives in La Grave. TC for the Swedish Mountain Guide Association (responsible for the education/training of future mountain guides). www.guidelagrave.com

Dick Johansson — UIAGM mountain guide. President of the Swedish Mountain Guide Association and member of the training committee. Former member of the Swedish mountain rescue team in northern Sweden. Skied in Chamonix at the end of the seventies and now lives in Kiruna. www.vertikal.se

Jan Stenström — UIAGM mountain guide and military mountain guide trained in the Austrian army. Responsible for all mountain and rope related activities in the Swedish Army. Vice chairman of the Swedish Mountain Guide Association. www.sbo.nu

Mark Diggins — UIAGM mountain guide, member of the British Mountain Guides and Swedish Mountain Guide Association. Former TC (responsible for the education/training of future mountain guides) in the British Mountain Guides. One of the founders of the European Avalanche School. www.euro-avalanche.com

Hans Solmssen — UIAGM mountain guide, member of the Swiss Mountain Guide Association and the American Mountain Guide Association. Lives in Verbier. www.swissguides.com

Mike Porter — Former head of Vail Ski School. Has skied for his entire life. Lives in Vail and works for different companies in the ski industry.

Marcus Lindahl — Medical doctor.

Keith Durrans — Former meteorologist for the British army.

Erik Huss — Glaciologist, Swedish Museum of Natural History.

PHOTOGRAPHERS

Myriam Lang-Willar, Jancsi Hadik, Alex Klun, Bengt O. Pettersson (p. 70—82), Hans Solmssen, Marcus Lindahl, Carl Lundberg, Robert Bolognesi/Archives Air Glacier. SLF Archives Davos.

This book has by no means been a one-man job. In addition to all the people who have been directly involved in producing it, I would also like to thank everyone who has encouraged and supported me along the way. In particular Jessica Odén, Stefan Engström, Anders Norin, Pontus Kristiansson, Pia Davidsson, Mike Porter, Christer Lidslot, Gustaf Ström, Henrik Attorps, Christophe Berclaz, Myriam Lang-Willar and Jansci Hadik.

And last but by no means least, I'm deeply grateful to Laura Durrans for all her support and who, with great patience, has helped me with the language.

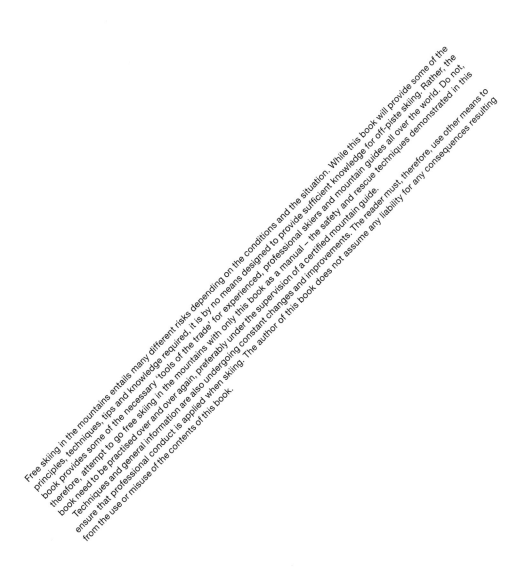

Free skiing in the mountains entails many different risks depending on the conditions and the situation. While this book will provide some of the principles, techniques, tips and knowledge required, it is by no means designed to provide sufficient knowledge for off-piste skiing. Rather, the book provides some of the necessary 'tools of the trade' for experienced, professional skiers and mountain guides all over the world. Do not, therefore, attempt to go free skiing in the mountains with only this book as a manual – the safety and rescue techniques demonstrated in this book need to be practised over and over again, preferably under the supervision of a certified mountain guide. Techniques and general information are also undergoing constant changes and improvements. The reader must, therefore, use other means to ensure that professional conduct is applied when skiing. The author of this book does not assume any liability for any consequences resulting from the use or misuse of the contents of this book.

PRODUCTION
© Choucas Förlag Stockholm 2005. © Text: Jimmy Odén/Choucas, Mats Ivarsson and Sebastian Bäckström/Public Speaking. © Photo: Myriam Lang-Willar, Jancsi Hadik, Alex Klun, Bengt O. Pettersson, Hans Solmssen, Marcus Lindahl, Carl Lundberg, Robert Bolognesi/Archives Air Glacier. SLF Archives Davos. © Art Director: Pontus Frankenstein/Frankenstein Stockholm/www.frankenstein.se. Producer: Cecilia Winbladh/Frankenstein Stockholm. Final artwork: Judith Wernholm/Kool. Illustrations: Fellow Designers. Editing: Write Right. Foreman: Eva Knapp. Pre-press, bookbinding and print: Fälth & Hässler, Värnamo 2005. ISBN 978-91-633-1313-4 www.freeskiing.nu